# AMERICA'S REGIONAL QUILTING

# AMERICA'S REGIONAL QUILTING

*by Marsha Evans Moore*

Photographs by Schecter Lee

Meredith® Press
New York

*Meredith® Press is an imprint of Meredith® Books:*
President, Book Group: Joseph J. Ward
Vice President, Editorial Director: Elizabeth P. Rice

*For Meredith® Press:*
Executive Editor: Connie Schrader
Editorial Assistant: Carolyn Mitchell
Copy Editors: Dina von Zweck, Vivien Fauerbach
Proofreaders: Northstar Productions; Guido Anderau
Production Manager: Bill Rose
Book Designer: Ulrich Ruchti
Photographer: Schecter Lee
Photo Stylist: Dina von Zweck

Cover Photograph: Schecter Lee
Illustrations: Marsha Evans Moore

*Credits:*
Quilt batting, Poly-fil polyester fiber stuffing, and
Pop-in-Pillows from Fairfield Processing Corporation,
Danbury, CT.

Ribbons from C.M. Offray and Sons.

Background fabrics on pages 79, 99, 133, 135, 139, 160,
165, and 178; teapots on pages 107 and 165; and lace panel
on page 107 from Laura Ashley.

"America the Beautiful" lyrics by Katherine Lee Bates, 1893.

ISBN: 0-696-02362-8
Library of Congress Card Number: 91-060641

Printed in the United States of America
10  9  8  7  6  5  4  3  2  1

Dear Quilter:

Editing and producing quilting books gives us a window into the past. *America's Regional Quilting* has been such a book. The color and joy of quilting, reflected in each of Marsha Evans Moore's traditional and adapted designs, leads us on a wondrous cross-country trip of America's history. It made me think of a passage in *Pioneer Women: Voices from the Kansas Frontier* by Joanna L. Stratton*: "In addition to sewing the family clothing, the housewife devoted a good deal of her spare time to making household blankets, linens, and coverlets . . ..Best of all were the beautiful handmade quilts pieced together with odd bits of calico, muslin, and other fabrics."

Kansas women, like other American women, struggled to bring warmth and beauty into the wilderness and into their homes. In this century, that tradition has continued, and we believe it will continue on into the 21st century. Meredith® Press has been publishing crafts books for years and we are dedicated to bringing you the best. We are proud that *America's Regional Quilting* provides what crafters value most: full-size color pictures, clear instructions, and easy-to-follow patterns. We hope you enjoy this book.

Sincerely,

*Connie Schrader*

Connie Schrader
Executive Editor

*Joanna L. Stratton, *Pioneer Women: Voices from the Kansas Frontier* (New York: Simon & Schuster, 1981), p. 69.

*O beautiful for spacious skies,*
*For amber waves of grain,*

# CONTENTS

*For purple mountain majesties*
*Above the fruited plain!*

*America! America!*
*God shed His grace on thee*

*And crown thy good with brotherhood*
*From sea to shining sea!*

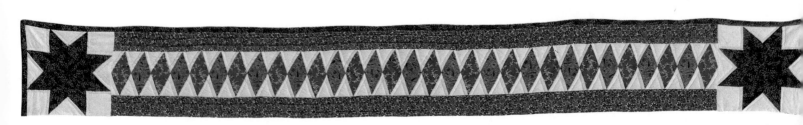

# INTRODUCTION

e've created this book to celebrate the rich heritage of American quilting. The projects presented here will give you an opportunity to use your skills to make everything from large quilts that are truly heirlooms to smaller projects that are decorative and fun. *America's Regional Quilting* is a treasury of ideas—for you, your home, your family, and friends. Quiltmaking is an art you always can learn more and more about. And the clear, step-by-step instructions will instill confidence, no matter what your level of expertise.

Quilts have always been a symbol of warmth and comfort in the home. However, to America's pioneers, home was not just a house but the surrounding countryside. The quilts that these quilters made reflected the lives they led and the natural beauty of the landscape. Over the last 20 years, I have been inspired by the patterns and colors of American quilts that I've seen in museums, antique shops, and private collections. Between the covers of this book, you will find a unique collection of the best of the quilt patterns and ideas that pay tribute to our country, its regions, and its states.

Women have been making quilts for centuries. By putting a layer of fluffy material between two layers of fabric and holding them together with tiny stitches, they devised a very practical combination that could be used to make warm clothing and bed-coverings.

When the first European settlers came to this country, they brought the art of quilting with them. They also brought a wealth of beautiful quilting designs that were popular in the 17th and 18th centuries. Feathered medallions, wreaths and borders, leaves and flowers, cables and cross hatchings were among the patterns used to quilt plain-colored clothing and to decorate large bed-covers and hangings in the style we now call "Whole Cloth Quilts."

Toward the end of the 18th century, trading ships brought beautiful floral print fabrics to our shores. Because these imported chintz fabrics were expensive, needleworkers began to cut out the designs. They arranged the cutouts to make trees, wreaths, vines, and baskets or urns of flowers. They appliquéd them on solid color fabrics to make a little decoration go a long way. A few women, who couldn't afford even a little piece of printed fabric, began to cut shapes from solid-color fabrics to make flowers, trees, and baskets. By the first decade of the 19th century, a truly unique American style of appliqué was born.

At the same time, patchwork techniques developed as a way for needlewomen to make leftover scraps of fabric into something useful. When necessary, they even salvaged the good portions of worn-out clothing and recycled them into patchwork. Wool and flax were used for batting in the North, while cotton was used in the South. Worn blankets or clothes also could be used for batting when nothing else was available. At first, the patterns were simple repetitions of squares, triangles, and diamonds. The *Lone Star Quilt* (page 86), originally known as the "Star of Bethlehem" pattern, is an example of this type of quilt. Composed of many diamonds, it is one of the full-size quilts in this book.

Soon these simple shapes were combined in every way possible to make the quilt blocks, and each was given a name. Quilters were inspired by the beauty of the land—by the wildflowers that grew near their homes in the East and by the mountains they crossed to establish homes in the West. They gave their patterns names such as "Carolina Lily" and "Rocky Road to Kansas." As pioneer women traveled westward to make homes in lonely places, they took their quilting with them. Making quilts to keep their families warm in winter was the difference between life and death. Some patterns reminded them of everyday things, like the log cabins they lived in or the churns they used to make butter, and so we have patterns named "Log Cabin" and "Churn Dash."

Quilting provided both a creative outlet and a quiet task to look forward to during days of physically hard work. It provided, through sewing circles and quilting bees, a chance to socialize and form friendships. As the women quilted, they often discussed famous people, daily events, and current political happenings. They named the patterns they exchanged "Clay's Choice" or "Old Tippecanoe." Hundreds of star patterns were designed. I used some of the patchwork stars named in honor of the states to make the *Stars of the States Quilt* (page 52).

Many different religious, ethnic, and regional groups added diversity to American quiltmaking. The Amish of Pennsylvania, Ohio, and Indiana created simple geometrically patterned quilts using both brilliant and dark colors that were inspired by their religious beliefs. The *Amish Mini-Quilts* (page 92) are examples of four of their classic patterns. The Pennsylvania Dutch made bright red and yellow quilts using the folk art symbols they brought from Germany. They used these "distlefink" designs to decorate household items like the *Pennsylvania Dutch Chair Seat* (page 114). Many Indian tribes made beaded sashes, and the Navaho Indians of the Southwest made beautiful woven textiles. I've used their traditions as inspiration for the *Hopi Kachina Sash* and the *Navaho Patchwork Vest* (pages 176 and 158).

During the Civil War, women made quilts and organized fairs and raffles to raise money to build hospitals. They also made quilts for soldiers. The patriotic color scheme of red, white, and blue was often used—and stars and stripes were prominent. Later in the century, in 1876, the country celebrated its Centennial. Many new states joined the Union around this time, and commemorative quilts were made to celebrate these events. Once again red, white, and blue quilts were popular. I've included several projects using this color scheme: the *American Eagle Pillow*, the *Star-Spangled 4th of July Picnic Cloth*, and the *Betsy Ross and Uncle Sam Dolls* (pages 187, 170, and 117).

In the latter part of the 19th century, many women had leisure time to devote to needlework of a very decorative nature. The "crazy quilt" style of patchwork reflects the highly embellished style of that era. Abstract shapes of velvets, silks, and satins were stitched together and elaborately embroidered to make quilts which were often displayed in the parlor rather than used as bed-coverings. You, too, can make the *Rocky Road to Kansas Pillow* using "crazy quilt" techniques to ornament a cozy corner of your home.

As a new century began, quilting was already a tradition in small towns and rural areas of our country. Women's magazines and even newspaper columns featured quilt patterns. New patchwork blocks and appliqué patterns were designed. Pastel colors were now more popular than the stronger contrasting colors and calico fabrics of the previous century. With two world wars and the Depression of the 1930's, there were plenty of hard times to get through. Once again, American women economized by making quilts using scraps of fabrics. Many women made quilts to earn extra money for household expenses.

My great-grandmother made wonderful quilts. When I was small, in the 1950's and 60's, each bed in our house had one of her quilts to keep us warm in winter. But, during that time, quiltmaking was not so popular as it once had been. After all, there were plenty of blankets to buy in the stores, decorating styles had changed, and most homes had central heating. I'm sorry that I did not learn quiltmaking at my great-grandmother's knee.

During the 1970's, quiltmaking, along with other crafts, experienced a revival. Antique quilts were shown in museums and galleries, and there was renewed interest in this art. I made my first quilt in 1972 when I was a college student. I used scraps of cotton prints and corduroy left over from clothes I had made to create a simple nine-patch design which was tied, not hand-quilted. Years later, when this quilt was well-worn, I used it in the yard for my baby. He played on it while I worked in my garden. Since then, I've made a number of quilts for myself and as gifts. I've learned patchwork, appliqué, and quilting techniques from books and magazines, from classes I've taken, and from many friends with a common interest in quilting.

The most recent revival of quiltmaking was fueled by the bicentennial celebrations in 1976. In many areas of the country, groups of women came together (as they had 100 years before) to make commemorative quilts to celebrate our country's heritage. Many of these quilts depicted events that reflected local history. National quilting organizations have since been formed, and quilt shows are held all year long, all over the country. Shops sell fabric designed especially for quilting, along with all the other tools and materials we need to make quilts. Thanks to new techniques that make quiltmaking easier, these days we can finish our projects fairly quickly.

I have tried to include some of the new techniques for quick-piecing and appliqué in my instructions. You can try them. For the patchwork enthusiasts, there are projects for every level of skill, from the quick-and-easy *Indiana Puzzle Pot Holders*, *Lincoln's Platform Place Mats*, and *Magnolia Bud Sachet*, to more ambitious ones such as the two full-size quilts, *The Stars of the States Quilt* and the *Lone Star Quilt*. I used machine-appliqué on some projects like the *Montana Mountain Bear Cub Quilt* and the *Pennsylvania Dutch Chair Seat*. It's a great time-saver, especially for children's quilts and gifts. Many of the other appliqué projects in this book can be adapted for machine techniques.

There has been a renewed interest in the art of hand-appliqué. I wanted to include several of these projects because hand-appliqué is a lovely technique. If you don't have much experience with this aspect of quiltmaking, try starting with the *Kentucky Rose Pillow* or the *Prairie Flower Table Runner* (pages 138 and 44). The simple shapes that form these designs are repetitive and allow time to practice making small invisible stitches. After a few projects such as these, you will gain sufficient confidence to tackle the *Appalachian Wildflower Quilt* (page 36).

In the chapter on the basics of quiltmaking, you will find helpful information on patchwork, appliqué, quilting, and finishing techniques for your projects. Whether you're a beginner or an expert, I recommend reading this chapter.

Quilts will brighten your home with warmth, color, and exciting designs—just as they did in homes 100 or 200 years ago. In this modern world full of high-tech uncertainties, quilts remain a source of security and comfort. I've included several other projects for your home: *Maine Woods Autumn Pillow* (page 83) and the *Wisconsin Churn Dash Wall Hanging* (page 64). Quilted clothing is also popular once again, and today's quilters enjoy making clothing to show off their needlework skills. So I've included the *Iowa Harvest Apron* (page 141) and the *Navaho Patchwork Vest* (page 158).

Traditionally, quilts were made and given as gifts to mark the important events of life: a couple's engagement, marriage, anniversary, birth of a baby, and so on. This tradition can be part of our lives today. By planning ahead and working a little bit at a time, making that special gift can be very rewarding. For birthdays and other holidays, smaller gifts such as pillows, wall hangings, tote bags, or even a small pincushion or sachet are appropriate. They are truly gifts of love. You can get together with your friends and plan a gift for another friend who is about to celebrate a special occasion. Some of the most original quilts were presentation quilts made by a group of people and given to someone who had made a valued contribution to the community.

I know you will enjoy making the quilts and other projects in this book for your home and for the people you love. A quilt made today is tomorrow's treasured heirloom.

Marsha Evans Moore

# QUILTING BASICS

## BASIC TOOLS AND MATERIALS

Here are the basic tools and materials you should have on hand to work on the projects in this book. All other required tools and materials are listed at the beginning of each project.

Tracing or Wrapping Paper, for enlarging patterns.

Tracing paper is best because you can see through it and thus trace directly from the book.

Graph or Quadrille Paper, for enlarging patterns or drafting your own designs.

Masking Tape and/or Scotch Tape, for holding paper and fabric in place.

Template Plastic or Cardboard, for making templates (reusable pattern pieces).

Bridal Tulle, for making templates for quilting patterns.

Pencils and Pens, for drawing patterns and marking fabrics.

Compass or Circle Templates, for drawing circles.

Ruler, preferably a 2″ by 18″ see-through plastic ruler, for enlarging and drawing patterns, measuring fabric, and marking straight quilting lines.

Tape Measure, for measuring lengths longer than 18″ or lengths that are not straight or flat.

Yardstick, for measuring lengths longer than 18″ and marking long lines of quilting.

Dressmaker's Shears, sharp, for cutting fabric.

Paper Scissors, for cutting paper, so you don't dull shears.

Craft Knife (X-acto), for cutting plastic or cardboard templates.

Embroidery Scissors, with sharp pointed tips, for cutting small pieces of fabric, for appliqué and trimming threads.

Rotary Cutting, a wheel-shaped cutting tool that will save you a lot of time when cutting strips of fabric.

Cutting Board, a plastic mat to place under fabric when using a rotary cutter.

Large Plastic Ruler, made of thick plastic and marked with a grid, for use with a rotary cutter.

Pins, for holding patterns in place while cutting and holding fabrics in place while sewing.

Quilting Pins, long pins for pinning the layers of a quilt together. Safety Pins, for machine quilting.

Sewing Machine, for machine-piecing and quilting.

Needles, for hand-sewing. You will need an assortment of different-size sharps for hand-sewing, piecing, and appliqué; embroidery needles for embroidering, and different weights of floss and quilting needles or betweens for hand-quilting.

Iron and Ironing Board, for pressing fabric.

Seam Ripper, for pulling out stitches, if necessary.

Thimbles, made of metal or leather to protect your fingers while hand-sewing or quilting.

Quilting Hoop or Frame, for holding fabrics smooth and taut while you quilt them.

Embroidery Hoop, for holding fabrics taut while you embroider.

Dowel or Chopstick, for turning fabric tubes and pushing in stuffing.

Bias Bars and/or Knitting Needles, for making fabric tubes for appliqué stems.

## FABRICS

The fabrics listed for each project are shown in the photograph of the project. All yardage estimates in this book are based on fabric 45″ wide, unless otherwise indicated. In all cases, the yardages include a little extra since it is better to have some left over for the scrap-basket than to run out of fabric before the project has been completed.

Always choose the best quality fabrics you can afford for your quilts, since you will be investing your valuable time in these projects. For most patchwork, 100 percent cotton fabrics work best: they are strong, durable, and easy to manipulate. Cotton blend fabrics also can be used if the design does not contain intricate patchwork or hand-appliqué. Sometimes you will wish to use fabrics such as silks, satins, or decorating fabrics to achieve special effects. Just remember that they will be harder to work with and, in most cases, the finished project will need to be dry-cleaned.

Even more important, choose fabrics that you love and wish to live with. Work in colors that are pleasing to you and that will fit into the decor of your home. Be sure to use fabrics with patterns that are appropriate for the overall design of the project and that the scale of the fabric is appropriate for the size of the pieces to be cut

**FABRIC   DIAGRAM 1**

CROSSWISE GRAIN

LENGTHWISE GRAIN

SELVAGE

SELVAGE

BIAS

**MARKING AND CUTTING   DIAGRAM 2**

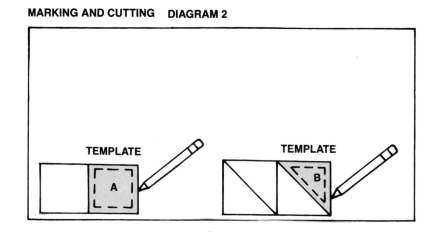

TEMPLATE

TEMPLATE

A

B

from it. Choose the main fabric for the project and then coordinate the other fabrics around it.

Always wash and dry your fabrics before beginning to cut or sew. This preliminary washing not only pre-shrinks the fabric but removes excess dyes and sizing, thus making it easier to work with. Press the fabric until it is smooth.

The *selvage* of any given fabric is the woven finished edge along each side of the fabric. The *grain* is the lengthwise and crosswise threads of a woven fabric. The *lengthwise grain* runs parallel to the selvages. The *crosswise grain* runs perpendicular to the selvage and has more stretch to it. The *bias* is the diagonal of the fabric at a 45-degree angle to the grain; it stretches easily (see Diagram 1). Place the arrows that appear on the patchwork templates parallel to the lengthwise or crosswise grain of the fabric. Do not include the selvage edge in patchwork or appliqué pieces or in any other pattern pieces.

## ENLARGING PATTERNS

When a pattern or design for a project is too large to fit on the pages of this book, it is shown reduced on a grid.

Use a piece of tracing or wrapping paper large enough to accommodate the final design, piecing two sheets of paper together if necessary. With a pencil and ruler, draw a grid on the paper, spacing the lines ½″ apart, 1″ apart, or whatever measurement is indicated on the pattern. Be sure to draw the right number of squares for a given project. Copy the pattern, square by square, first marking dots on your grid where the pattern lines intersect corresponding lines on the reduced grid in the book. Then sketch in the lines between the dots. Use a ruler to draw straight lines. Include any other pattern markings.

Instead of drawing a grid, you can use a large sheet of printed blue graph (quadrille) paper. This can be purchased in pads and comes in several sizes. Some sewing supply stores carry special grid paper marked with 1-inch squares for enlarging patterns.

If you are planning to enlarge several patterns using grids of the same scale, it saves time to make a master grid on heavy paper. Tape a sheet of tracing or tissue paper over the grid and draw the pattern as you would on the grid itself. When the pattern is complete, remove the paper from the grid and save the grid for future use.

Patterns on grids can also be photostated or photocopied to the scale given on the pattern. Photostats are usually somewhat expensive. Photocopiers that both enlarge and reduce are now inexpensive to use, and a large design can sometimes be enlarged in sections for a rea-sonable fee. Check your local photocopy shop or printer.

## TEMPLATES

Templates are full-size plastic or cardboard pieces that are used to trace the pattern pieces onto the fabric. For most of the patchwork patterns in this book, the solid outer line is the cutting line, and the long, broken inner lines usually ¼″ from the cutting line indicate the seam-line. Shorter broken lines within the pattern piece indicate quilting lines and are usually marked as such. To make a plastic template, place the clear or translucent plastic sheet over the pattern in this book. Then, using a sharp pencil, trace the cutting and sewing lines accurately.

To make a cardboard template, trace the cutting and sewing lines of the pattern onto tracing paper, and using carbon paper, transfer the lines to the cardboard. Cut out both plastic and cardboard templates carefully and accurately with paper scissors or a craft knife.

For hand-piecing, make template same as above. After you cut out the pieces, mark the stitching line with a ruler and pen or pencil. Or make your template by tracing only the broken sewing line and cutting out the template along this line; add seam allowance when you cut out your fabric pieces later.

## MARKING AND CUTTING

A wide variety of pencils and markers are available for tracing templates onto your fabric. I recommend a soft or a regular lead pencil for light fabrics, and a white-colored pencil or dressmaker's chalk pencil for marking dark fabrics. Test all pens and pencils on a scrap of each fabric before marking your project.

Place your template on the wrong side of the fabric and trace around the shape accurately. If your pattern requires more than one piece of that shape, reposition the template on the fabric and trace that shape again (see Diagram 2). Most patchwork templates include a ¼″ seam allowance; most appliqué patterns do not include a seam allowance. If your templates do not include a seam allowance, be sure to leave at least ½″ between pieces when you trace around them. Then cut out carefully, simultaneously adding a seam allowance beyond the drawn line on all edges. Add ¼″ to patchwork pieces and ⅛″ to ¼″ to hand-appliqué pieces. Machine-appliqué pieces do not need a seam allowance. For triangles and other shapes, fit the shapes together to save fabric. Again, accuracy is the key. Cut out carefully along the marked lines.

Sometimes you will have to cut shapes for which you will not have templates, as is the case with border strips, sashing strips, background squares for appliqué, and the like. In that case, measure and draw the shape with a pencil and ruler; then cut out accurately with scissors. Sometimes, even if you try to sew patchwork pieces together accurately, your finished block may be a slight bit smaller or larger than the actual block size. Therefore, if you cut pillow border and sashing pieces before stitching patchwork blocks, I recommend adding an extra inch to sashing strips and pillow borders. Add 2″ to 4″ to wall hangings and quilt borders, the exact measurement depending on their length and the number of blocks the project requires. Stitch these pieces in place, then trim the ends even with the pillow or quilt center.

Rotary cutters make cutting strips and simple shapes quick and easy. Fold your fabric in half, matching selvages, and place it on the cutting board. Line up the heavy plastic ruler so one long edge is perpendicular to the fold; cut along the right edge (see Diagram 3). Reverse right and left if you are left-handed. Then turn the fabric around and place the ruler on it so the marking for the desired width of strip is even with the cut edge of the fabric. Cut along the right side of the ruler (Diagram 4). You can cut the strip into squares, rectangles, and triangles as desired (Diagram 5).

**DIAGRAM 3**

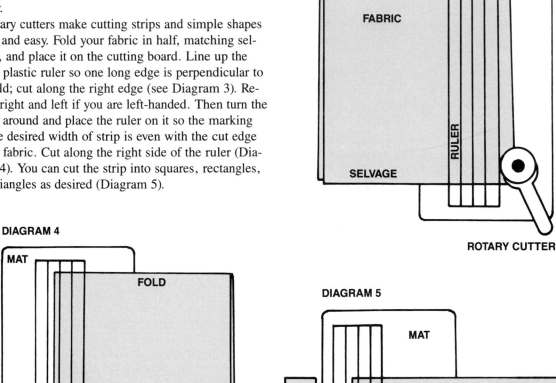

**DIAGRAM 4**

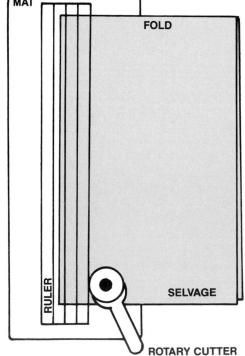

**DIAGRAM 5**

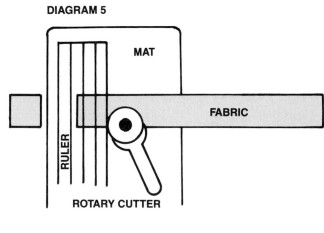

## PATCHWORK BASICS

### Machine-Piecing

Use a clean, oiled machine in good working order. Set the stitch length for 8 to 10 stitches per inch (2.5 on European machines). Thread your machine and bobbin with a good cotton or cotton-covered thread that matches your fabrics. Pin the pieces together with right sides in. Using a ¼" seam allowance, stitch the pieces together, backstitching at the beginning and end (see Diagram 6). Or set the stitch length to 12 to 15 stitches per inch (2 on a European machine) to eliminate the backstitching.

### Hand-Piecing

Place seamlines together, right sides in; place a pin at the beginning and end of seam. Pin remaining length of seam. Thread a needle with a 14" to 18" length of thread, and knot one end. Make a row of running stitches along the drawn line (see Diagram 7). When the stitching is complete, knot the thread by making several tiny stitches in the same place; trim thread.

### Pressing

Pressing your patchwork as you work keeps your blocks smooth and allows you to match seams easily and accurately. To strengthen the seams, always press them to one side. Do not press them open. Use an up-and-down motion when pressing to avoid stretching the fabric out of shape. Press the seam allowance toward the darker fabric to avoid creating a shadow on the right side of the block.

### Quick-Piecing Triangles

This technique will save you a lot of time when sewing triangles together in pairs to make a square. Accurately measure the cut size of your triangles by measuring the length of the shorter sides. These should be ⅞" larger than the finished size (see Diagram 8).

Determine the number of pairs of triangles you need and divide by 2. Draw that number of squares on one of the fabrics. Draw a line to divide the squares in half diagonally (Diagram 9).

Cut out fabric ½" larger than squares, and cut a piece of the other fabric the same size. Pin fabrics together, right sides in, along diagonal lines. Using 12 to 15 stitches per inch, stitch ¼" on each side of diagonal line.

**QUICK-PIECING TRIANGLES**  **DIAGRAM 8**

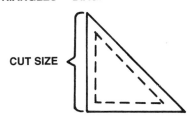

CUT SIZE

**DIAGRAM 9**

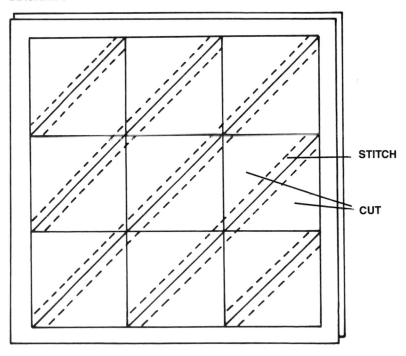

STITCH

CUT

**MACHINE-PIECING**
**DIAGRAM 6**

BACKSTITCH

**HAND-PIECING**
**DIAGRAM 7**

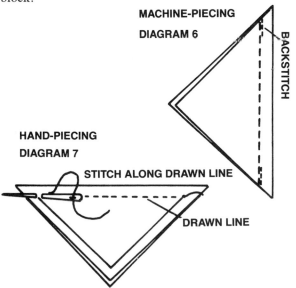

STITCH ALONG DRAWN LINE

DRAWN LINE

**DIAGRAM 10**

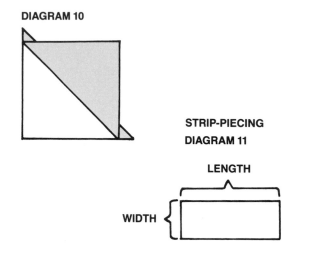

**STRIP-PIECING**
**DIAGRAM 11**

**DIAGRAM 12**                    STITCH

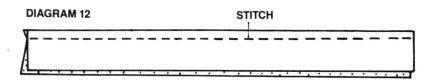

**DIAGRAM 13**

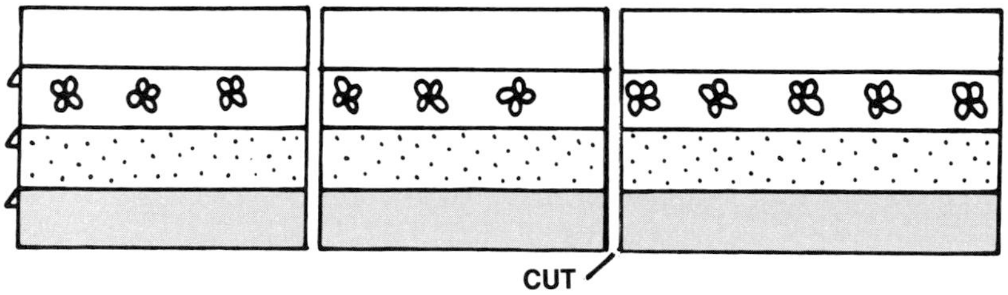

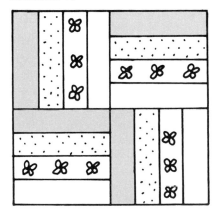

CUT

Cut the triangles apart along diagonal lines between the stitching. Remove extra stitching at points. Open out triangles to form the square and press the seam allowance toward the darker fabric (Diagram 10).

*Strip-Piecing*

This technique will save you a lot of time when piecing blocks that are made up of a series of strips.

Measure the finished width of the strip needed and add ¼″ seam allowance to each side. Then measure the length of the block and add ¼″ seam allowance to each end (see Diagram 11). Multiply that number by the number of blocks you need to determine the length of strip you will cut.

Cut strips of each fabric required, following your measurements. When you need many blocks, cut the strips across the entire width of your fabric.

Arrange the strips in the required sequence. With right sides in, sew them together using 12 to 15 stitches per inch (2 on European machines) and ¼″ seam allowance (see Diagram 12). Press the seam to one side, then join the next strip in the same manner.

When all the strips have been joined and pressed, place the fabric right side up on your cutting surface. Use either a rotary cutter and plastic ruler to measure the length of the blocks, or measure them with a regular ruler and pencil and cut along the lines with scissors (Diagram 13). Then arrange the blocks as they appear in the design and stitch them together using ¼″ seams (Diagram 14).

**DIAGRAM 14**

**DIAGRAM 15**

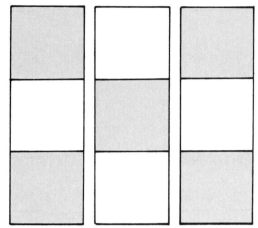

**DIAGRAM 16** STITCH

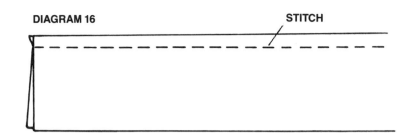

**DIAGRAM 17**

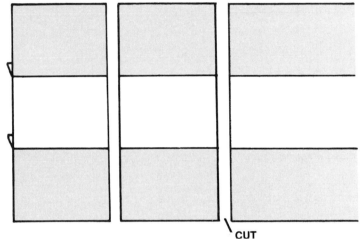

CUT

*Quick-Piecing Squares*

For blocks made up of square or rectangular pieces, such as the nine-patch block, divide the block into three rows of smaller blocks (see Diagram 15). Cut your strips the width of each block plus seam allowance. Stitch them together, and press as described on page 17 (see Diagram 16).

Then cut the strips to the required length plus seam allowance (see Diagram 17). Make strips for each row of blocks. With right sides in and seams matched, stitch the rows together (see Diagram 18).

## APPLIQUÉ BASICS

Appliqué designs are made by cutting out shapes of fabric and stitching them to a background fabric.

*Hand-Appliqué*

For hand-appliqué, I recommend using the freezer paper method. Because it does not require much basting, it saves time and is less tedious than any other method. Freezer paper, which is polyethylene-coated, can be purchased in rolls at the grocery store. Other medium-weight paper can be used if you baste it to the appliqué fabric instead of pressing it in place with an iron.

Trace the actual-size pattern from this book or from your enlarged pattern onto tracing paper. Then trace the design to your background fabric as indicated in the instructions for the individual project.

There are two ways to use freezer paper to make the patterns for the appliqué pieces. The first technique is the easiest to use, but requires some basting. Turn your

**DIAGRAM 18**

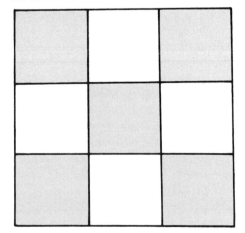

tracing paper pattern to the wrong side. Trace the shapes for each appliqué piece in reverse onto the dull side of a piece of freezer paper. Cut out each piece accurately.

Move to your ironing board and set your iron to a medium temperature setting, turning off the steam. Place the shapes shiny side down on the wrong side of fabric and press them with the iron to fuse them in place (see Diagram 19).

**HAND-APPLIQUÉ**
**DIAGRAM 19**

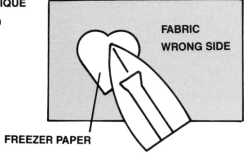

FABRIC
WRONG SIDE

FREEZER PAPER

Then cut out the pieces, adding a scant ¼″ around all edges. For very small pieces you may wish to add only ⅛″ around the edges (see Diagram 20).

**DIAGRAM 20**

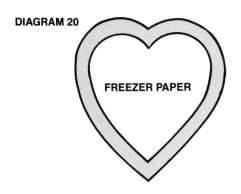

FREEZER PAPER

Clip to any inner corners on the shape. Fold the fabric over the edge of the paper and baste it in place, using running stitches. Sew through both fabric and paper (see Diagram 21). If another shape will cover one side of the appliqué piece, do not turn under that edge.

**DIAGRAM 21**

SEW

The second technique works best for large shapes with smoothly curved edges, such as large petals or simple leaves. It is a little bit harder to do because it requires skillful ironing. First, trace the shapes from the right side of your pattern onto the dull side of the freezer paper. Cut them out carefully.

Pin the shapes dull side down onto the wrong side of the appliqué fabric. Cut out the fabric pieces adding ⅛″ to ¼″ around the entire shape. Clip to any inner corners on the shape (see Diagram 22).

**DIAGRAM 22**

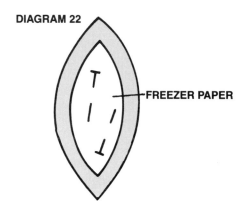

FREEZER PAPER

Set your iron temperature to medium and turn off the steam. Using the tip of your iron, press the fabric edge over the paper. It will stick to the shiny side (Diagram 23). Again, if another shape will cover one side of the appliqué piece, do not turn under that edge.

**DIAGRAM 23**

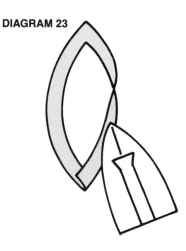

Place the shapes that should be positioned directly on top of the background fabric or those which have other shapes on top of them on the background first. Begin with the stems, if there are any. Pin them in place or baste them to the background fabric. Then slipstitch or whipstitch along the edges of the appliqué to hold each shape in place.

To slipstitch, bring needle up through background fabric along the edge of the appliqué shape. Take a small (⅛″ or less) stitch in the appliqué fabric, beginning directly above this point. Then take a small stitch in the background fabric beginning just below the end of the first stitch. The thread should not show on the right side of the fabric (see Diagram 24).

**SLIPSTITCH    DIAGRAM 24**

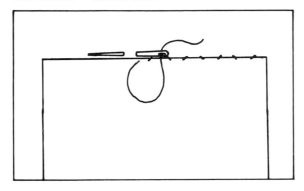

To whipstitch, bring the needle up through the background fabric and the appliqué, about ¹⁄₁₆″–⅛″ from the edge of the appliqué. Insert the needle at the outer edge of the appliqué and make a small diagonal stitch. The stitch that shows on top should be perpendicular to the edge of the appliqué (see Diagram 25). Use this stitch at the inner corners of shapes to secure the edges of the appliqué where there is no fabric (or very little fabric) to be turned under.

Continue stitching the shapes in place until the design is complete. Then turn the design to the wrong side. Cut

**WHIPSTITCH    DIAGRAM 25**

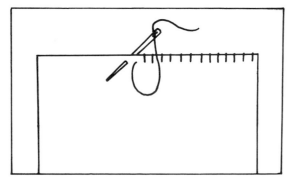

out the background fabric to within ¼″ of the stitching line, and remove the paper patterns. On very small shapes, simply cut a tiny slit and pull the paper through it (Diagram 26).

Turn the block right side up and press lightly.

**DIAGRAM 26**

*Stems*

Stems can be made easily from bias strips of fabrics. Cut a ⅞″-wide bias strip to match the length of the stem you need. Or, if you are making several stems, cut one long bias strip and divide it into sections later. Fold the bias strip in half lengthwise with right sides together, and stitch ⅛″ to ¼″ from the fold (see Diagram 27).

**STEMS    DIAGRAM 27**

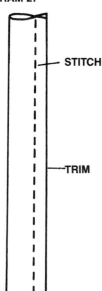

STITCH

TRIM

21

Insert a bias bar or a knitting needle into the tube so the seamline is centered on one flat side (see Diagram 28). Steam press both sides of the tube and remove the bias bar. If you are using a knitting needle, remove the needle and re-press the tube so it is flat.

*Machine-Appliqué*

Machine-appliqué is very easy if you use fusible webbing to hold your pieces in place while you stitch. Paper-backed fusible webbing is easiest to use. Trace the full-size pattern from this book onto tracing papers, then trace the design to your background fabric as indicated in the instructions. Turn your tracing paper pattern to the wrong side and trace each shape onto the page backing, leaving room between each shape. Add ⅛" to ¼" to all edges that will be overlapped by other shapes. Group together all the shapes that are to be cut from one fabric.

Cut out the patterns roughly. On your ironing board, place the patterns paper side up on the wrong side of the appliqué fabric. Following the manufacturer's directions, fuse them in place (see Diagram 29). Cut out shapes along the drawn lines.

Fusible webbing adds stiffness to the appliqué pieces which can partially be removed with one washing. Repeated washings may eliminate even more of the stiffness. If you wish to eliminate the stiffness without having to wash your project, cut out the center of each shape about ⅛" to ³⁄₁₆" from the outline. Then leave a little extra room around the shape when you rough-cut the shape (see Diagram 30). Carefully flatten the fusible webbing on the wrong side of the fabric and fuse it in place (Diagram 31). Cut out shapes along the drawn lines, the same as before.

Make stems following instructions under *hand-appliqué* (page 21) and slipstitch them in place by hand. Or outline the stem portion of the design with a row of wide zigzag stitches.

When all appliqué pieces are fused in place, zigzag-stitch around the shapes, using matching thread. Use the widest zigzag stitches for large shapes and narrower stitches for smaller shapes.

Draw or transfer additional lines in the design for machine- or hand-embroidery. For machine-embroidery, zigzag-stitch along lines, using the color thread indicated. Hand-embroider small details and features using the color and embroidery stitch suggested in the instructions.

**DIAGRAM 28**

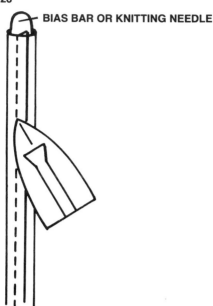

BIAS BAR OR KNITTING NEEDLE

**MACHINE-APPLIQUÉ    DIAGRAM 29**

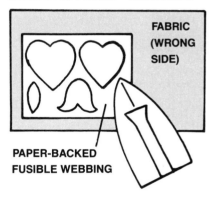

FABRIC (WRONG SIDE)

PAPER-BACKED FUSIBLE WEBBING

**DIAGRAM 30**

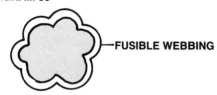

FUSIBLE WEBBING

**DIAGRAM 31**

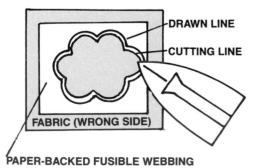

DRAWN LINE

CUTTING LINE

FABRIC (WRONG SIDE)

PAPER-BACKED FUSIBLE WEBBING

## QUILTING BASICS

### Marking

When the top layer of your quilted project is complete, it is time to mark the quilting lines on your project. I recommend using a sharp lead or silver pencil to mark quilting lines on a light-colored fabric. These lines will usually rub off while you are quilting, or you can rub them out with a kneaded eraser when you are finished. For dark-colored fabrics, use a dressmaker's chalk-marking pencil or a white-colored pencil. When you are finished, excess colored pencil can be removed with a damp cloth. Special blue-marking pens work well on light-colored fabrics or prints. They disappear when washed or simply moistened with water. Test all pens and pencils on a scrap of each fabric before marking your project.

Outline quilting is done along the lines of the patchwork or appliqué design. Quilting that is done right on the seam (called "stitching in the ditch") does not have to be marked. Quilting stitches also can be made ⅛" or ¼" from the seam. You can sew these stitches by eye or mark them with a ruler and pencil or pen.

Background quilting usually fills large fabric shapes with straight or diagonal lines or with a grid. Use a ruler and pencil or pen to mark these lines.

Designs which are given in the patterns can also be quilted in portions of your quilt top. Enlarge the patterns or trace them from the book. On light-colored fabrics you can sometimes place your fabric over the quilting design and trace it through the fabric. To make templates for simply shaped quilting designs, follow the directions for templates (page 15) and trace around them on the fabric.

For more complex quilting designs, cut a piece of bridal tulle slightly larger than your quilting motif and center it over your pattern. Using a permanent marking pen, trace the design onto the tulle. Place the tulle over the section of the quilt you wish to mark, and trace over the lines to mark them on the fabric.

To mark borders, first mark the corners as indicated on the pattern and then measure the repeat of the quilting design. Measure across the border, marking the repeat intervals with pins. If the repeat does not fit evenly, stretch or shrink each repeat a little to fit it evenly between the corners.

### Backing

The piece of fabric, either a solid or print fabric, used on the underside of a quilt or pillow top is called backing fabric. Some fabrics, such as muslin, are available in the wide widths required for backing large projects. Bed sheets made from 100 percent cotton also can be used. Otherwise, backing is made from two or more lengths of fabric seamed together. Quilt backing should be made 2" larger than the quilt top on all sides. For smaller projects, such as pillows or place mats, ½" to 1" larger is fine.

Prewash and dry backing fabrics exactly the same as fabrics for the top. Remove the selvages. Cut one length of fabric for the center panel. Then cut two side panels that are each half the width needed to complete the desired width of backing. Stitch the side lengths of fabric together, using a ¼" seam allowance; then press the seam open.

### Assembling The Quilt

Place the backing on your working surface wrong side up, and smooth it out. If you are working on a full-size quilt or large wall hanging, you will probably be working on the floor. Hold the backing in place on a carpet with T-pins or quilting pins. Hold the backing in place on a wood or tile floor with masking tape. Smaller pieces for other projects do not need to be pinned or taped. Place batting on top of the backing. Then place the quilt top on the batting and smooth it out. Pin the layers together with quilting pins or straight pins.

Using a large needle and a contrasting light-colored thread, baste the layers together as shown in Diagram 32. Baste from the center to the midpoint of each side. Baste from the center to the four corners. If you are planning to place this quilt in a frame, you can stop here and baste around the edges. If you are using a quilting hoop, continue to make rows of stitching from near the center out to the edges. Then baste the layer together around the edges.

For small projects, baste along the vertical and horizontal centers and diagonally across the project; then baste the edges together (see Diagram 33), page 24.

### Hand-Quilting

Place your quilt in a frame or hoop. Thread a needle with an 18" to 24" length of quilting thread and make a small knot on one end. You can use a short needle called a "between," which makes taking small, even stitches easy, or you can use whatever needle you feel comfortable with. Use sewing thread if you cannot find quilting thread to match the color of your fabric. For small decorative sections you can also use two strands of embroidery floss.

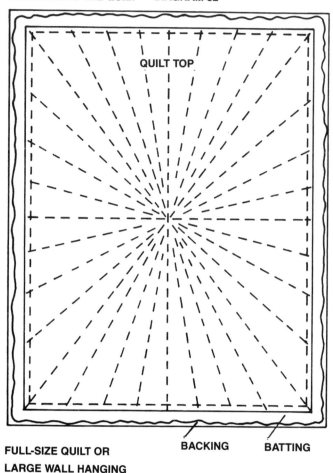

**FULL-SIZE QUILT OR**
**LARGE WALL HANGING**

DIAGRAM 33

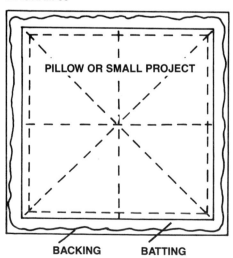

Always begin to quilt in the center of your project and work out toward the edges. Insert the needle into the layers of the quilt about one needle length away from your starting point and bring it up at the starting point (see Diagram 34). Pull the knot through the fabric to bury it in the layers of the quilt (Diagram 35). Then make a row of small, even running stitches along the quilting line as shown in Diagram 36.

When you are one stitch from the end of the quilting line, or have about 3″ of thread left, make a knot in your thread and pull it with the tip of your needle to ⅛″ above the quilt top (Diagram 37). Repeat to make another knot on top of this one. Insert the needle into the quilt to make the last stitch and bring it up a needle's length away. Pull to bury the knot in the layers of the quilt and trim the end of the thread.

*Machine-Quilting*

Place batting between backing and quilt top, as described above. Pin the layers together with 1″-long safety pins placed every 4″. Try to avoid placing the pins along the lines where you plan to stitch. Instead of using pins, you can baste the layers together.

There are two types of machine-quilting: straight-line quilting and free-motion quilting. Straight-line quilting, which is used for quilting along the seam, or "in the ditch," uses the feed dogs of the machine to move the fabric through the machine. Use your regular presser foot or an even feed presser foot, which helps move the top layer of fabric through the machine. Insert the needle into the fabric at the end of the seam or line that you wish to quilt, and backstitch to knot the thread. Then set your stitch length to 8 stitches per inch (or 3 on a European machine). When stitching in the ditch, use your hands to spread the seam slightly to help the needle stitch in the ditch. Push any excess fullness of fabric into the presser foot, but do not pull on the seam to ease in the fabric. Backstitch at the end of the line of stitching.

Free-motion quilting, which is used to create curved quilting designs, uses a darning foot to hold the fabric as the needle passes through it. You move the fabric through the machine instead of the feed dogs. Drop the feed dogs when using this technique. Again, insert the needle into fabric at the beginning point on your design, and make a few small stitches backward and forward to knot the threads. Place your hands on the fabric on either side of the needle, and move fabric so the needle stitches along the lines of the design as a pen would. Keep your machine stitching at a slow, constant speed,

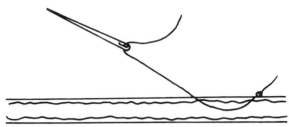

**DIAGRAM 35**

**DIAGRAM 36**

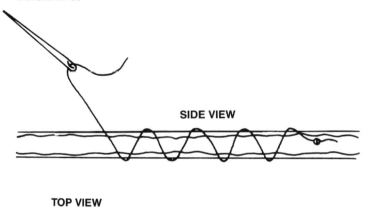

**SIDE VIEW**

**TOP VIEW**

**PULL**

**DIAGRAM 37**

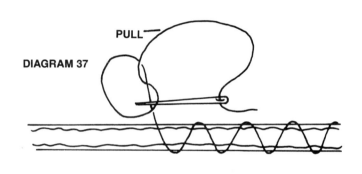

and keep your stitches even. Do not turn the block. Knot the end of the thread by stitching back and forth with small stitches at the end of the design. This technique requires practice to master, so try some sample pieces first.

Stippling (see Diagram 38) is a type of free-motion quilting that is used to fill in backgrounds. Find a starting point and meander back and forth at random, creating a curved line. The stitching looks very organic and develops from the starting point. Do not cross over any lines to make loops or figure eights. Keep the lines evenly spaced—about ⅛″ to ¼″ apart.

**MACHINE-QUILTING** **DIAGRAM 38**

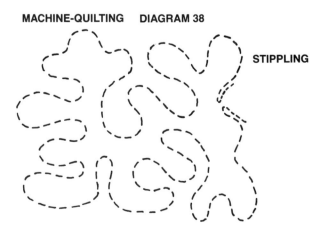

**STIPPLING**

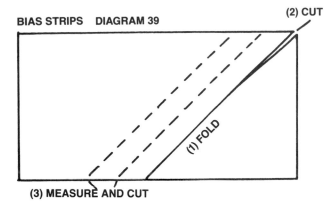

BIAS STRIPS    DIAGRAM 39

(2) CUT

(1) FOLD

(3) MEASURE AND CUT

### Bias Strips

Bias strips—strips of cloth cut diagonally across the grain of the fabric—are cut at a 45-degree angle to the grain. First, spread out a large piece of fabric on a flat surface with the grain of the fabric running up and down. Fold the fabric diagonally from one corner so that the corner touches the long edge opposite. Press along the fold. Open the fabric out and cut along the fold. Parallel to the diagonal, measure and mark strips to the width indicated in the project instructions (see Diagram 39).

To the required length of each strip, add a ¼″ seam allowance on each end. Place right sides together, with two strips at right angles to each other, and stitch across the seamlines (Diagram 40) to make longer strips. Press seams open.

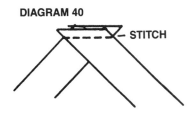

DIAGRAM 40

STITCH

### Binding

Binding for square or rectangular projects can be made from strips of fabric cut on the straight grain. Straight grain bindings are easier for the beginner to work with. With fabric folded in half, measure and cut strips perpendicular to the fold. Trim off selvages and sew ends of strips together, using ¼″ seams. Press seams open.

Bias bindings are used on projects with curved edges, but they can also be used on square or rectangular-shaped pieces. Cut bias strips and piece them together as shown in Diagram 40.

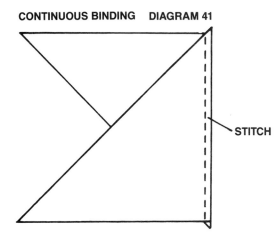

CONTINUOUS BINDING    DIAGRAM 41

STITCH

### Continuous Binding

To make a continuous bias binding for large quilts, cut a large square of fabric in half diagonally. Placing right sides together, sew the two triangles together with a ¼″ seam (see Diagram 41). Press seam open.

Working parallel to the bias edge, draw bias strips of the required width (see Diagram 42). Cut along the first line for 5″. With the right side in, fold the fabric into a tube, matching the drawn lines along the stitching line

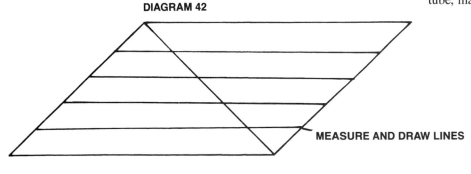

DIAGRAM 42

MEASURE AND DRAW LINES

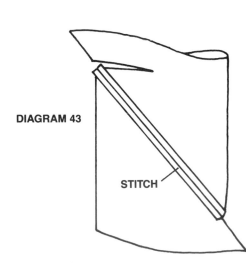

DIAGRAM 43

STITCH

**TO ATTACH BINDING**

**DIAGRAM 44**          **DIAGRAM 45**

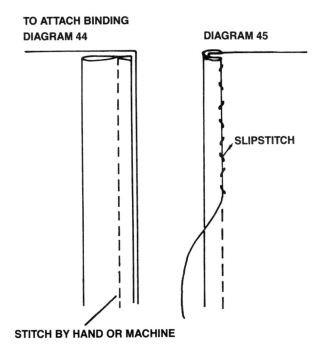

SLIPSTITCH

**STITCH BY HAND OR MACHINE**

**MITERING CORNERS**

**DIAGRAM 46**

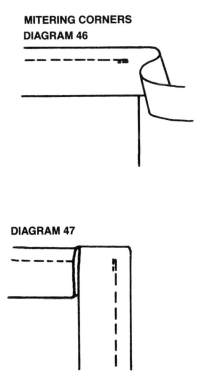

**DIAGRAM 47**

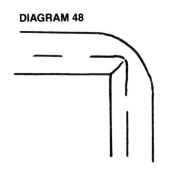

**DIAGRAM 48**

**DIAGRAM 49**

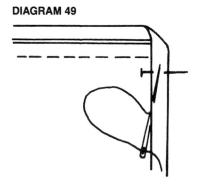

¼″ from the edge (Diagram 43). Pin, then stitch together. Press the seam open. Cut along the drawn lines to form one long bias strip.

*To Attach Binding*

Fold the binding strip in half lengthwise and press. Place the binding on the right side of your quilted project, with raw edges even. Stitch along the seamline as indicated in the instructions (Diagram 44), noting that the binding will be double thickness.

Fold the binding to the backing side of the quilted project so that the fold is along the stitching line. Then slipstitch the folded edge in place (Diagram 45).

*Mitering Corners*

To miter a corner, place right sides together and pin and stitch the binding strip to one edge of the project, backstitching at the corner (see Diagram 46). Fold the binding strip diagonally to bring it around the corner, and pin it in place. Pin the binding along the adjacent edge. Beginning at the backstitched corner, stitch to the next corner (Diagram 47). Continue stitching around all edges.

Fold binding over the edge of fabric, making a diagonal fold at the corner (Diagram 48). On the backing side, pin the folded edge of the binding in place along the stitching line. Form a miter at the corners on the wrong side by making a diagonal fold, tucking the excess fabric in the opposite direction to the fold on the right side. Slipstitch the binding to the wrong side, and then slipstitch the edges of the miter together (Diagram 49).

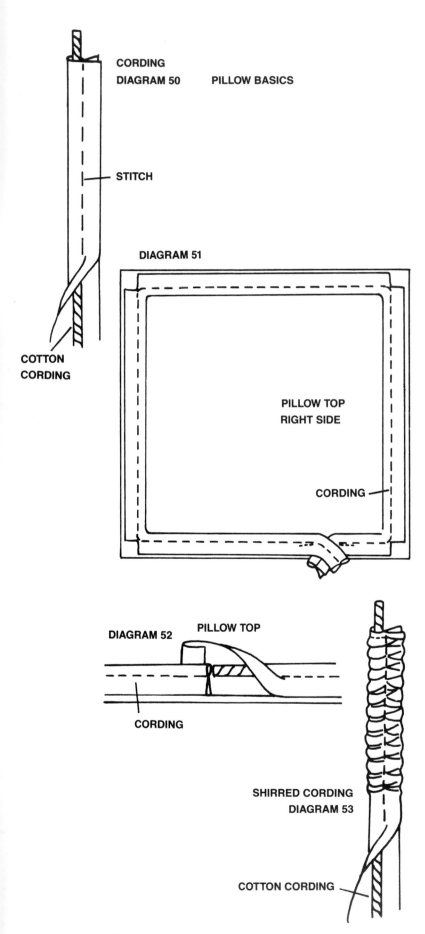

CORDING

**DIAGRAM 50**   PILLOW BASICS

STITCH

COTTON
CORDING

**DIAGRAM 51**

PILLOW TOP
RIGHT SIDE

CORDING

**DIAGRAM 52**   PILLOW TOP

CORDING

SHIRRED CORDING
**DIAGRAM 53**

COTTON CORDING

## PILLOW BASICS

*Cording*

To make bias strips for your project, follow the directions on page 26. Piece strips together, if necessary, to make a strip of the desired length. Then fold the strip in half lengthwise, wrong sides together, inserting cotton cording inside along the fold. Using a zipper foot, machine-baste along the edge of the cording (Diagram 50).

With right sides together, pin the cording to the pillow top along the seamline, beginning 1″ from end of cording. Clip seam allowance of cording to turn corners. Stop stitching 2″ from the point where the cording will meet (Diagram 51). Remove basting from end of cording. Trim ends of cotton cording so they just meet. Turn under end of fabric on cording and slip under beginning of cording (see Diagram 52). Baste ends in place.

*Shirred Cording*

To make bias strips, follow the instructions on page 26. Piece bias strips to make a length two to three times as long as the finished length of piping. Fold the strip in half lengthwise, wrong sides together, inserting cotton cording inside along the fold. Using a zipper foot, machine-baste across end of piping and then along the edge of cording for about 6″. Raise presser foot and pull cording, pushing fabric back behind the needle to shirr or gather it to the desired fullness (Diagram 53). Continue stitching 6″ and shirring until all cording is covered. Stitch across end.

*Ruffles*

Cut strips to make ruffles, following the instructions in your pattern. Right sides in, piece the strips together at ends, using ¼″ seam allowance. Fold in half lengthwise and press.

Set your stitch length to 6 stitches per inch (4 on European machines). Make rows of gathering stitches ¼″ and ½″ from the raw edges (see Diagram 54). Fold ruffles into quarters, with ends of thread at one fold. Mark the folds with pins. Pull the thread at the ends and at the pins to gather ruffle (Diagram 55).

Place ruffle around pillow top, evenly adjusting gathers, and pin in place. Arrange a little more fullness at corners. Secure the thread ends around pins in a figure eight (Diagram 56). Baste ruffle to pillow top just inside the inner row of gathering stitches.

28

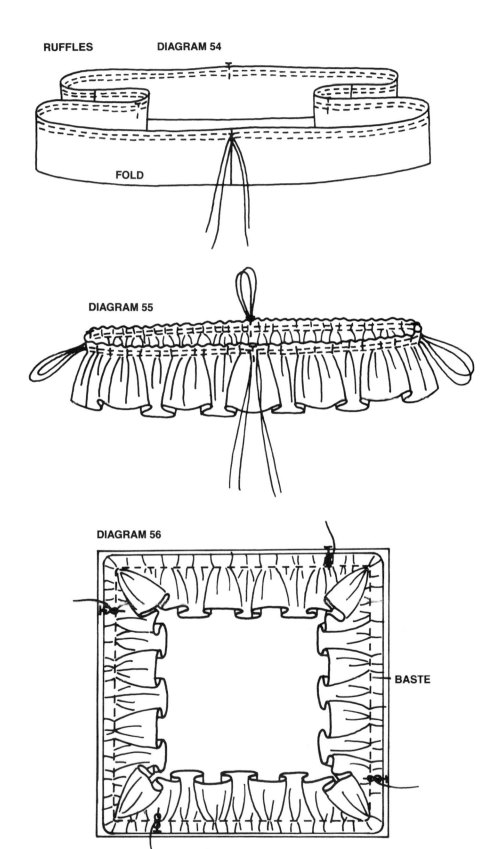

**RUFFLES**     **DIAGRAM 54**

**FOLD**

**DIAGRAM 55**

**DIAGRAM 56**

**BASTE**

**SIMPLE PILLOW BACK
DIAGRAM 57**

**DIAGRAM 58**

## PILLOW BACKS

*Simple Pillow Back*

The easiest way to make a pillow back is to cut it from a single piece of fabric. The drawback to using this method is that, once the pillow form or stuffing is inserted, it cannot be easily removed for laundering.

Cut the fabric for the pillow back following the measurements given in the project instructions. Pin the pillow front to the back, right sides together. If you are using a pillow form, stitch around three sides only (see Diagram 57). If you are using stuffing, stitch around four sides, leaving an opening along one edge (Diagram 58). Turn pillow cover right side out and insert pillow form or stuffing. Turn seam allowance of opening to inside and slipstitch the edges of the opening together. Lap other piece over other side of zipper so fold is along stitching line on first half. Pin, then stitch, fabric to zipper about ½″ from fold (Diagram 60). Stitch each end of zipper as shown in Diagram 61.

## PILLOW BACK WITH ZIPPER

Purchase a zipper 2″ shorter than the finished length of the pillow. Divide the pillow back into two halves. For a 10″ square, the two halves should be 5″ by 10″, plus ¾″ for a zipper seam to make a cut size of 5¾″ by 10″. Cut two pillow backs this size. Press under ¾″ on one long edge of each piece. Lap edge of one piece centered over edge of zipper with edge of fold along coils of zipper. Pin, then stitch, along the edge (see Diagram 59).

**PILLOW BACK WITH ZIPPER
DIAGRAM 59**

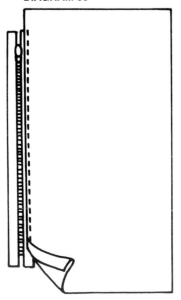

30

## LAPPED PILLOW BACK

Divide the pillow back into two halves. For a 10″ square, the two halves would measure 5″ by 10″. Add 4″ to the width of each half for the 4″ overlap and cut each half to measure 9″ by 10″. Turn 1″ twice along the 10″ center edge and stitch hem in place (see Diagram 62). Overlap hemmed edges so that the width of the back measures 10″. Baste backs together ½″ from edges (Diagram 63).

**DIAGRAM 60   PILLOW BACK WITH ZIPPER**

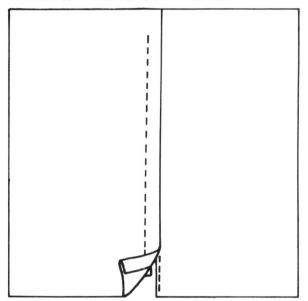

**DIAGRAM 61**

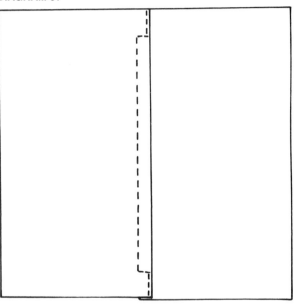

**LAPPED PILLOW BACK**
**DIAGRAM 62**

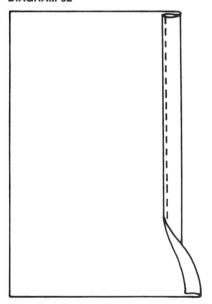

**DIAGRAM 63**

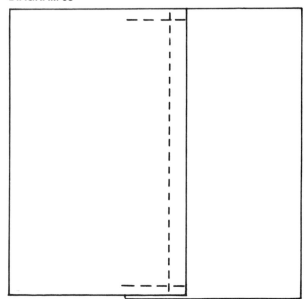

31

## EMBROIDERY BASICS

Place fabric in an embroidery hoop and work stitches, using the color of floss and the number of strands that are indicated in your pattern.

### Backstitch

**BACK STITCH**

Bring the needle up from the underside of the fabric and insert it one stitch length to the right. Bring it out again one stitch length ahead, to the left. Repeat, keeping stitch lengths even.

### Blanket Stitch

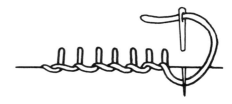

**BLANKET STITCH**

Working from left to right, bring the needle out on the line or close to the hemmed edge. Take an upright stitch to the right with the needle pointed down, keeping thread under the needle and coming out on line or edge.

### Bullion Stitch

**BULLION STITCH**

Bring the needle out to the right side of fabric. Take a short stitch to the right, and bring needle out at the same place as before. Wrap thread around needle several times to fill the length of the stitch taken. Hold the wrapped thread while pulling thread through so stitch will be smooth and even.

### Buttonhole Stitch

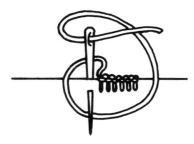

**BUTTONHOLE STITCH**

Place needle through background fabric at edge of the appliqué piece, bringing the needle out about ⅛″ from edge of appliqué. Wrap thread around needle. Pull needle through fabric, so a little knot is formed at the appliqué's edge. Repeat, keeping stitches even and close together.

### Chain Stitch

Bring the thread out on the line. Insert the needle where the thread came out and take a short stitch on the line, keeping the thread under the needle. This makes a loop that lies flat against the fabric. Insert the needle where thread came out and take another stitch. Tack last stitch with a short straight stitch.

**CHAIN STITCH**

### Feather Stitch

Make a blanket stitch to the right of a straight vertical line. With the thread under the needle, make a blanket stitch to the left. Repeat along line.

**FEATHER STITCH**

### French Knot

Hold the needle in your right hand. With your left hand, wrap the thread around the needle two or more times, depending on the size of knot you want to make. Be sure the needle points away from the fabric when you wrap the thread around it, and wrap close to where the thread comes through the fabric. Insert the needle close to where it came out. Holding knot in place, pull the needle to the wrong side to secure the knot.

**FRENCH KNOT**

### Herringbone Stitch

Work from left to right along two parallel lines (imaginary or lightly drawn). Bring needle out on line at upper left. Take a short backstitch on lower line a little to the right, keeping the thread under the needle. Take a short backstitch on upper line a little to the right with the thread under the needle. Continue keeping stitches even.

**HERRINGBONE STITCH**

## Lazy Daisy Stitch

Bring thread from wrong side of fabric at the inner edge of the petal. Insert needle where the thread came out, making a short loop. Bring needle through the fabric at outer edge of the petal, and catch the loop under the needle's point. Insert needle again just outside the loop to hold it in place.

**LAZY DAISY STITCH**

## Running Stitch

Insert the needle into the fabric and bring it out again, making stitches of even length. This is also a basic sewing and quilting stitch. Make stitches long for basting and short for sewing seams by hand.

**RUNNING STITCH**

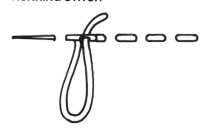

## Satin Stitch

Work parallel, straight stitches close together across the entire area of the shape to be filled.

**SATIN STITCH**

## Stem Stitch

Working from left to right along the line of a design, make stitches of equal length, keeping the thread on the same side of the needle. Bring the needle out each time at the point where the last stitch went in.

**STEM STITCH**

## Straight Stitch

This stitch is used for occasional single stitches scattered in a design. Each stitch is separated from the next one.

**STRAIGHT STITCH**

Shown here, *Rocky Road to Kansas Pillow*, incorporating the blanket, chain, feather, herringbone, and satin stitch.

# APPALACHIAN WILDFLOWER QUILT

The colorful flowers found in the fields and woodlands of the Appalachian Mountain states, here form a delicate hand-appliquéd wreath in the center of a single bed-sized quilt. Clockwise (starting from top right) the quilt features day lilies, bluebells, Jack-in-the-Pulpit, Dutchman's breeches, violets, wild geraniums, trillium, wild hyacinths, Johnny-jump-ups, columbine, lady slipper, spring beauties and mayflowers that are hand-appliquéd and embellished with embroidery. The quilt has a pastel sashing around the top and a double border of print and off-white fabrics. The entire quilt is generously quilted with leaf, vine, and graceful swag motifs. This quilt, an ambitious project for the advanced appliqué needleworker, is a very special heirloom to make for a wedding or anniversary present.

*Size: 67" by 94½" before quilting*

**MATERIALS**

45"-wide cotton fabrics
    4¾ yards off-white
    2⅜ yards peach print
    2½ yards yellow print
    ⅛ yard each bright green, green, and light green
    ⅛ yard or scraps bright pink, pink, rose, maroon, purple, lavender, light blue, white, yellow, mauve, light peach, and peach
    5⅝ yards backing fabric
    72" by 99" piece low-loft quilt batting
    Sewing thread to match solid color fabrics
    Embroidery floss: 1 skein each of yellow, lavender, light green, medium green, bright green, orange, rust, violet, brown, and white.
    Off-white quilting thread

**DIRECTIONS**

## Background Fabric

Enlarge each of the four patterns for the appliqué center on pages 38–42 on an 18" by 24" piece of tracing paper. Matching horizontal center lines, tape each half together and trace leaf quilting pattern to right half of wreath. Then tape halves together to make entire wreath.

Cut a 39½" by 81" piece of off-white fabric. By hand, mark lengthwise vertical center with a basting thread. Mark a horizontal line 31¼" from lower edge. Matching lines, center fabric over wreath pattern and lightly trace outlines of appliqué wildflowers and leaf-quilting motif to fabric. Leave basting lines in place as guide for marking quilting lines later.

## Appliqué Flowers

Following directions under *Hand-Appliqué* (page 19), make patterns for shapes of each flower and leaf, and cut from each fabric as indicated below. Make lengths of stems ¼" and ⅛" wide from each of three green fabrics, following directions on page 21. Transfer embroidery marking to appliquéd flowers. (See *Embroidery Basics*, page 32, for embroidery stitches.) Begin at upper center with the mayflowers and appliqué each flower along left side of wreath. Then appliqué day lily and other flowers along right side of wreath. End at lower center with trillium.

## Mayflowers (also known as Trailing Arbutus)

Cut leaves with dots from bright green, and remaining leaves from green. Cut small petals with dots from white. Cut remaining petals, whole flowers, and bud from pink. Cut calyxes from light green.

Place a piece of ¼"-wide green stem along line between spring beauties and trailing arbutus and slipstitch edges in place. Slipstitch ⅛"-wide light green stem in place. Slipstitch leaves in place. Appliqué pink petals and bud, then small white petals. Slipstitch calyxes to lower edge of bud and flower. Slipstitch whole flowers in place. Using 3 strands of floss, embroider centers with light green satin stitch and stamens with yellow satin stitch.

## Spring Beauties (also known as Hepatica)

Make a pattern for each petal individually. Cut bud and 10 petals from white. Cut leaves and calyx pieces from green. Place pieces of ⅛"-wide green stem along upper stem lines and a ¼" piece along stem line below flowers. Slipstitch stems in place. Appliqué leaves, petals, bud, and calyx pieces in place.

Draw 7 lines on each petal as indicated on pattern. Embroider lines, using backstitch with 2 strands of violet floss. Using 3 strands of floss, embroider stamens with a white straight stitch along seamlines of petals, with a violet bullion stitch across top to make a T-shape. Using 2 strands of yellow floss, make ¼"-long straight stitches around center between violet lines.

## Lady Slipper

Cut large leaf from green. Cut shapes with dots from light green. Cut pouch-shaped pieces from pink, long narrow petals from rose, and center of pouch from

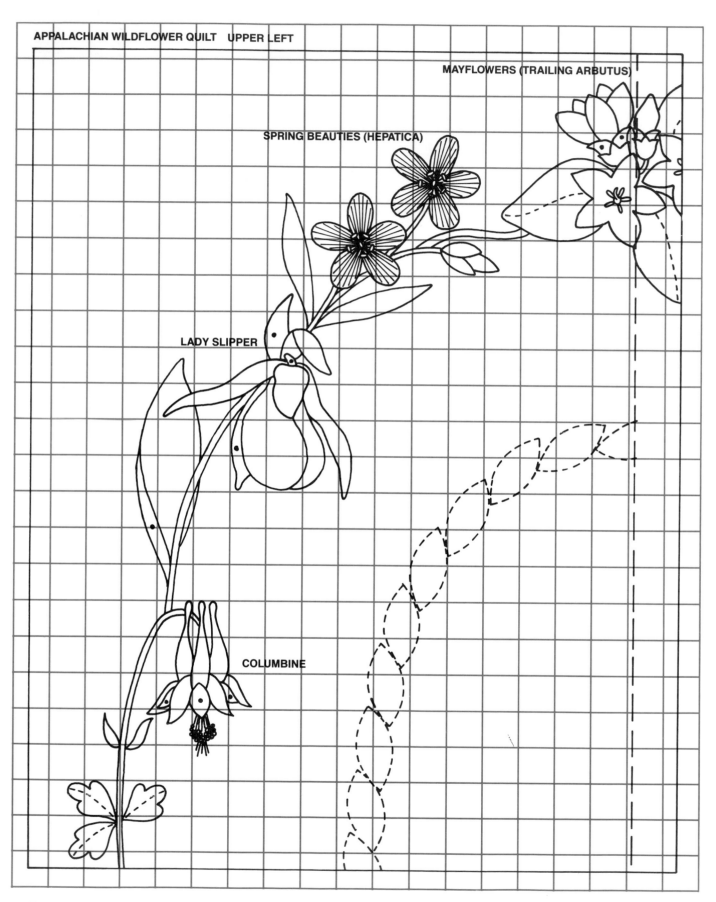

APPALACHIAN WILDFLOWER QUILT   UPPER LEFT

MAYFLOWERS (TRAILING ARBUTUS)

SPRING BEAUTIES (HEPATICA)

LADY SLIPPER

COLUMBINE

EACH SQUARE = 1"

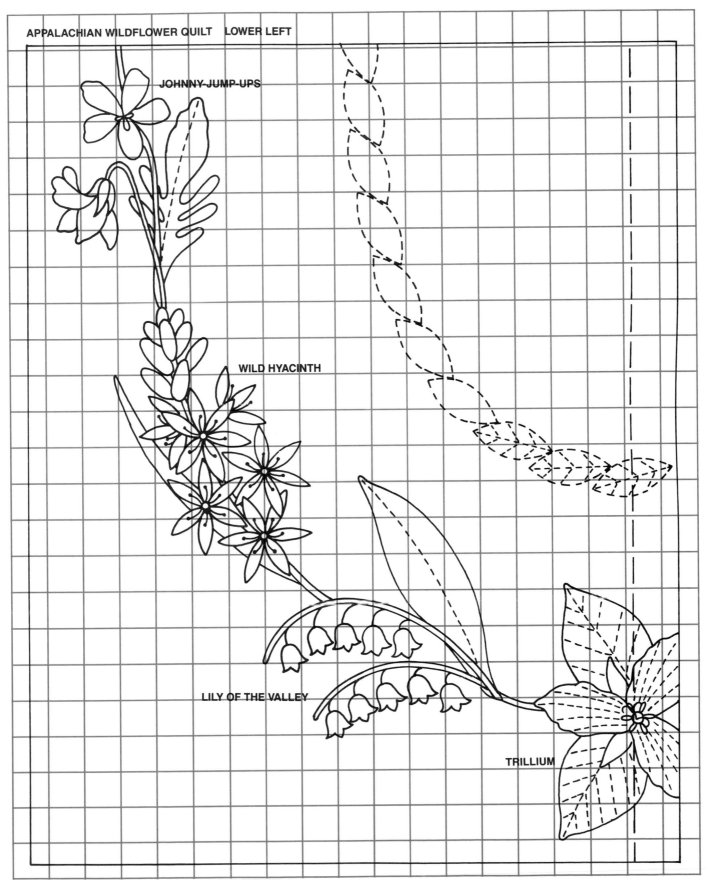

APPALACHIAN WILDFLOWER QUILT    LOWER LEFT

JOHNNY-JUMP-UPS

WILD HYACINTH

LILY OF THE VALLEY

TRILLIUM

39

**EACH SQUARE = 1″**

bright pink. Slipstitch large green leaf in place. Slip-stitch ¼"-wide light green stem along stem line. Slip-stitch light green leaves in place. Slipstitch pouch-shaped pieces to flower. Appliqué rose petals in place. Stitch stem, then center to flower.

## Columbine

Cut 3 large leaves from bright green and 2 small ones from light green. Cut petal pieces with dots from yellow and remaining petal shapes from bright pink. Place a piece of ¼"-wide light green stem along stem line and slipstitch it in place. Appliqué leaves to background. Appliqué upper side petals first. Then lower side petals, small yellow petals, lower pink petals, upper center pe-tal and yellow center petal. Using 3 strands of yellow floss, embroider upper stamens with straight stitches and French knots. Embroider lower lines with 3 strands of light green floss.

## Johnny-Jump-Ups

Cut leaf from bright green, calyx pieces from green, and petals from yellow.

Appliqué leaf in place. Place ⅛"-wide green stems along stem lines and slipstitch them along edges. Slip-stitch petals in place on flowers. For calyx, slipstitch side pieces, then center, in place. Embroider center of flower with lazy daisy stitches, using 3 strands of or-ange floss.

## Wild Hyacinth

Cut leaf from green and petals and buds from lavender. Slipstitch ¼"-wide green stem along lower section of stem line. Place ⅛"-wide pieces of green stem along other portions of line and slipstitch them in place. Slip-stitch leaf in place. Beginning at top, slipstitch buds in place. Slipstitch petals of side flowers, then petals of lower 4 flowers, in place. Embroider centers with satin stitch, using 3 strands of yellow floss. Embroider sta-mens with stem stitch, using 2 strands of lavender floss. Make French knots at the ends of stamens with 3 strands of yellow floss.

## Lily of the Valley

Cut leaf from green and flowers from white. Place a piece of ¼"-wide green stem along stem line between lily of the valley and trillium, and slipstitch edges in place. Appliqué leaf to background. Slipstitch ⅛"-wide light green stems along main stem lines. Appliqué flowers in place. Using 3 strands of light green embroi-dery floss, embroider curved lines between main stem and flowers with stem stitch.

## Day Lily

Cut leaf, flower calyx, and bud calyx from green. Cut petals and buds with dots from light peach and remain-ing petals and buds from peach. Slipstitch buds to back-ground. Appliqué bud calyx over lower edge of buds. Place ¼"-wide green stem along line and slipstitch edges in place. Appliqué leaf to position. Slipstitch ca-lyx, light peach petals, and then peach petals to flower. Using 3 strands of rust embroidery floss, work stamens with stem stitch. Using 3 strands of brown thread, make a French knot at the end of each stamen.

## Bluebells

Cut calyxes with dots from light green. Cut remaining calyxes and leaves from bright green. Cut bluebells from light blue and buds from mauve. Slipstitch pieces of ⅛"-wide stem along stem lines. Appliqué leaves in place. Appliqué bluebells and buds to background. Then slipstitch calyxes in place. Using 3 strands of yel-low, embroider tips of stamens with Lazy Daisy stitch.

## Jack-in-the-Pulpit

Cut stem from mauve. Cut leaves and upper section from green, inner section from rose, and stamen from maroon. Cut remaining sections from light green. Slip-stitch stem and leaves to position on background. Slip-stitch lower left sections in place. Appliqué inside section, then stamen, in place. Slipstitch lower right, then upper right, section in place. Appliqué upper sec-tion in place. Embroider lines on inner section with backstitches, using 3 strands of light green floss. Em-broider lines on remaining sections with backstitches, using 3 strands of white floss.

## Dutchman's Breeches

Cut leaf from light green, petals from white, and centers from yellow. Slipstitch leaf in place on background. Place pieces of ¼"-wide green stem along stem lines and slipstitch edges in place. Appliqué petals, then cen-ters, in place. Using 3 strands of light green embroidery floss, embroider narrow stem lines from stem to flowers with stem stitch.

## Violets

Cut leaves from green, petals from purple, and calyx from light green. Place ¼"-wide stem along lower sec-tions of stemline and ⅛"-wide stem along all other stem lines. Slipstitch in place along edges. Slipstitch leaves and calyx in place. Then appliqué petals on flowers. Using 2 strands of white floss, embroider center of flowers with straight stitches.

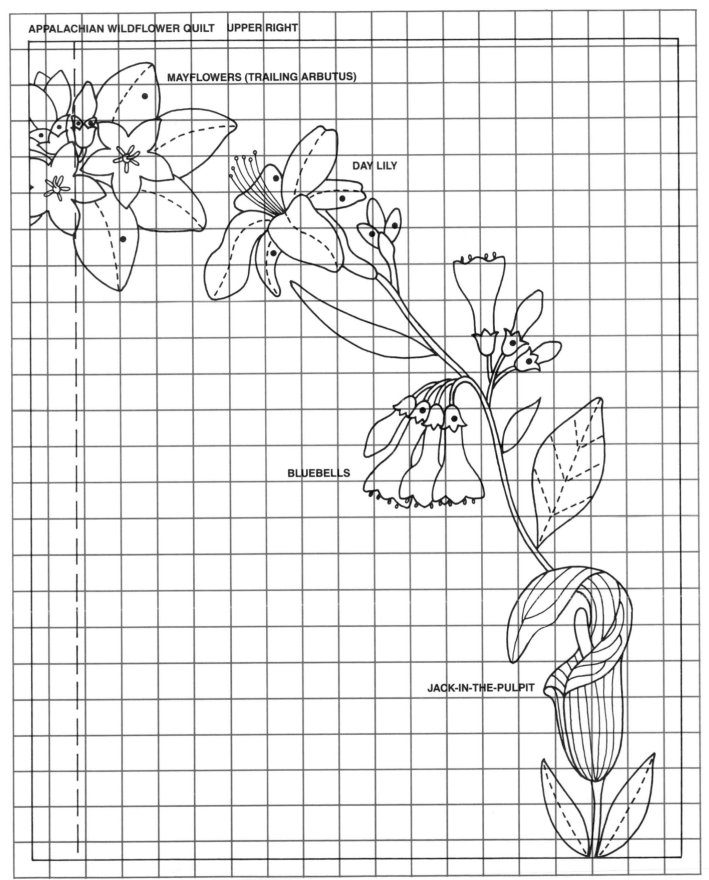

APPALACHIAN WILDFLOWER QUILT    UPPER RIGHT

MAYFLOWERS (TRAILING ARBUTUS)

DAY LILY

BLUEBELLS

JACK-IN-THE-PULPIT

**EACH SQUARE = 1″**

41

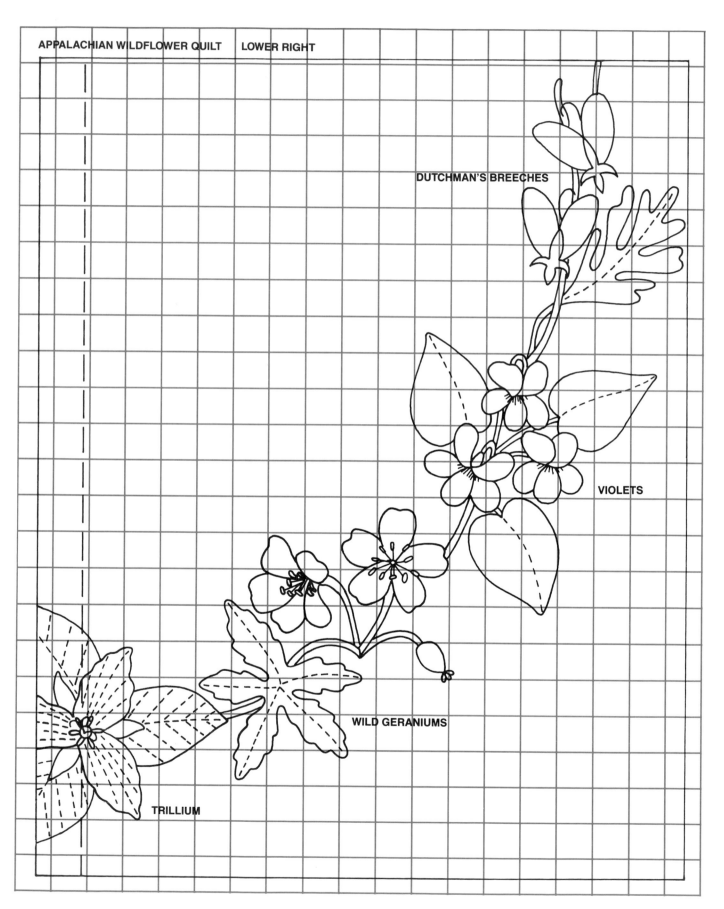

APPALACHIAN WILDFLOWER QUILT     LOWER RIGHT

DUTCHMAN'S BREECHES

VIOLETS

WILD GERANIUMS

TRILLIUM

EACH SQUARE = 1″

## Wild Geraniums

Cut leaf from green, bud from light green, and petals from bright pink. Place ¼″-wide stem along lower stem section and pieces of ⅛″-wide stem along remaining stem lines. Slipstitch in place along edges. Appliqué leaf and bud in place. Slipstitch petals to flowers. Using 3 strands of light green floss, embroider tip of bud with Lazy Daisy stitches. Using 3 strands of white floss, embroider stamens with backstitch. Make a bullion stitch at the end of each stamen.

## Trillium

Cut large leaves from bright green, small leaves from light green, petals from white, and center from yellow. Slipstitch large leaves to background. Slipstitch small leaves to large leaves. Appliqué petals on flower. Using 3 strands of floss, embroider straight stamens with yellow satin stitch and curved with white stem stitch.

## Quilt Top

From peach print, cut 2 inner side borders 3″ by 81″ and lower inner border 3″ by 44½″. From off-white, cut 2 side borders 5½″ by 83½″ and lower border 5″ by 54½″. From yellow print, cut 2 side borders 7″ by 88¼″ and lower border 7″ by 67½″.

For inner border, stitch sides to appliquéd top with ¼″ seams. Stitch lower inner border to lower edge of top. Stitch off-white side borders to inner border. Stitch off-white lower border to lower inner border. Stitch yellow print border to off-white side border. Then stitch yellow print lower border to lower edge.

### Quilting

Enlarge leaf and swag quilting motifs from pattern below and make templates following directions on page 15. Make another row of horizontal basting 31″ above line marking center of wreath. Using a ruler and pencil, lightly mark a diagonal line from center of quilt to lower corners. Lightly mark a diagonal line from center to corner of upper basting line. In each quarter of top, draw diagonal lines 1¼″ apart that meet at vertical and horizontal center lines. In center of wreath inside leaves, extend diagonal lines to make a grid.

Beginning 7″ from top edge, trace leaf motif across upper section of quilt top. Extend diagonal lines into upper section. Following directions on page 23, mark leaf motif on off-white border and swag motif on yellow print border. Mark quilting lines on inner borders ½″ from edges. Mark quilting lines on leaves and petals as indicated by broken lines on appliqué patterns.

Make backing following directions on page 23. Place batting between backing and top with right sides out. Pin, then baste, the layers together. Quilt ⅛″ from edges of appliqué flowers, stems, and leaves with off-white thread. Quilt along lines on leaves and flowers with 2 strands of matching embroidery floss. Quilt remaining marked lines with off-white thread.

### Binding

Following directions on page 26, make a 3½″-wide continuous binding from a 35½″ square of peach print. Using ½″ seam allowance, stitch binding to edges of quilt.

**BORDER QUILTING**

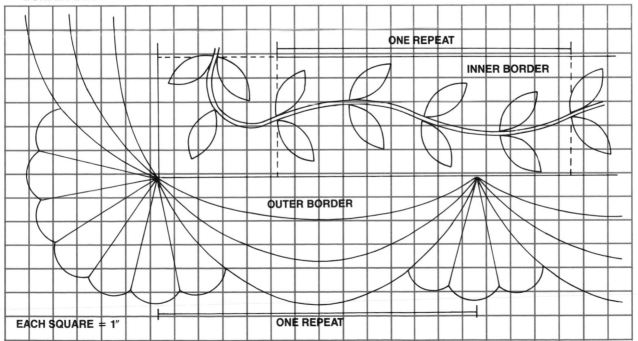

ONE REPEAT

INNER BORDER

OUTER BORDER

EACH SQUARE = 1″

ONE REPEAT

# PRAIRIE FLOWER TABLE RUNNER

The prairie beckoned men and women of the 19th century to open and free land. In the tall grasslands of the Plains states, they built cabins and began to farm. The women who traveled west in covered wagons brought their needlework skills with them. In their sparsely furnished homes, they made quilts for warmth and decoration, often using the traditional prairie flower pattern inspired by the wildflowers near their new homes.

*Size: 18″ by 48″*

## MATERIALS

45″-wide cotton fabrics.
   1½ yards muslin for background and backing
   ¾ yard light blue print
   ⅜ yard pink print
   ¼ yard solid pink
   ½ yard small green print
   ¼ yard green floral print
   3″ scrap of pale yellow
   50″ by 20″ piece low-loft quilt batting
   Sewing thread to match fabrics
   Off-white quilting thread

## DIRECTIONS

*Marking and Cutting*

Matching centers, enlarge the placement pattern for the end section (see page 15) to one half of a piece of tracing paper. Fold the tracing paper in half and trace design to make entire pattern. Cut two 18″-square pieces of muslin. Trace placement lines onto muslin, keeping straight edge of section ¼″ from edge of fabric.

Enlarge the placement pattern for the center square on page 47. Cut a 12″ square of muslin. Fold it into quarters and finger-press folds. Open out fabric and trace the placement lines onto each quarter. Following directions in *Appliqué Basics* (page 19) for making templates, make templates from appliqué patterns shown below.

From solid pink, cut 2 large rose petals and 6 tulip center petals (2). From pink print, cut 2 small rose petals and 6 tulip centers (3). From blue print, cut 12 tulip side petals (3). From green floral print, cut 50 leaves. Cut 2 rose centers from yellow. From small green print, make two 21″ stems, two 10″ stems, and two 5″ stems (see directions under *Stems*, page 21). Make all stems ¼″ wide.

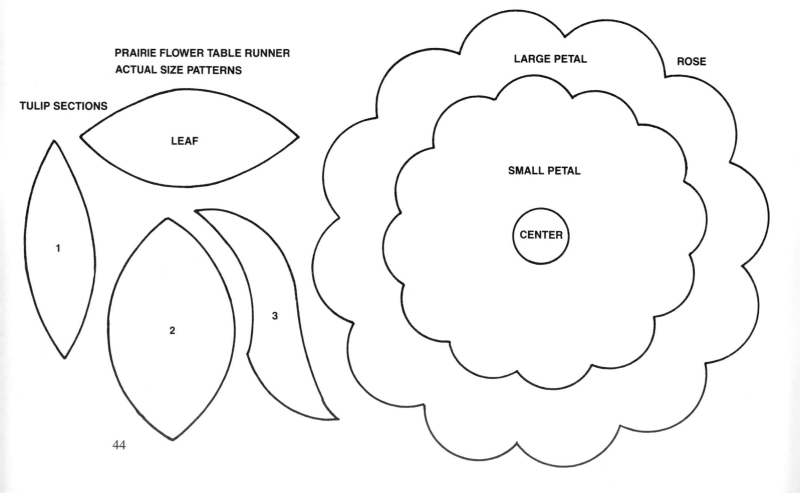

**PRAIRIE FLOWER TABLE RUNNER
ACTUAL SIZE PATTERNS**

**TULIP SECTIONS**

LEAF

1

2

3

**LARGE PETAL**

**ROSE**

**SMALL PETAL**

**CENTER**

PRAIRIE FLOWER TABLE RUNNER    END SECTION

EACH SQUARE = 1″

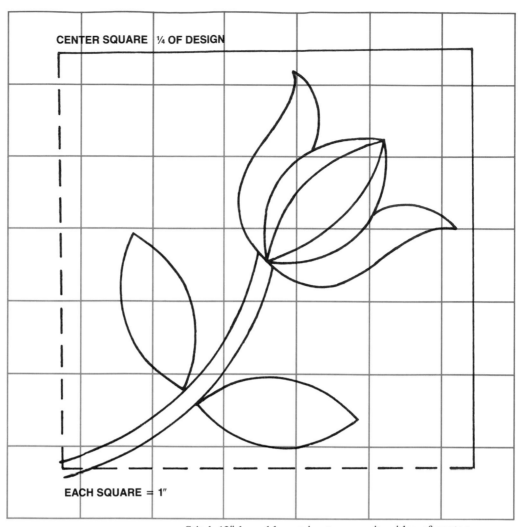

CENTER SQUARE | ¼ OF DESIGN

EACH SQUARE = 1″

## Center Square

Pin 10″ stems to background fabric, trimming ends ¼″ inside lines of tulips. Slipstitch them in place along edges. To make tulips, slipstitch side petals (1) to background, then stitch center petals (2) in place. Slipstitch tulip centers (3) to center petals. Slipstitch leaves in place.

## End Sections

Pin 5″ stems along center stems, trimming ends ¼″ inside lines of flowers. Slipstitch them in place along edges. Pin long stem in place along curved line, and slipstitch it in place. To make tulips, follow directions given above for Center Square.

Pin large rose in place and slipstitch around edges. Then slipstitch small rose in center of large rose. Slipstitch center to small rose. Slipstitch leaves in place. Trim fabric from behind appliqué pieces, and remove paper patterns. Press appliqué sections.

### Assembling Table Runner

From blue fabric, cut 2 strips ⅞″ by 12″ and 2 strips ⅞″ by 13″. From small green print, cut 2 strips ⅞″ by 18″. Draw two 9¾″ squares on wrong side of pink print fabric; divide them in half diagonally to make 4 triangles. Cut out triangles along lines.

Stitch 12″-long blue strips to opposite sides of center square. Press seam allowance toward strips. Stitch 13″-long blue strips to remaining sides of center square. Press seams toward strips. Stitch a triangle to each strip along sides of center square. Center green print strips along opposite sides of center block and stitch in place. Stitch straight edge of end sections to remaining side of green strips.

### Quilting and Finishing

Draw a template for a right triangle with two edges that are 3½″ long. Using template, mark a triangle on pink print triangles 1½″ from finished edges. Cut a 20″ by 50″ piece of muslin for backing. Following directions under *Quilting Basics* (page 23), place batting between backing and table runner top. Pin, then baste, the layers together.

Quilt ⅛″ from edges of appliqué designs. Quilt ⅛″ from outer edge of center square, from straight edge of end sections, and from seamed edges of pink triangles. Quilt along marked lines on triangles. Trim batting and backing even with top, cutting along curved edges of end sections. Following directions under *Binding* (page 26), cut a 23½″ square of blue fabric and make a 3¼″-wide continuous bias binding. Bind edges of table runner, using a ⅜″ seam allowance.

# KENTUCKY LOG CABIN WALL HANGING

 he quilters of the last century looked to their surroundings for inspiration. This simple pattern was formed with interlocking strips of light and dark fabrics sewn to a center square, which often was cut from turkey red fabric. It reminded the early settlers of the log cabins they lived in and made warm and cozy with quilts. The 12″ blocks are arranged as a frame around a center square that features a pieced log cabin. The log cabin design is based on the popular schoolhouse pattern and is decorated with quilted details and surrounded with appliquéd pine trees.

*Size: 48″ square*

## MATERIALS

45″-wide cotton fabrics
   1½ yards brown print
   ⅜ yard rust print
   ⅜ yard gold print
   ¼ yard beige
   ½ yard green
   ⅝ yard light green
   ⅜ yard blue
   ⅝ yard light blue
   ¼ yard red
   ⅛ yard dark brown
   ⅛ yard beige
   Scraps of dark green, medium brown, rust, and light
     blue solids
   3 yards backing fabric
   52″ square traditional-weight quilt batting
   Off-white, red, green, and medium brown sewing
     thread
   Off-white quilting thread

## DIRECTIONS

Following directions for enlarging on page 15, enlarge pattern for Log Cabin Center. Make patterns or templates for sky, side sky, side ground, ground, tree trunk, house front, roof, chimney, house side, walk, roof strip, and side strip. Add ¼″ seam allowance to all edges. Make appliqué pattern for tree, following directions on page 19.

### Cutting

From red, cut sixteen 2½″ squares, a door 1⅞″ by 3½″, and a chimney. From beige print, cut sixteen A strips 1¾″ wide by 2½″ and 16 B strips 1¾″ by 3¾″. From light blue print, cut sky triangle, sky side, reverse sky side pattern and cut another piece. Then cut 12 C strips 1¾″ by 3¾″, 12 D strips 1¾″ by 5″, and 18 Q strips 1¾″ by 4¼″ for center blocks.

From gold print, cut 16 E strips 1¾″ by 5″ and 16 F strips 1¾″ by 6¼″. From blue print, cut 12 G strips 1¾″ by 6¼″ and 12 H strips 1¾″ by 7½″. From rust print, cut 16 I strips 1¾″ by 7½″ and 16 J strips 1¾″ by 8¾″. From light green, cut ground triangle, side ground; then reverse side ground pattern and cut another piece. Cut 12 K strips 1¾″ by 8¾″, 12 L strips 1¾″ by 10″, and 14 Q strips 1¾″ by 4¼″ for center blocks.

From brown print, cut a 28½″ square for binding, cut 16 M strips 1¾″ by 10″, and 16 N strips 1¾″ by 11¼″. From green print, cut 12 O strips 1¾″ by 11¼″ and 12 P strips 1¾″ by 12½″. From blue, cut 2 windows 1⅝″ by 2¼″ and small window 1⅜″ by 1½″. From medium brown, cut walk and 2 tree trunks. From beige, cut roof strip and side strip. Cut 2 trees from dark green. Cut roof from rust. Cut 2 strips 1″ by 44″ from dark brown and 2 strips ¾″ by 44″ from beige for cabin.

## Log Cabin Center

Stitch all seams right sides together, using ¼″ seam allowance unless otherwise indicated. For cabin front, from both dark brown and beige strips, cut nine 4¾″ strips. Alternating colors, stitch 8 strips together. Cut this piece into two 2″-wide pieces and stitch them, beige side up, to each side of door. Stitch 3 more strips to top of door piece. Stitch a beige strip along each side of a brown strip. Cut this piece into two 2¼″-wide pieces; stitch to each side of small window. Stitch window piece to front; stitch remaining strips to top of window piece. Using template, cut out cabin front. Stitch side strip, then roof strip, to right side of cabin front.

For cabin side, from both dark brown and beige strips, cut six 6¾″ strips. Stitch 3 beige and 2 brown strips together, alternating colors. Cut joined pieces into three 1¾″ pieces. Stitch together alternately with side windows. Alternating colors, stitch 2 brown and 1 beige strip to lower edge of window piece. Stitch 2 brown and 2 beige to upper edge of window strip. Stitch to edge of side strip. Stitch roof to cabin.

Stitch side sky to side ground. Stitch side pieces to cabin, clipping seam allowance at inner corner. Turn under curved edges of walk and place walk on ground triangle. Slipstitch edges in place. Stitch ground to lower edge of cabin piece. Turn under upper and side edges of chimney and place it on sky triangle. Slipstitch edges in place. Stitch sky to cabin piece. Place tree trunk, then tree, on sides of cabin and slipstitch edges in place.

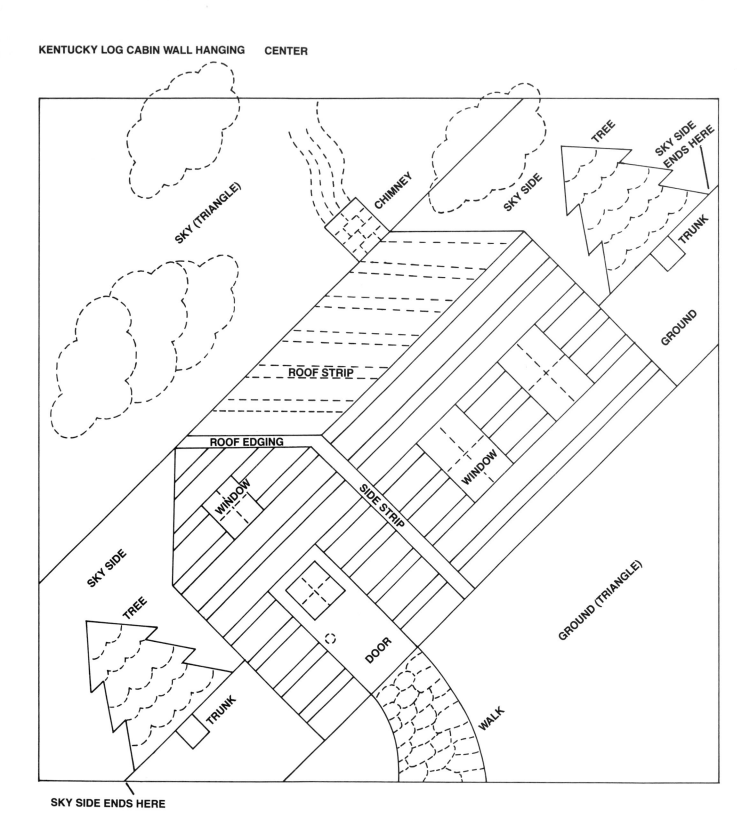

SKY (TRIANGLE)

CHIMNEY

SKY SIDE

TREE

SKY SIDE ENDS HERE

TRUNK

GROUND

ROOF STRIP

ROOF EDGING

WINDOW

WINDOW

SIDE STRIP

SKY SIDE

GROUND (TRIANGLE)

TREE

DOOR

TRUNK

WALK

SKY SIDE ENDS HERE

## Center Blocks

Following piecing diagram for Center Block, make 2 blocks using light blue Q strips only and 2 blocks using green Q strips only. Stitch A and B strips to center square. Stitch 2 Q strips to remaining sides. Stitch E and F strips to edges with A and B strips, then join 2 more Q strips. Stitch I and J strips to edges and 2 more Q strips. Join M and N strips.

Join light blue Q strips to remaining sides of 2 blocks with light blue Q strips. Place center blocks around Log Cabin Center. Stitch remaining light blue Q strips to top edges at sides. Stitch remaining green Q strips to lower edges at center. Trim edges of Q strips diagonally as shown in diagram. Stitch center blocks to edges of log cabin block, beginning and ending stitching ¼" from ends of seam. Stitch center blocks together at corners of log cabin block.

## Log Cabin Blocks

Following piecing diagram for Log Cabin Block, stitch strips A and B to center square. Stitch strips C and D to remaining edges of center. Continue joining strips E-P in alphabetical order. Arrange log cabin blocks around center so edges with brown strips meet. Stitch 4 blocks together for side strips. Stitch remaining blocks together along center seam. Stitch pairs of blocks to upper and lower edges of center. Stitch side strips to center, matching seams.

### Quilting and Finishing

Following directions under *Marking* (page 23), mark quilting lines indicated on patterns for Log Cabin Center. Mark vertical rows of quilting on ground ¾" apart. Draw lines diagonally across center to form an X. If you desire, mark quilting lines on log cabin blocks and center blocks ¼" in from outer edge of each row of strips.

Cut two 26½" by 52" pieces of backing fabric. Stitch them together along one long edge. Press seam open. Following directions in *Quilting Basics* (page 23), place batting between backing and wall hanging, right sides out. Pin, then baste, the layers together. Quilt by hand along lines mentioned in first paragraph above. Trim batting and backing ⅛" larger than top.

Following directions under *Binding* (page 26), make a 3¼"-wide bias binding from square of brown print. Stitch binding to edges of top ¼" from edge of top, ⅜" from edge of batting and backing.

**CENTER BLOCKS    PIECING DIAGRAM**

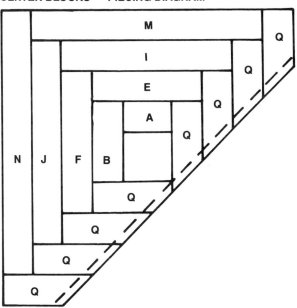

**LOG CABIN BLOCKS    PIECING DIAGRAM**

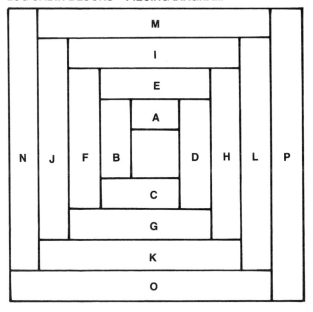

# STARS OF THE STATES QUILT

**P**atchwork stars can be made from diamonds, triangles, and squares. The possibilities are endless. Patchwork stars have been designed for all 50 states. In the Stars of the States Quilt, the Lemoyne Star of Louisiana and stars honoring the states of North Carolina, Virginia, Tennessee, Missouri, and Kansas surround a medallion featuring the popular Ohio star in the center of a feathered California star.

The quilt is pieced in dark red, unbleached muslin and blue print fabrics. Hand quilting accentuates the lines of the star motifs, and wreathes and grids fill in the blocks and borders. Sharpen your piecing skills by accurately constructing these challenging blocks to create a quilt which fits a double bed. The quilt makes a splendid heirloom gift or a warm and welcoming addition to your own home.

*Size: 80" square before quilting*

## MATERIALS

45"-wide cotton fabrics
  4 yards unbleached muslin
  2 yards dark blue print
  2 yards dark red print
  1 yard red, off-white, and blue print
  ¼ yard red on off-white print
  ¼ yard blue on off-white print
  4⅞ yards backing fabric (or 2⅜ yards 90"-wide muslin)
  84" square quilt batting
  Dark blue, dark red, and off-white sewing thread
  Off-white quilting thread

## DIRECTIONS

Following directions under *Templates* (page 15), make templates for all pattern pieces on pages 58–62. For Kansas Star, make template for inner border F, using inner border pattern from Kansas Sunflower Pillow (page 136. Trace each template to wrong side of fabric and cut out each piece. See directions under *Quick-Piecing-Triangles* (page 17). Stitch all seams right sides together, using ¼" seam allowance.

## Center Medallion

### Cutting

From muslin, cut four 7½" corner squares. Draw two 7" squares and divide them in half diagonally. Cut out these 4 triangles for sides. Cut 8 triangles (A), 4 large

squares (B), and 72 small triangles (D). Or cut 16 small triangles and quick-piece the rest. Cut one large square (B) from dark red print. Cut 8 triangles (A) from red on off-white print. From dark blue print, cut 4 small squares (C), 8 large triangles (E), 8 diamonds (F), and 60 small triangles (D). Or cut 4 small triangles and quick-piece the rest.

## Ohio Star

Matching edges, stitch each off-white triangle (A) to a print triangle (A) along one short edge. Stitch pairs of triangles together to form a square unit, matching seams in center and alternating colors. Stitch off-white edge of a square unit to each of two opposite sides of dark red center square (B) for center strip. Stitch each small square (C) to the corner of muslin squares (B) for corner squares. Following piecing diagram, stitch a corner square to each print edge of each square unit to make two side strips. Stitch side strips to center strip, matching seams.

## California Star

Stitch each of 56 off-white small triangles (D) to a dark blue small triangle (D) to form a square unit, or quick-piece triangles. Following piecing diagram, make 4 feathered star units, as follows: Stitch 3 square units together with dark blue triangle in lower left corner. Stitch an off-white small triangle to lower edge of this piece. Stitch to right-hand side (r) of large triangle E (#1).

Stitch 4 pairs of triangles together with dark blue triangles in lower right corner. Stitch an off-white triangle to lower edge. Then stitch a diamond (F) to long side of this off-white triangle. Stitch strip to long edge of large triangle E and end of first strip to form star point.

Stitch side triangle to long edge of star point. Stitch 3 square units together with dark blue triangle in lower right corner. Stitch an off-white small triangle to lower edge of this piece, stitch to left-hand side (l) of large triangle E (#2).

Stitch 4 square units together with dark blue triangles in lower left corner. Stitch an off-white triangle to lower edge. Stitch a diamond (F) to side of off-white triangle. Then stitch a dark blue triangle to other end of this piece. Stitch to long edge of a large triangle (#2). Stitch this star point to side triangle to make feathered star unit.

Stitch feathered star unit to two opposite sides of Ohio Star for center strip. Stitch corner squares to end of remaining feathered star units for side strips. Stitch side strips to sides of center strip.

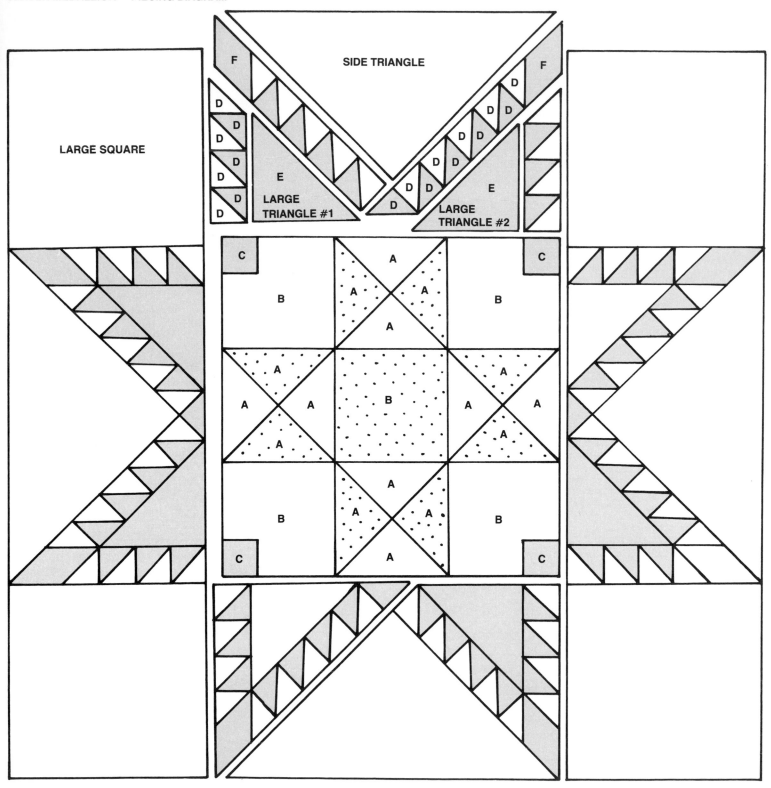

## Missouri Star

### Cutting

From muslin, cut 16 C pieces, 8 D pieces, and 8 G pieces. Cut 8 B pieces from dark red print. Cut 16 A pieces from dark blue print. From red on off-white print, cut 8 E pieces and 16 F pieces.

*Make two Missouri Star blocks as follows:*

Following piecing diagrams, stitch A pieces together in pairs along one edge. Stitch two C pieces to each long edge of B. Stitch D pieces to E pieces. Clip seam allowance at inner corner of B and stitch CB to DE. Stitch A units to CE units. Stitch two F pieces to adjacent sides of G pieces to form a triangle. Stitch piece A-E together in pairs along edge of A pieces. Stitch a triangle (FG) between them. Stitch half stars together along edges of A pieces. Stitch a triangle (FG) to each side.

## Kansas Star

### Cutting

Trace inner border to muslin four times, matching ends to make a square shape with a circle inside it. Cut out shape as one piece, then cut out center. Then cut 16 B pieces. Reverse pattern and cut out 16 more B pieces.

Cut 16 A pieces from blue on off-white print. Cut 8 C pieces from red print. Cut 8 D pieces from dark blue print. Following directions under *Appliqué Basics* (page 19), make a pattern for center and cut from red on off-white print.

*Make each of two Kansas Star blocks as follows:*

Stitch B pieces to outer edges of A pieces. Stitch an AB unit to each edge of C pieces. Stitch an AC unit to each side of four D pieces. Stitch a remaining D unit to each edge of one half-star unit. Stitch remaining edges of D pieces to edges of another half star. Slipstitch appliqué center to center of star. Matching curves, stitch inner border around star. Clip inner edge of inner border if necessary.

## North Carolina Star

### Cutting

From muslin, cut 8 D pieces. Reverse pattern and cut out 8 more. Cut two A pieces from dark blue print. Cut 8 pieces each C and E from red on off-white print. Cut 8 F pieces from blue on off-white print.

*Make each of two North Carolina Stars as follows:*

Following piecing diagram, stitch B pieces to E pieces. Stitch a C piece to each side of two BE units along B edge. Stitch remaining BE units to opposite side of A. Stitch BCE units to opposite sides of ABE unit to form star. Set in D pieces between E and C pieces around star. Stitch F pieces to each corner.

## Iowa Star

### Cutting

From dark blue print, cut 16 A pieces and 4 B pieces. Cut 48 A pieces from red on off-white print. From muslin, cut 16 C pieces.

*Make four Iowa Star blocks as follows:*

Following piecing diagram, stitch 2 red on off-white print A triangles to sides of each blue print A triangles. Then stitch another red on off-white print triangle to end of blue triangles to form a large triangle. Stitch a large triangle to each side of B pieces. Set in C pieces between large triangles.

**NORTH CAROLINA STAR   PIECING DIAGRAM**

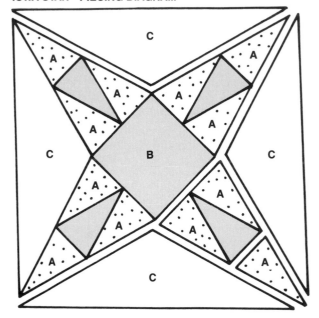

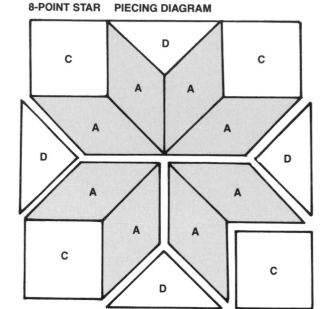

## Louisiana Star, Virginia Star, and Tennessee Star

### Cutting

From muslin, cut 24 squares and 24 triangles. For Louisiana Star, cut 16 half-diamonds each from dark blue print and red on off-white print. For Virginia Star, cut 32 A pieces from dark blue print and 64 B pieces from red print. For Tennessee Star, cut 16 diamonds from red print. Following directions under *Appliqué Basics* (page 19), make patterns for center and petals. Cut 16 petals and 2 centers from blue on off-white print.

### Make two of each star, as follows:

For Louisiana Star, stitch each dark blue print half-diamond to a red on off-white half-diamond. For Virginia Star, stitch two B pieces to edges of each A piece to make a triangle as shown in piecing diagram. Stitch triangles together in pairs, matching seams to make diamonds. For each block, following 8-point star piecing diagram above, stitch diamonds together in pairs, ending stitching at side ¼″ from edge of fabric. Stitch a square between points of diamonds. Stitch pairs of diamond units together in same manner. Stitch a triangle in center space between points of diamonds. Stitch half stars together. Stitch a triangle between remaining points of diamonds to complete square. For Tennessee Star, center a petal over the seamline between dia-

monds. Following directions under *Appliqué Basics* (page 19), slipstitch petals in place. Slipstitch center to center of block.

## Quilt Top

### Cutting

From red print, cut center borders 2½″ by 28½″ (or length of edges of center medallion), 4 inner borders 2½″ by 64″, and 8 inner border ends 2½″ by 10″. From red, off-white and blue print, cut four 10½″ squares. Draw six 10⅞″ squares and divide them in half diagonally; cut out to make 12 side triangles. Draw two 8″ squares and divide them in half diagonally; cut out to make four corner triangles. Cut 8 corner squares 2½″ by 2½″ from dark blue print. From muslin, cut 4 borders 10¼″ by 62″.

### DIRECTIONS

Stitch center borders to two opposite sides of center medallion. Stitch corner squares to each end of remaining center borders. Stitch these borders to remaining sides of center medallion. Arrange 2 side triangles along opposite sides of each Louisiana Star. Place a corner triangle along the edge between them to make a triangle. Stitch triangles to sides of blocks.

To each of 2 print squares, stitch a Missouri Star and a Kansas Star to opposite sides to form strips. Stitch a

**MISSOURI STAR   PIECING DIAGRAM**

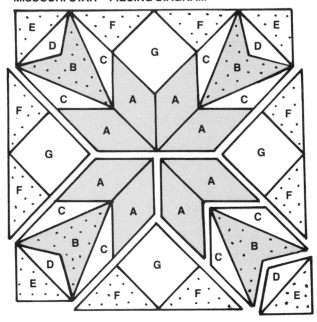

**KANSAS STAR   PIECING DIAGRAM**

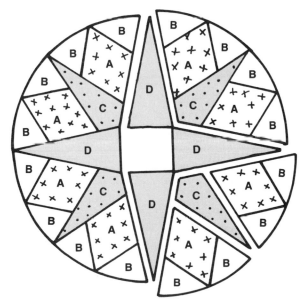

strip to long edge of Louisiana Star unit to form a large triangle. Stitch large triangles to 2 opposite edges of center medallion. Arrange 2 side triangles along opposite sides of each Virginia Star. Place a corner triangle along the edge between them to make a triangle. Stitch triangles to sides of blocks.

To each of 2 print squares, stitch a Tennessee Star and a North Carolina Star to opposite sides to form strips. Stitch side triangles to ends of this piece. Stitch to long edge of Virginia Star piece to form a large triangle. Stitch these large triangles to 2 remaining edges of center medallion.

*Borders*

Trim inner border and inner border pieces to the same length as edges of quilt center. Stitch two inner borders to opposite sides of quilt center. Stitch corner squares to ends of remaining inner borders. Stitch these pieces to quilt center.

Stitch inner border end along end of each muslin border. Stitch a border unit to 2 opposite sides of quilt top. Stitch an Iowa Star block to each end of remaining 2 border units. Stitch these units to remaining edges of quilt, matching seams.

*Marking Quilting Lines*

See directions under *Quilting Basics* (page 23) and mark quilting lines on top, as follows: Enlarge patterns for medallion, cable, and 5-point star. Trace feathered wreath to four corners of a piece of tracing paper to make pattern for feathered medallion. Make templates for each quilting design, following directions on page 15.

On Ohio Star, connect midpoints of sides of red center square to make a square. Repeat to make a square within a square. Mark quilting lines ¼″ from edges of off-white triangles. Mark a quilting line diagonally across center of off-white squares. Then mark quilting lines ⅜″ apart on half of square closest to center parallel to this line. Mark lines ¼″ from outer edges of small blue squares.

On California Star, trace medallion to center of corner squares and one half of medallion to side triangles. Mark quilting lines ¼″ from outer edges of large triangle, diamond, and blue triangles. Draw another line on large triangles ¼″ from first line. Mark quilting lines on off-white pieces ¼″ from outer edges of star. Mark cable along center borders, inner borders, and border ends. Mark a square in center of corner squares.

**VIRGINIA STAR
PIECING DIAGRAM**

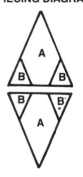

Mark quilting lines on remaining star blocks ¼″ from edges of pieces, as desired. On Iowa Star, draw lines from center of off-white triangle to outer edges. Mark diagonal lines 1¼″ apart across print squares, side triangles, and corner triangles to make a grid.

*Quilting and Binding*

Following directions under *Backing* (page 23), piece backing from lengths of 45″-wide fabric if necessary. Place batting between backing and batting right sides out. Pin, then baste, the layers together. Quilt along all lines mentioned under *Marking Quilting Lines* (page 57) using off-white quilting thread. Following directions under *Binding* (page 26), make a continuous binding 3½″ wide from 35½″ square of dark blue print fabric. Stitch binding around edges of quilt, using a ½″ seam allowance.

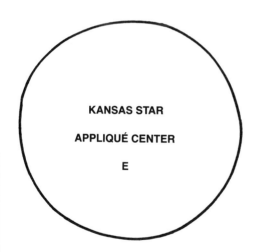

**ACTUAL SIZE PATTERN**

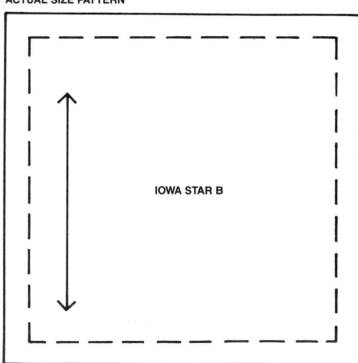

STARS OF THE STATES QUILT ACTUAL SIZE PATTERNS CENTER MEDALLION

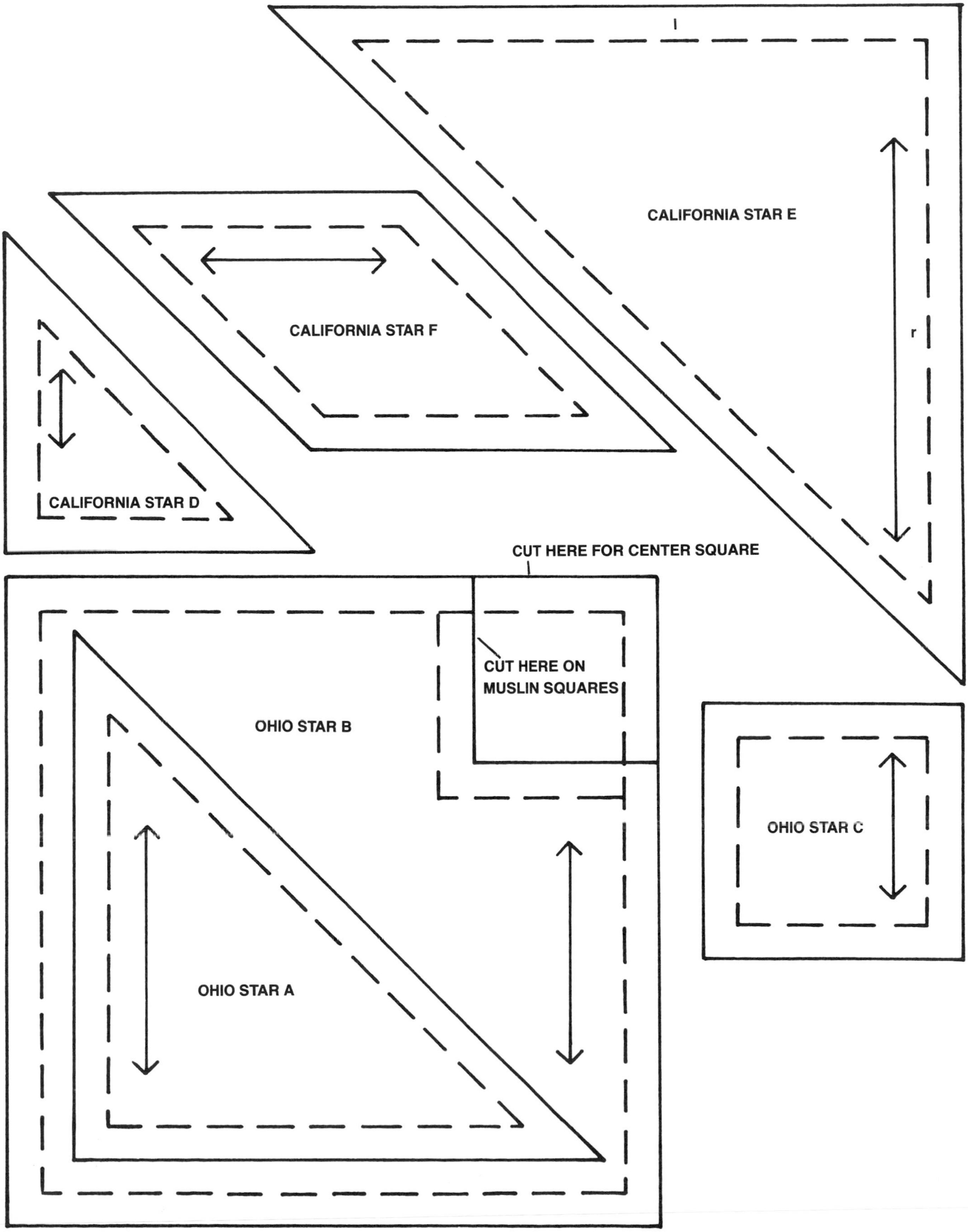
l
CALIFORNIA STAR E
r
CALIFORNIA STAR F
CALIFORNIA STAR D
CUT HERE FOR CENTER SQUARE
CUT HERE ON
MUSLIN SQUARES
OHIO STAR B
OHIO STAR C
OHIO STAR A

STARS OF THE STATES QUILT    ACTUAL SIZE PATTERNS

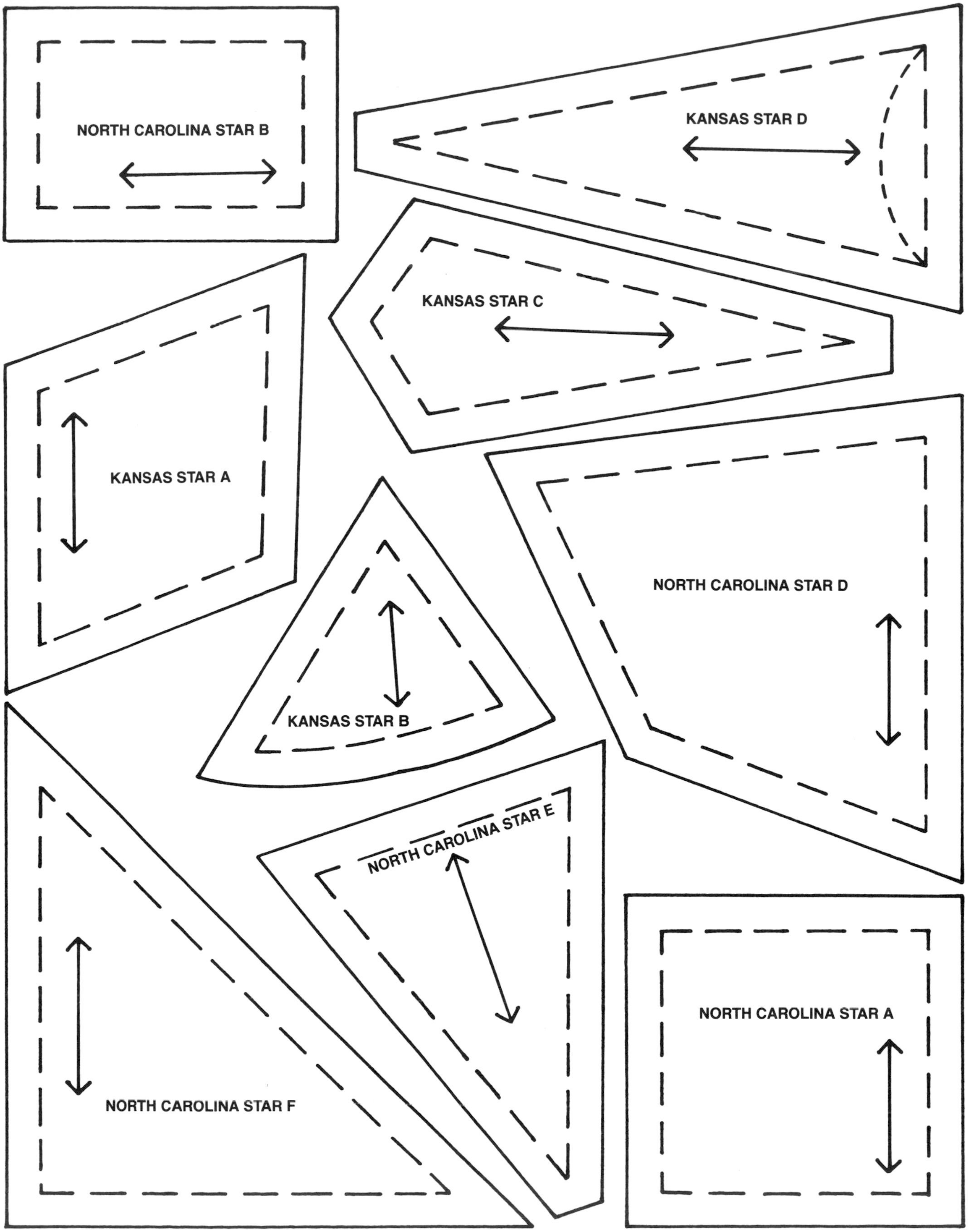

NORTH CAROLINA STAR B

KANSAS STAR D

KANSAS STAR C

KANSAS STAR A

NORTH CAROLINA STAR D

KANSAS STAR B

NORTH CAROLINA STAR E

NORTH CAROLINA STAR F

NORTH CAROLINA STAR A

STARS OF THE STATES QUILT   ACTUAL SIZE PATTERNS

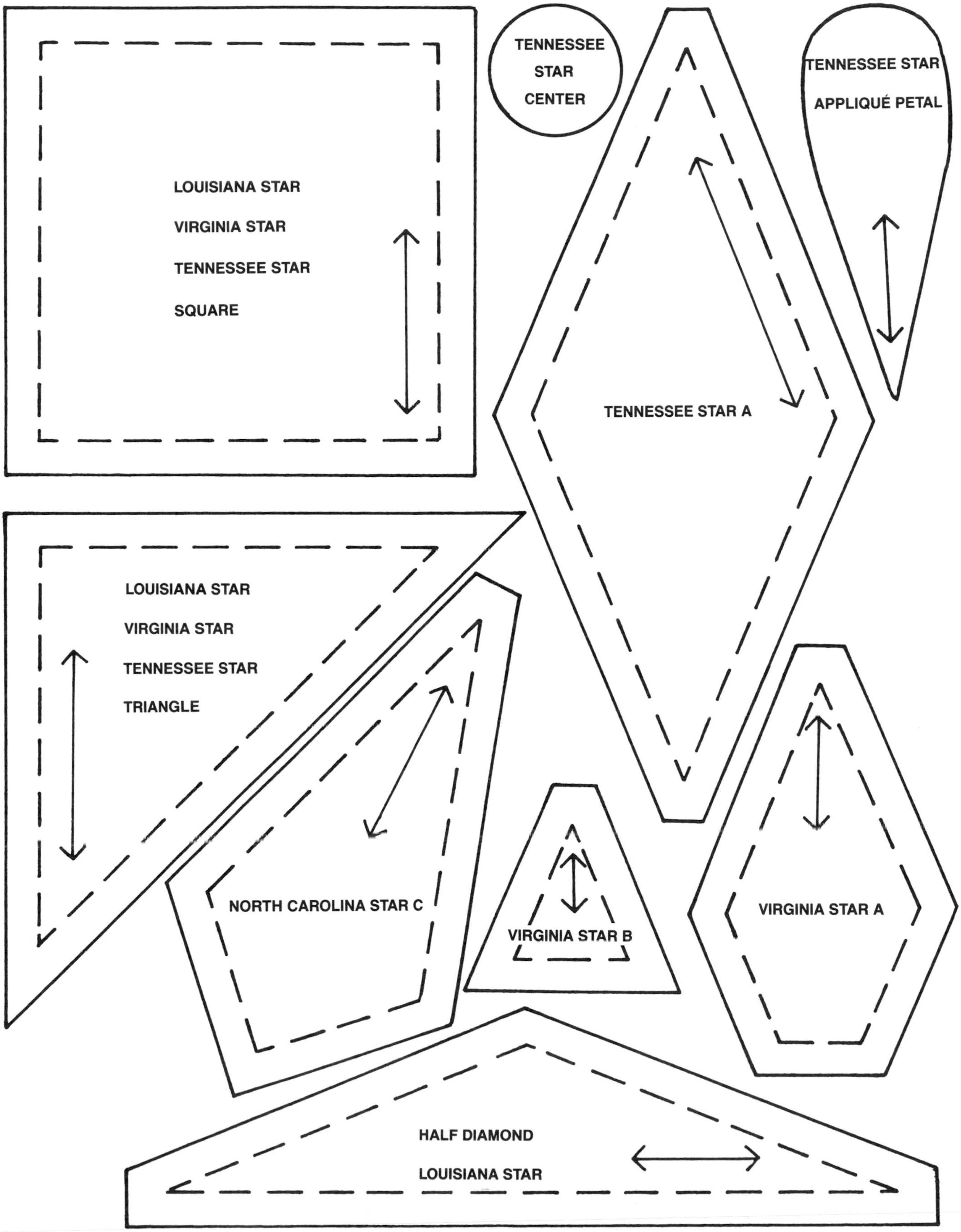

TENNESSEE
STAR
CENTER

TENNESSEE STAR
APPLIQUÉ PETAL

LOUISIANA STAR

VIRGINIA STAR

TENNESSEE STAR

SQUARE

TENNESSEE STAR A

LOUISIANA STAR

VIRGINIA STAR

TENNESSEE STAR

TRIANGLE

NORTH CAROLINA STAR C

VIRGINIA STAR A

VIRGINIA STAR B

HALF DIAMOND

LOUISIANA STAR

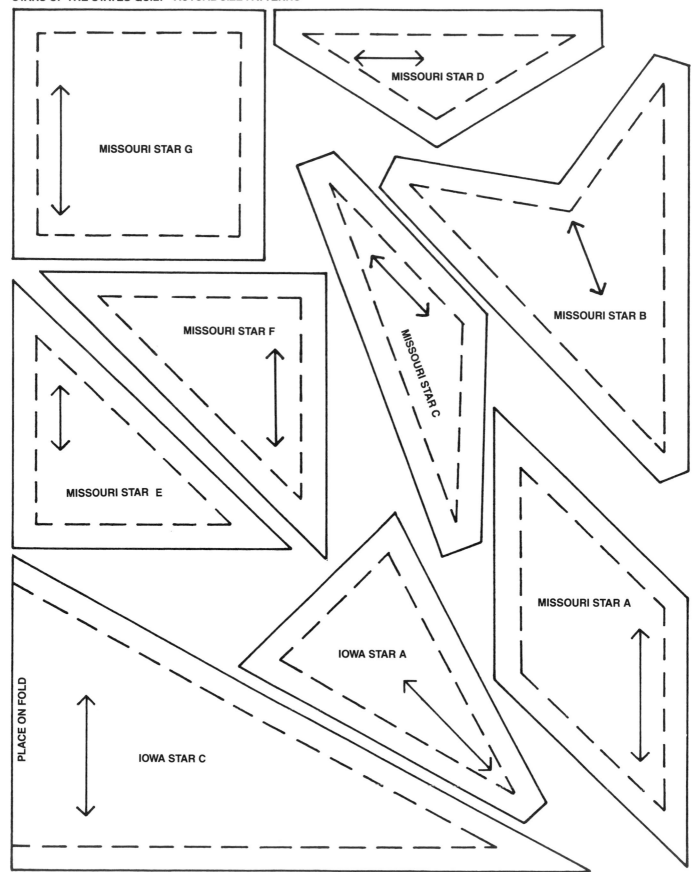

**STARS OF THE STATES QUILT   QUILTING PATTERNS**
**½ OF MEDALLION**

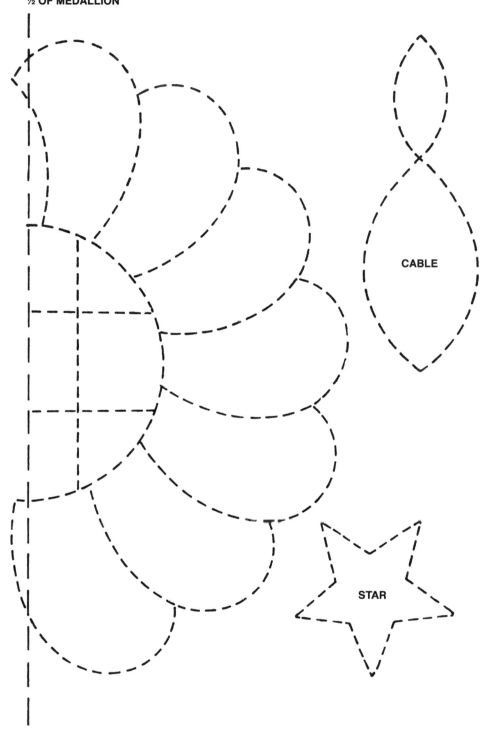

CABLE

STAR

# WISCONSIN CHURN DASH WALL HANGING

**W**isconsin is famous for its dairy products. This wall hanging combines the churn dash block so popular with beginning quilters with blocks of simple machine-appliquéd cows. This colorful 43″ square project would look perfect hanging in your kitchen or dining area. Because free motion machine-quilting techniques are very easy to learn, you can finish your wall hanging in no time at all.

*Size: 43″ square*

## MATERIALS

45″-wide cotton fabrics
   1 yard off-white print
   1 yard red and off-white vertical stripe or ½ yard of
      other print fabric
   1¼ yards red print
   ½ yard green print
   ¼ yard muslin
   ⅛ yard black
   2⅝ yards backing fabric
   ½ yard fusible webbing
   47″-square quilt batting
   Black, off-white, red, and green sewing thread
   1 yard each, black and white embroidery floss

## DIRECTIONS

Following directions under *Templates* (page 15), make templates for patchwork pieces by tracing patterns on pages 66–67, or quick-piece triangles and squares for Wisconsin Churn Dash Block, following directions on pages 17 and 19. Do not cut triangles (A,C) and squares (B) if you plan to quick-piece them. Make patterns for cows by tracing cow on page 66 (see directions under *Machine-Appliqué*, on page 22). If desired, draw four cows with different spots as shown in photograph.

### Cutting

From off-white print, cut 2 top and bottom borders 5″ by 44″ and 2 side borders 5″ by 36″. Then cut 20 triangles (A) and 25 squares (B). From red, cut a 24″ square for binding, 20 triangles (A), 20 squares (B), and 4 small triangles (C). From green print, cut four 10½″ squares and 4 small triangles (C). From red and off-white stripe, cut 4 inner borders 2½″ by 31″. From muslin, cut 4 cows backed with fusible webbing. Cut hooves and spots from black, backed with fusible webbing. Cut tails from black or white, as desired.

## Appliqué Cows

Fuse muslin cows to center of large green squares. Fuse spots and hooves on cows. Using matching thread, zig-zag around appliqué pieces. Embroider thin line of tails, using thread to match tail. Following directions under *Embroidery Basics* (page 32), embroider eyes with satin stitch and nose with straight stitch, using 3 strands of floss and a color which contrasts with the face.

## Churn Dash Blocks

Stitch all seams right sides together, using ¼″ seam allowance. Stitch each off-white triangle (A) to a red triangle (A) to form a square, or quick-piece triangles. Stitch each of 10 red squares (B) to an off-white square, or quick-piece squares. Following piecing diagram, stitch pairs of triangles to each side of joined squares. Alternating colors, stitch 5 squares (B) together to form center of block, or quick-piece squares. Stitch pieces with triangles to each side of center strip, matching seams.

## Quilt Top

Arrange churn dash blocks alternately with appliqué blocks. Stitch blocks together in three vertical rows. Then stitch the rows together, matching seams to make center top. Trim ends of inner borders even with edges of center top. Stitch inner borders to side edges of center top. Stitch each red small triangle (C) to a green small triangle (C) to form a square, or quick-piece triangles. Stitch a square to each end of remaining inner borders. Stitch inner borders to top and bottom of center.

**CHURN DASH BLOCK    PIECING DIAGRAM**

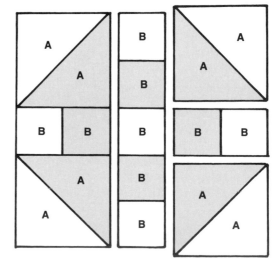

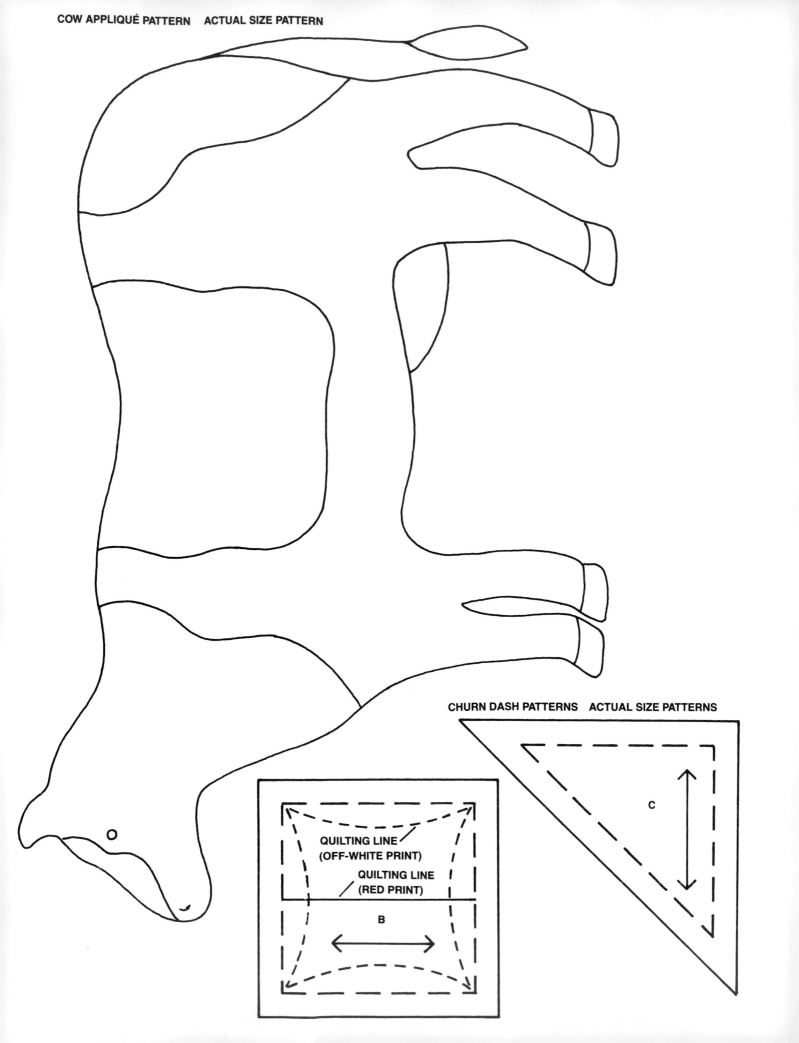

COW APPLIQUÉ PATTERN  ACTUAL SIZE PATTERN

CHURN DASH PATTERNS  ACTUAL SIZE PATTERNS

C

QUILTING LINE
(OFF-WHITE PRINT)

QUILTING LINE
(RED PRINT)

B

Stitch borders to side edges of inner borders. Trim ends even with top and bottom edge of corner squares. Stitch top and bottom border to quilt. Trim ends even with side edges.

## Quilting

Make templates for quilting off-white print squares and triangles by tracing short broken lines for quilting on templates. Mark quilting lines on red squares and triangles, following solid lines for quilting. Make template for cable and heart motif from pattern below. Following directions under *Quilting Basics* (page 23), mark quilting lines on churn dash blocks and cable and heart motif on borders.

From backing fabric, cut a 32″ by 48″ center piece and two 8″ by 48″ side pieces. Stitch side pieces to center. Press seams open. Place batting between backing and top with right sides out. Pin layers together with safety pins or baste them together. Following directions under *Machine-Quilting* (page 24), free-hand quilt along lines marked on churn dash blocks, using matching or invisible thread. Fill in background on appliqué blocks by stipple-quilting around cows, using green or invisible thread. Quilt along the lines of the cable on the border.

## Finishing

Baste layers of quilt together ½″ from edges. Following directions under *Binding* (page 26), make a 3½″-wide bias binding from the 30½″ square of red print. Stitch binding to quilt top ½″ from edges.

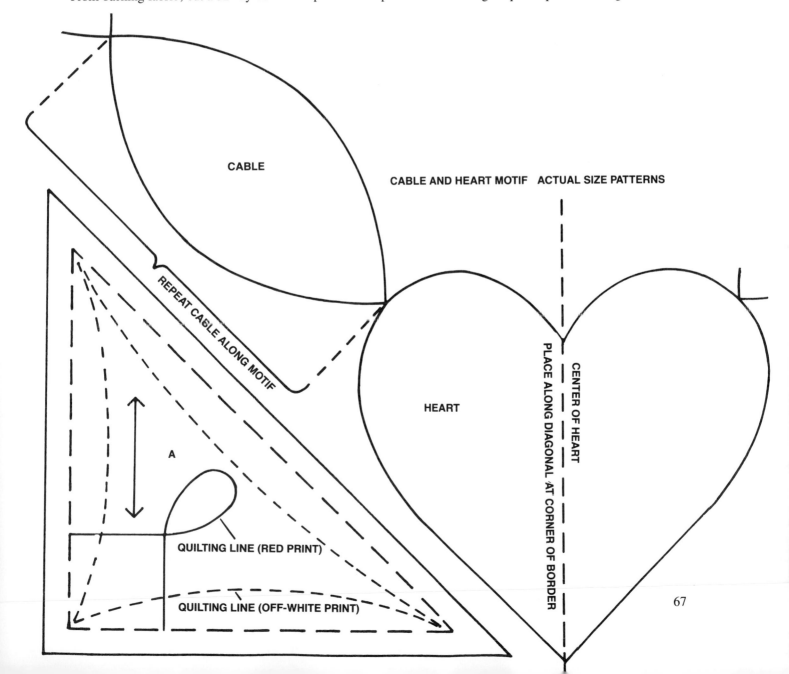

CABLE

CABLE AND HEART MOTIF ACTUAL SIZE PATTERNS

REPEAT CABLE ALONG MOTIF

HEART

PLACE ALONG DIAGONAL AT CORNER OF BORDER

CENTER OF HEART

A

QUILTING LINE (RED PRINT)

QUILTING LINE (OFF-WHITE PRINT)

67

# MONTANA MOUNTAIN BEAR CUB QUILT

This machine-appliquéd mountain scene features a bear cub, an ever-popular motif for children's quilts. The bear cub, shown climbing a tree, is similar to the bear in the famous Theodore Roosevelt political cartoon which led in 1903 to the first stuffed bears made in this country. The scene is surrounded by borders of pastel blue and lavender prints; cornerstones of the inner borders are patchwork bear's paw blocks. This quilt is perfect for a baby's crib or a child's wall hanging.

*Size: 38" by 46"*

## MATERIALS

45"-wide cotton fabrics
⅝ yard muslin
1¼ yards blue print
⅞ yard blue and purple print
½ yard off-white print
⅛ yard or 3" by 12" scrap gray floral print
¼ yard light green print
½ yard blue
¼ yard brown print
¼ yard or 8" by 11" piece light brown
⅛ yard or 6" by 8" piece white
⅛ yard or 4" by 78" piece green
1⅜ yards backing
42" by 50" low-loft quilt batting
¾ yard fusible webbing
Brown, white, light blue, light green, light brown, and green sewing thread
Brown, green, dark brown, and red embroidery floss
Light blue, blue, light green, brown, and off-white quilting thread

## DIRECTIONS

Enlarge pattern for center scene following directions on page 15. Following directions under *Machine-Appliqué* (page 22), make patterns for sky, mountain, hill, tree trunk, bear cub, clouds, snow, and pine trees. Make templates for patterns A-C and quilting motif on page 70, following directions on page 15.

### Cutting

Cut a 18½" by 26½" piece muslin for background. From light blue print, cut sky and 16 triangles (A). Do not cut triangles if you plan to quick-piece them. From off-white print, cut 2 inner borders 4" by 27" and 2 inner borders 4" by 19", 4 small squares (B), and 16 triangles. Do not cut triangles if you plan to quick-piece them.

From gray print, cut 4 large squares (C). From blue and purple print, cut side borders 6½" by 35" and top and bottom borders 6½" by 39". Cut mountain from blue and hill from light green. Cut the remaining appliqué pieces backed with fusible webbing as follows; tree trunk from brown print, bear cub from light brown, snow and clouds from white, and pine trees from green.

## Center Scene

Place sky along top of background, right side up. Place mountain over lower edge of sky, and baste along upper edge of mountain. Place hill over lower edge of mountain, and baste along upper edge of hill. Baste pieces to background, ¼" from outer edge.

Fuse remaining appliqué pieces in place as indicated on pattern. Zigzag along edges of each piece using matching thread. On bear cub, zigzag along inner lines of arm, leg, ears, and neck.

Draw or transfer bear's features, tree branches, and needles to center. Use 3 strands of embroidery floss for all embroidery. Embroider eyes and nose using dark brown satin stitch, lines of paws using dark brown straight stitches, and mouth using red backstitch. Embroider branches with brown backstitch and needles with green straight stitches.

### Borders

Stitch all seams right sides together, using ¼" seam allowance. Stitch each blue print triangle (A) to an off-white triangle (A) to make a square, or quick-piece triangles following directions on page 17. Following Bear Paw diagram, stitch 2 pairs of triangles together. Stitch a small square (B) to end of one of these pairs. Stitch remaining pair to edge or large square (C). Stitch pieces together, matching seams to make block.

**BEAR PAW
PIECING DIAGRAM**

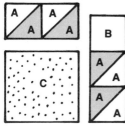

Stitch long inner borders to sides of center scene. Trim ends even with edges of center. Trim ends of remaining inner borders the same width as top and bottom edges of scene, plus ½″ for seam allowances. Stitch Bear Paw blocks to ends of top and bottom inner borders. Stitch inner borders to center and inner borders, matching seams. Stitch side borders to sides of inner borders. Trim ends even with edges. Stitch remaining borders to top and bottom edges. Trim ends even with edges.

*Quilting and Finishing*

Following directions under *Quilting Basics* (page 23), mark quilting lines ¼″ from outer edge of center scene, if desired. Mark cable quilting motif along inner bor-

ders. Mark quilting lines of Bear Paw block ¼″ from edge of large square and ¼″ from edges of off-white pieces. On outer borders, mark quilting lines ¼″ from inner edge, 2″ and 4″ from inner edge.

Place batting between backing and quilt top, right sides out. Pin, then baste, the layers together. Baste edges together ⅜″ in. Quilt along edges of appliqué pieces on center scene, using thread that matches the background. Quilt along lines mentioned in first paragraph above. Trim backing and batting even with edges of quilt top.

Following directions under *Binding* (page 26), make a continuous binding 3¼″ wide from a 28″ square of light blue fabric. Stitch binding around quilt top, using ⅜″ seam allowance.

**MONTANA MOUNTAIN BEAR CLUB QUILT   ACTUAL SIZE PATTERNS**

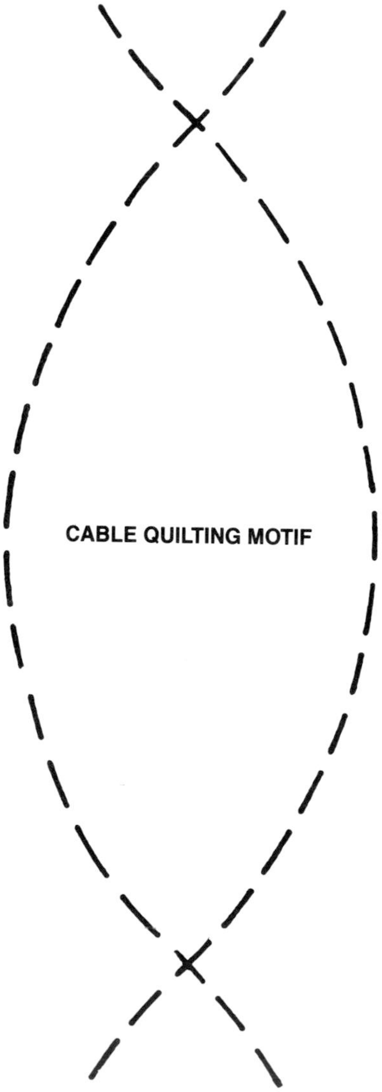

CABLE QUILTING MOTIF

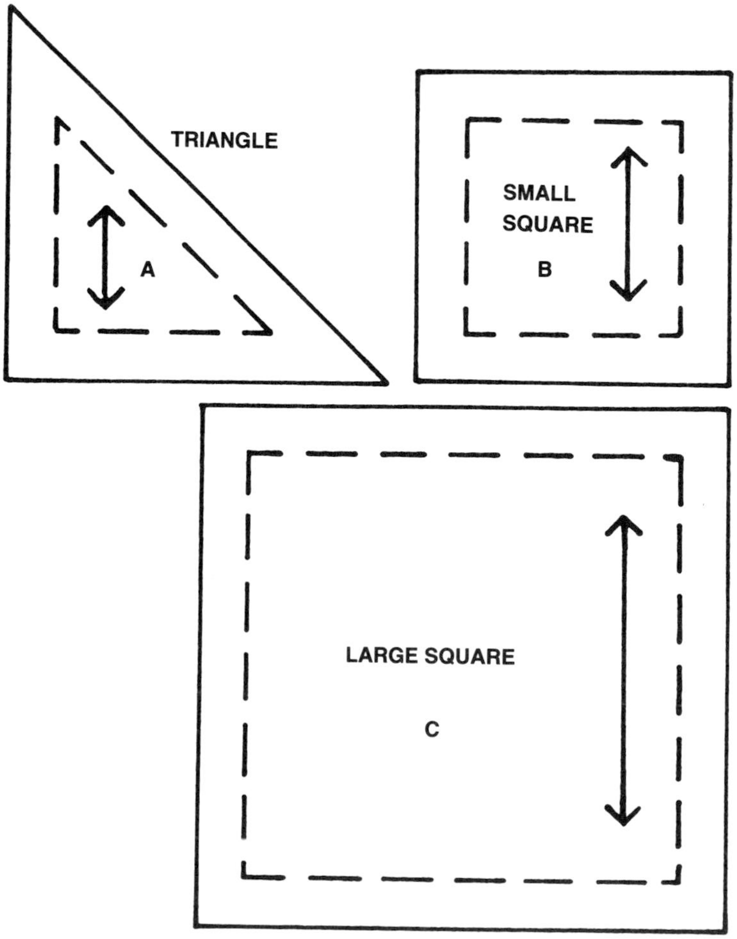

TRIANGLE

A

SMALL SQUARE B

LARGE SQUARE

C

MONTANA MOUNTAIN BEAR CUB QUILT    APPLIQUÉ PATTERN    CENTER SCENE

EACH SQUARE = 1"

# MONTANA MOUNTAIN PATCHWORK BEAR CUB

rom patchwork fabric left over from the quilt, you can make a matching bear. He's approximately 16″ high and has moveable arms and legs. Both projects are sure to delight the baby or toddler in your life. They're also perfect as a baby shower present.

*Size: 16″ high*

**MATERIALS**

45″-wide cotton fabrics
  ½ yard muslin
  ⅜ yard off-white print
  ⅛ yard each, blue print, blue and purple print, brown, light green print, and gray print
  3″ by 6″ piece quilt batting
  12-ounce bag polyester stuffing
  Two ½″-diameter brown buttons for eyes
  Four 1″-diameter shank-type buttons
  1″ square brown felt
  ½ yard red embroidery floss
  Off-white sewing thread
  3 yards carpet thread
  Long (4″) needle
  ¾ yard ⅝″-wide satin ribbon

**DIRECTIONS**

Enlarge patterns for bear cub on pages 76–77 (see directions under *Enlarging Patterns*, page 15). Stitch all seams right sides together, using ¼″ seam allowance.

## Patchwork Fabric

Cut thirty-six 2-inch squares from each of the following fabrics, or quick-piece squares following directions on page 19: light blue (A), off-white (B), blue and purple print (C), light brown (D), light green (E), and gray print (F). Arrange the squares in rows following Patchwork Diagram A, and stitch them together. Make 6 of each row.

Arrange Rows 1–6 following Patchwork Diagram A and stitch them together, matching seams. Repeat twice more so that 18 rows have been joined. Arrange Row 1 and Rows 2–6 following Patchwork Diagram B and stitch them together, matching seams. Repeat twice more so that 18 rows have been joined.

### Cutting

From one patchwork piece, cut front, back, outer arm, and leg. Reverse pattern and cut another leg. From second patchwork piece, reverse pattern pieces and cut front, back, outer arm, and leg. Reverse pattern and cut another leg. With muslin fabric folded in half, cut 2 fronts, 2 backs, 2 head sides, 2 outer arms, 2 inner arms, 4 legs, 2 foot pads, and 2 paw pads.

With off-white print folded in half, cut 2 head sides and 2 inner arms. From a single layer of fabric, cut 1 head center. With light blue fabric folded in half, cut 2 paw pads, 2 foot pads, and 2 ears. Cut 2 ears from each light brown and quilt batting.

**PATCHWORK DIAGRAM  A**

| 1 | 2 | 3 | 4 | 5 | 6 |
|---|---|---|---|---|---|
| A | F | E | D | C | B |
| B | A | F | E | D | C |
| C | B | A | F | E | A |
| D | C | B | A | F | E |
| E | D | C | B | A | F |
| F | E | D | C | B | A |

**PATCHWORK DIAGRAM B**

| 1 | 6 | 5 | 4 | 3 | 2 |
|---|---|---|---|---|---|
| A | B | C | D | E | F |
| B | C | D | E | F | A |
| C | D | E | F | A | B |
| D | E | F | A | B | C |
| E | F | A | B | C | D |
| F | A | B | C | D | E |

# MONTANA MOUNTAIN PATCHWORK BEAR CUB

### DIAGRAM 1

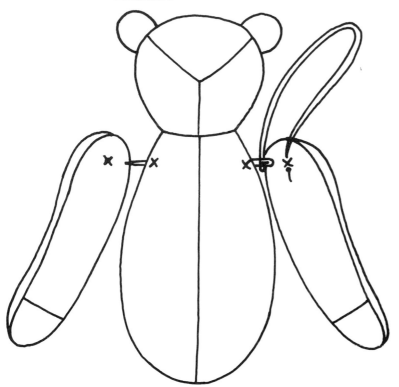

## Bear

Stitch all seams, right sides together, using ¼″ seam allowance. Clip seam allowance along curves before turning pieces right side out. Use thread doubled in needle for all hand-sewing. Place each patchwork or fabric piece, except ears, on a corresponding muslin piece. Machine-baste pieces together a scant ¼″ from edge. Matching notches, stitch fronts to backs along side seam. Stitch body halves together along curved edge. Turn under seam allowance along neck edge; baste edge in place. Stuff body.

Stitch darts in head pieces, slash along center of dart and press darts open. Stitch head sides together along center front below nose. Pin and baste head center to

### DIAGRAM 2

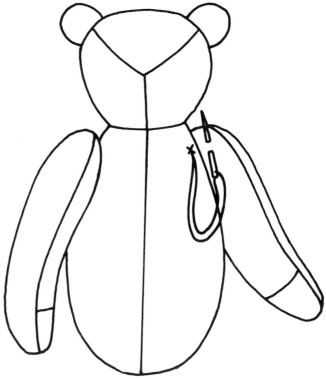

**DIAGRAM 3**

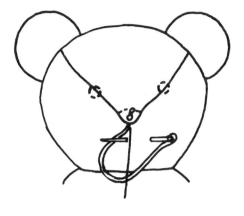

**DIAGRAM 4**

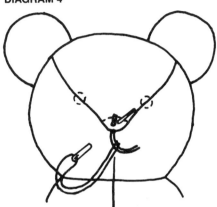

sides along top curved edge. Machine stitch seam. Turn under seam allowance along lower edge and baste it in place. Stuff head. Place head on body, matching center front seams, and slipstitch head to body. Stitch paw pads to inner arms. Stitch inner arms to outer arms, leaving an opening between dots. Turn under seam allowance along opening and baste edge in place.

Sew legs together in pairs, leaving straight edge and area between dots open. Pin and baste foot pad to straight edge of legs, matching dots. Machine-stitch seam. Turn under seam allowance along edge of opening and baste it in place. Stuff arms and legs, inserting a large button inside inner arm and inner leg and positioning shank under x. Pin shank in place through fabric. Slipstitch edges of arm and leg openings together. Thread a large needle with a long length of carpet thread, double it, and knot the ends together. Insert needle through button shank in one arm. Push needle through body between x's (see Diagram 1).

Insert needle through button shank in second arm and then back through body at x's, but not necessarily at the

exact same spot as before. Pull thread very tightly so body is a little indented around x's. Stitch through fabric of first arm close to x and knot thread securely (see Diagram 2). Bring the needle out through the arm and trim off end of thread so it doesn't show. Attach legs in same manner.

Baste quilt batting to wrong side of light blue ears. Stitch light blue ears to brown ears along upper curve. Turn right side out. Turn under seam allowance along lower edge and slipstitch edges together. Slipstitch ears to head centered over darts on head sides and center. Securely sew buttons to position for eyes.

To make mouth, using 6 strands of embroidery floss, insert needle from the top of the nose area and bring it up at top of center seam. Insert needle on right-hand side of mouth and bring it up on center seam ¾" below nose (see Diagram 3). Insert needle on left-hand side of mouth and bring it out again on top of nose (see Diagram 4). Knot thread securely. Cut nose from brown felt. Glue or whipstitch nose to position on head center. Tie ribbon around neck and make a bow.

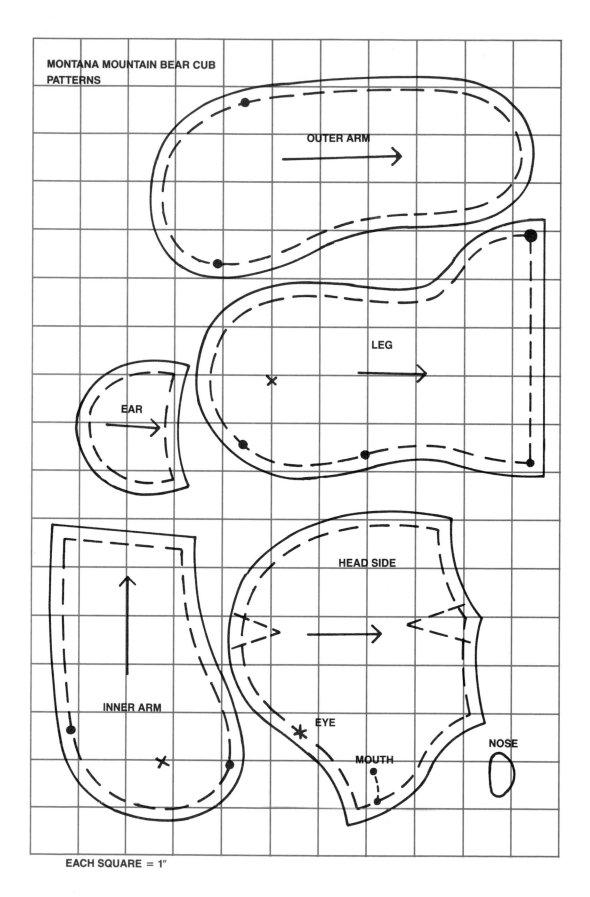

MONTANA MOUNTAIN BEAR CUB
PATTERNS

OUTER ARM

LEG

EAR

INNER ARM

HEAD SIDE

EYE

MOUTH

NOSE

EACH SQUARE = 1"

76

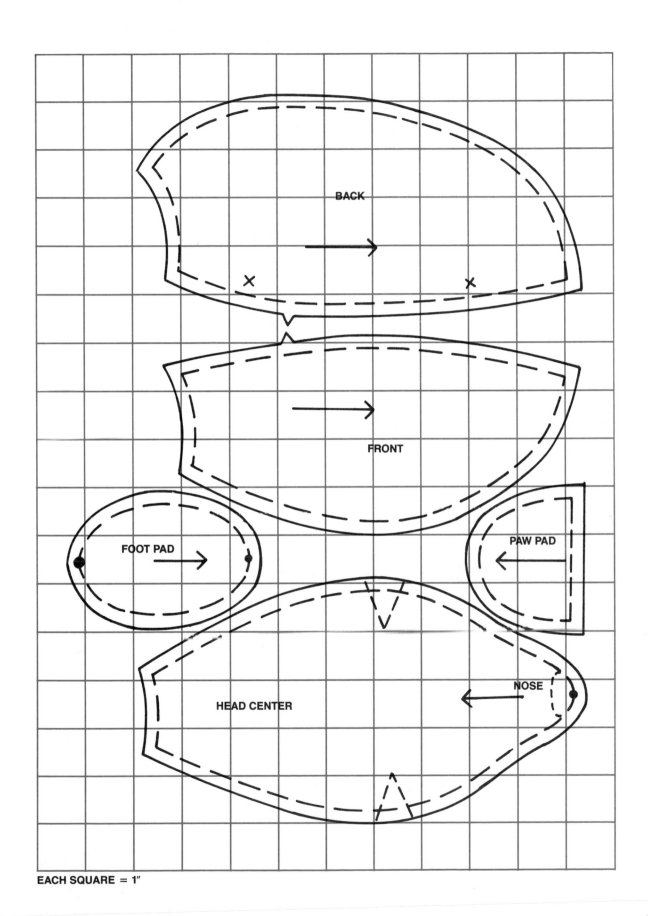

BACK

FRONT

FOOT PAD

PAW PAD

HEAD CENTER

NOSE

EACH SQUARE = 1"

# MAGNOLIA BUD PILLOW AND SACHET

The magnolia blossom is the state flower of both Alabama and Mississippi, and it's also a traditional symbol of the Deep South. This simple patchwork representation of the magnolia bud is a charming motif for a feminine bolster pillow that is stitched in mauve and rose. Off-white lace and rose grosgrain trim the 14″-long pillow. A smaller bud is stitched and trimmed with lace to make a matching 5″-square sachet. You can stuff it with sweet-smelling potpourri to use in your own boudoir or to give as a gift.

*Size: 14″-long pillow, 5″-square sachet*

## MATERIALS

45″-wide cotton fabrics
  1 yard muslin
  ½ yard pink print fabric
  ¼ yard mauve
  Scraps of both dusty green and rose
  Lace edging for pillow: 2½ yards ⅞″ wide, 2½ yards ½″ wide
  Lace edging for sachet: ¾ yard ⅞″ wide, ½ yard ¼″ wide
  1¾ yards ⅞″-wide rose grosgrain ribbon for pillow
  Traditional-weight quilt batting: 16″ by 26″ piece for pillow, 7″-square for sachet
  Large roll of extra-loft quilt batting to stuff pillow
  1 cup potpourri and small amount of polyester stuffing to fill sachet
  Off-white sewing thread
  Off-white, pink, and mauve quilting thread

## DIRECTIONS

### Pillow

Make templates for pieces A–F by tracing patterns on pages 81–82 (use patterns without dots).

#### Cutting

Cut 1 small square A from rose. From muslin, cut 2 pillow sides 8½″ by 25″, 1 small square (A), 1 rectangle (B), 2 triangles (C); reverse template and cut 2 more triangles (C) and 3 medium squares (D). From pink print, cut upper section 12″ by 14½″ and lower section 5½″ by 14½″, 1 large square (E), and 1 triangle (C); reverse template and cut another triangle (C). Cut a triangle (C) from dusty green; reverse pattern and cut another triangle (C). From mauve, cut 2 side sections (F), ignoring superimposed pattern for E.

### Pillow Top

Stitch all seams with right sides together, using ¼″ seam allowances. Following diagram for Magnolia Bud block, stitch the two small squares (A) together. Stitch rectangle (B) to sides of small squares. Stitch pink print and dusty green triangles (C) to muslin triangles. Stitch pieces together in 3 rows. Then stitch rows together, matching seams.

Make a row of reinforcement stitching (12 to 15 stitches per inch, 2 on European machines) along seamline at inner corner of side sections (F). Clip to stitching at inner corners. Stitch side sections to side edges of Magnolia Bud block. Stitch upper section to upper edge

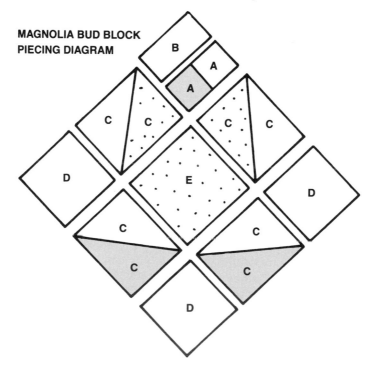

**MAGNOLIA BUD BLOCK
PIECING DIAGRAM**

## MAGNOLIA BUD PILLOW AND SACHET
### DIAGRAM 1

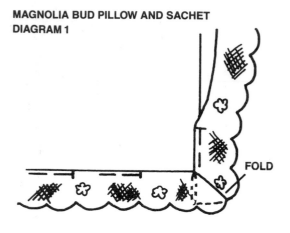

FOLD

### DIAGRAM 2

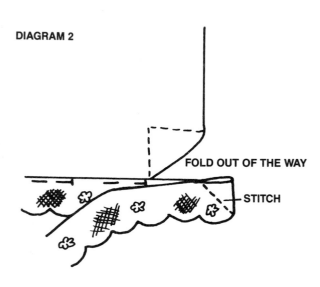

FOLD OUT OF THE WAY

STITCH

### DIAGRAM 3

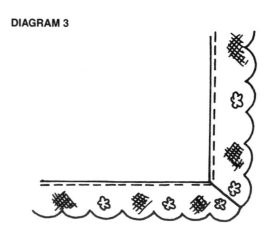

of side sections and lower section to lower edge. Pin straight edge of ½″ lace to upper and lower edge of side sections. Hand-baste, then stitch, lace in place. Pin straight edge of ⅞″-wide lace around Magnolia Bud block, folding lace diagonally at corners to form a miter. Finger-press foldline to mark it (see Diagram 1).

Unpin lace from corner. Pin the miter in, keeping the extra fold of lace on the wrong side. Stitch along fold of the miter by hand or machine (see Diagram 2). Trim the seam allowance close to the stitching. Overcast or zigzag-stitch the seam allowance to keep the trimmed edge from fraying. Re-pin lace to edge of block, hand-baste, and stitch lace around block (see Diagram 3).

Mark quilting lines on Magnolia Bud block ¼″ from edges of muslin sections and pink print magnolia bud. Mark quilting lines on side sections along lines indicated on pattern. Draw lines 2″ apart across upper and lower sections and perpendicular to side edges. Place batting between backing and pillow top with right side up. Pin, then baste, layers together. Using matching thread, quilt along marked lines and along edges of side sections just inside straight edge of lace.

### Finishing Pillow

For hem, turn under ⅛″ twice on one long edge of each muslin side piece. Hand-baste ½″-wide lace along hemmed edge. Stitch along straight edge of lace. Stitch opposite edge of sides to side edges of quilted pillow top. Remove batting from seam allowance and zigzag-stitch edge, if desired. Hand-baste ⅞″-wide lace along edge of pillow top; then stitch along straight edge of lace.

Matching seams and lace, stitch unfinished edges of pillow together to form a tube. Zigzag-stitch edge of seam allowance, if desired. Roll up quilt batting to fit inside pillow. Cut two 28″ lengths of ribbon. Gather muslin side and tie with ribbon. Make a bow.

## Sachet

Make templates for pieces A–G by tracing patterns with dots on pages 81–82.

### Cutting

Cut 1 small square (A) from rose fabric. From muslin, cut 1 small square (A), 1 rectangle (B), 2 triangle (C); reverse template and cut 2 more triangles (C), 3 medium squares (D), and a backing piece 7″ square. From pink print, 1 large square (E) and 1 triangle (C); reverse template and cut another triangle (C). Cut a triangle (C) from dusty green; reverse pattern and cut another triangle (C). From mauve, cut corners (G).

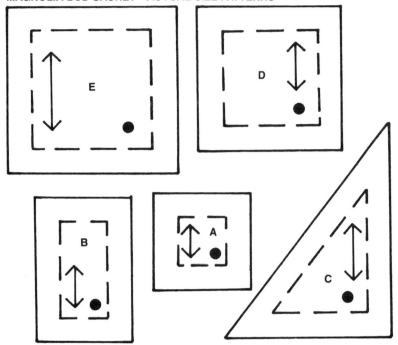

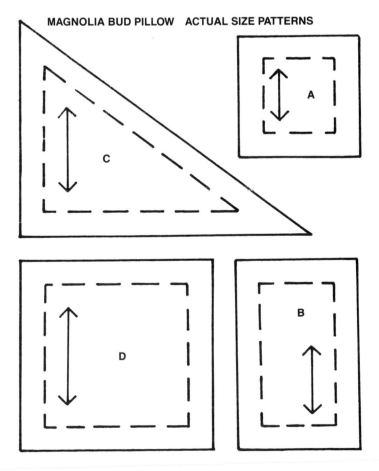

## Sachet Top

Piece Magnolia Bud block, following directions in first paragraph under *Pillow Top* (page 78). Stitch corners (G) to sides of block. Mark quilting lines on corners as indicated on pattern G. Place batting between backing and sachet top with right sides up. Using matching thread, quilt ⅛″ from edge of muslin sections and pink print magnolia bud and along lines on corners. Trim batting and backing even with sachet top.

### Finishing Sachet

Using top as a pattern, cut back from pink print fabric. With right sides together, stitch front to back, leaving an opening on one side for turning. Turn right side out. Stuff corners and edges of sachet with batting, then pour potpourri into center. Place a little stuffing just inside opening. Turn under edges of opening and slip-stitch them together. Hand-stitch ⅞″-wide lace around edge of sachet, following instructions for mitering under *Pillow Top* (page 78). Then stitch ¼″-wide lace around Magnolia Bud block, but do not stitch and trim miter at corners on such narrow lace.

**MAGNOLIA BUD SACHET   ACTUAL SIZE PATTERNS**

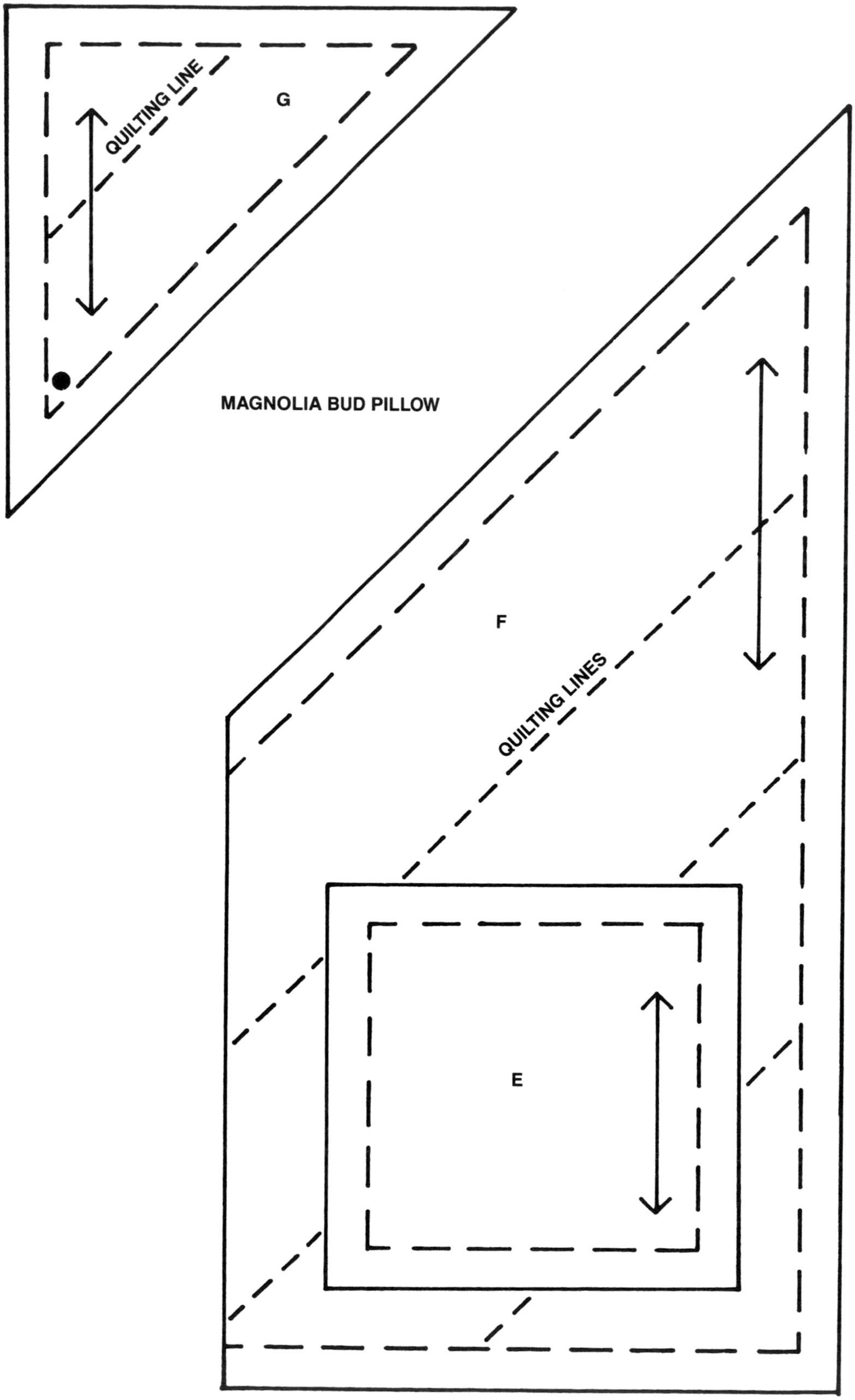

QUILTING LINE

G

**MAGNOLIA BUD PILLOW**

QUILTING LINES

F

E

# MAINE WOODS AUTUMN PILLOW

**T**he Maine woods are alive with color every autumn. Maine is known as the "Pine Tree State," and the pine cone and tassel are its official symbols. This pillow, a very portable, hand-appliqué project, will bring fall's splendid colors into your home all year long. Hand-quilting and embroidery add detail to the leaves, acorns, and pine cone. The tassel of pine is embroidered in outline stitch.

*Size: 15" square*

## MATERIALS

45"-wide cotton fabrics
  ½ yard plum
  ⅜ yard bright purple
Cotton fabrics
  7"-square dark red
  8" by 10" piece reddish brown
  4" by 11" piece brown
  3" by 5" piece rust
  4" by 8" piece gold
  18"-square muslin for backing
  Green, dark red, brown, rust, gold, and beige
    embroidery floss
  18"-square traditional quilt batting
  2 yards cotton cording
  Sewing thread to match fabrics
  Plum quilting thread or embroidery floss
  14" pillow form

## DIRECTIONS

### Appliqué and Embroidery

Enlarge appliqué pattern on page 85, following directions on page 15. Cut a 16" square from plum fabric for pillow front. Trace outline of leaves, acorns, pine cone, and tassel to pillow front.

Following directions under *Appliqué Basics* (page 19), make patterns for pine cone, leaves, acorns, and acorn caps. Cut pine cone and acorn caps from brown fabrics, maple leaf from dark red, birch leaves from gold, beech leaf from rust, and oak leaf and acorns from reddish brown. Pin leaves and pine cone to positions on pillow top and slipstitch them in place with matching thread. Pin acorns to position and slipstitch them in place. Then slipstitch acorn caps in place.

Use two strands of embroidery floss for all stitching. Embroider stems of beech leaf, maple leaf, oak leaf, and acorns, using rows of stem stitches with matching embroidery floss. For birch leaves, using rows of stem stitches, embroider main stem with brown and stems to leaves with gold. Embroider stem of pine tassel with rows of brown stem stitches, and needles with a single row of stem stitch. Cut out background fabric behind appliqué shapes.

### Quilting

Following directions under *Quilting Basics* (page 23), mark quilting lines on leaves and pine cone. Place batting between backing and pillow top with right sides out. Pin, then baste, the layers together. Quilt around each shape ⅛" from the edges with plum quilting thread or 2 strands of embroidery floss. Quilt along lines on leaves with 2 strands matching floss. Quilt lines on pine cone with 2 strands beige floss.

### Finishing

Following directions under *Cording* (page 28), cover cotton cording with bright purple fabric. Stitch cording around pillow top ½" from edges. Cut a 16"-square of plum fabric for pillow back, or use other fabric as desired (see directions under *Pillow Backs*, page 30). Stitch front to back, leaving opening for turning if necessary. Insert pillow form or stuff pillow. Slipstitch edges of opening together if necessary.

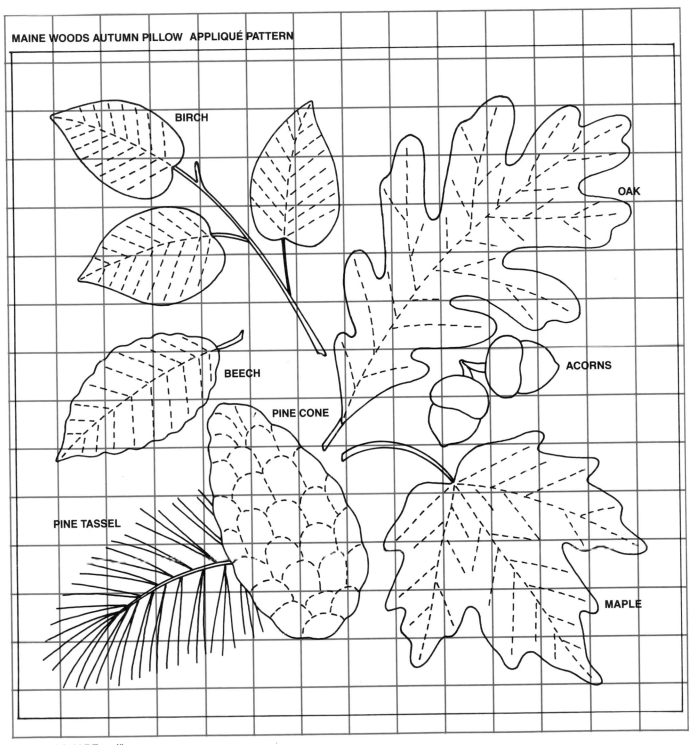

MAINE WOODS AUTUMN PILLOW  APPLIQUÉ PATTERN

BIRCH

OAK

BEECH

ACORNS

PINE CONE

PINE TASSEL

MAPLE

EACH SQUARE = 1"

# LONE STAR QUILT

This large star, also known as the star of Bethlehem, was a pattern popular with early American quiltmakers. As quilters moved westward, it seems appropriate that Texans (at that time the largest state and known for "big things") adopted this large star made of many small diamonds. They gave it their nickname—the "Lone Star," after the single star on their flag.

You can piece this star from individual diamonds, or you can follow quick-piecing instructions to make a fast and easy quilt. You'll want to choose and coordinate six of your favorite patterns and colors to make this star with diamond borders and 8-point star corners. A dramatic gift, the Lone Star quilt will be treasured and admired for many years by friends and relatives.

*Size: 78" by 88" before quilting*

## MATERIALS

45"-wide cotton fabrics
  4 yards white
  2½ yards blue floral print
  2 yards dark blue print
  1⅛ yards bright blue
  1 yard blue and gray print
  ½ yard light blue print
  ½ yard blue-on-white print
  5¼ yards backing fabric (or 2⅝ yards 90"-wide backing fabric)
  82" by 94" piece quilt batting
  White and blue sewing thread
  White, light blue and dark blue quilting thread

## DIRECTIONS

Directions are given for both traditional piecing and quick-piecing diamonds and borders. Use whichever method you feel most comfortable with. Stitch all seams, right sides together, with ¼" seam allowance.

### Traditional Piecing

Make templates for patterns A-D on page 91, following directions under *Templates* (page 15). Trace templates to wrong side of fabric and cut out each piece.

### Cutting

From white, draw two 19¾" squares and divide them in half diagonally to form large triangles. Cut out large triangles. Then cut 4 large squares 19" by 19", top and bottom inner borders 5½" by 62", 276 half diamonds (B), 16 small squares (C), and 16 small triangles (D). From dark blue print (1), cut 104 diamonds. From bright blue print (2), cut 132 diamonds. From blue floral print (3), cut 4 border strips for top and bottom 2½" by 62", 4 side border strips 2½" by 72", and 64 diamonds. From each light blue print (4) and blue-on-white print (5), cut 64 diamonds. From blue and gray print (6), cut 96 diamonds.

## Large Diamonds

Following large diamond piecing diagram (below), stitch diamonds together to make 16 of Row 1; then make 8 each of Rows 2–6. Stitch Row 1 to 2, matching seams. Stitch Rows 3–6 in place, following piecing diagram; then stitch another Row 1 to other edge of large diamond.

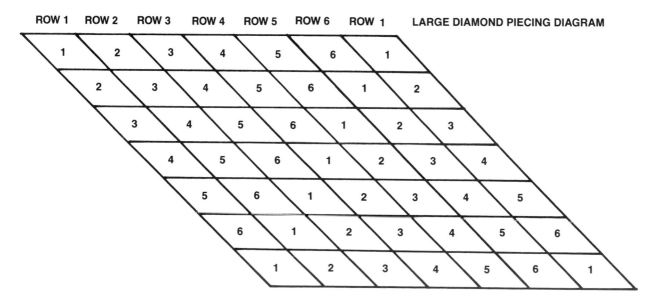

| ROW 1 | ROW 2 | ROW 3 | ROW 4 | ROW 5 | ROW 6 | ROW 1 | LARGE DIAMOND PIECING DIAGRAM |

## Diamond Borders

Stitch two half diamonds (B) to opposite sides of re-maining bright blue (2) and blue and gray print (6) dia-monds (A) (see border piecing Diagram 1). For top and bottom borders, alternating colors, stitch 31 diamond pieces together, beginning and ending with a bright blue diamond piece. Stitch two half diamonds to remaining corners of border strip. Trim ends perpendicular to long edges ¼″ from outer corners of diamonds.

For side borders, alternating colors, stitch 36 dia-mond pieces together. Stitch two half diamonds to re-maining corners of border strip. Trim ends perpendicular to long edges ¼″ from outer corners of diamonds.

### Quick-Piecing

Make templates for patterns B-D on page 91, following directions under *Templates* (page 15). Trace templates to wrong side of fabric and cut out each piece.

### Cutting

From white, draw two 19¾″ squares and divide them in half diagonally to form large triangles. Cut out large tri-angles. Then cut 4 large squares 19″ by 19″, top and bottom inner borders 5½″ by 62″, 14 strips 2¼″ by 45″ (or the width of the fabric), 8 half diamonds (B), 16 small squares (C), and 16 small triangles (D). From dark blue print (1), cut 9 strips 2¼″ by 45″ (or the width of the fabric); then cut 32 diamonds (A). From each bright blue print (2) and blue and gray print (6), cut 15 strips 2¼″ by 45″ (or the width of the fabric).

From blue floral print (3), light blue print (4), and blue on white print (5), cut 8 strips 2¼″ by 45″ (or the width of the fabric). From blue floral print (3), cut 4 border strips for top and bottom 2½″ by 62″, 4 side bor-ders strips 2½″ by 72″, and 64 diamonds.

## Large Diamonds

Following Quick-Piecing Diagram 1, stitch strips of print fabrics together for colors 1–6. Then stitch another strip of color (1) to the lower edge. Indent each strip 2″ from the edge of the preceding strip. Measure and cut 2¼″-wide strips from this piece at a 45° angle, following Quick-Piecing Diagram 2. Cut 16 strips for Row 1.

For each Row 2–6, arrange the strips in the color or-der indicated on the large diamond piecing diagram on page 86, and stitch them together in the same manner. Cut 8 strips from each piece. Stitch Row 1 to Row 2, matching seams. Stitch Rows 3–6 in place, following

piecing diagram; then stitch another Row 1 to other edge of large diamond.

## Diamond Borders

Stitch a white strip to the top and bottom edges of each remaining bright blue and blue and gray print strips. In-dent each strip 2″ from the preceding strip. Measure and cut 2¼″-wide strips from these lengths at a 45° angle, following border Quick-Piecing Diagram 1. Cut 68 strips from bright blue print lengths. Cut 66 strips from blue and gray print lengths.

For top and bottom borders, alternating colors, stitch 31 diamond pieces together, following border Quick-Piecing Diagram 2. Begin and end with a bright blue diamond piece. Trim upper and lower edges ¼″ from points of diamonds to make a strip about 5¼″ wide. Stitch two half diamonds (B) to remaining corners of border strip, following border Quick-Piecing Diagram 3. Trim ends perpendicular to long edges ¼″ from outer corners of diamonds.

For side borders, alternating colors, stitch 36 dia-mond pieces together. Trim upper and lower edges ¼″ from points of diamonds to make a strip about 5¼″ wide. Stitch two half diamonds to remaining corners of border strip. Trim ends perpendicular to long edges, ¼″ from outer corners of diamonds.

## Quilt Top

To make the Lone Star you may wish to baste the large squares and triangles in place first. Check to make sure the Lone Star is flat and the outer edges are not wavy. Make any adjustments necessary, and then stitch the seams with a smaller stitch. The large squares and trian-gles are cut a little larger than needed to accommodate variations in the piecing of the large diamonds.

Following the 8-point star piecing diagram shown un-der Stars of the States Quilt on page 56, and matching seams, pin large diamonds together in pairs. Stitch the seam from the center to the end of the seamline on the last small diamond (A) ¼″ from edge of fabric. Stitch a large square between the outer points. There may be some excess fabric on the outer edge of the squares.

Matching seams, stitch two pairs of diamonds to-gether in the same manner. Stitch a large triangle be-tween the outer points. There may be some excess fabric on the outer edge of the triangles.

Matching seams, pin the halves of the Lone Star to-gether. Stitch the seam, beginning and ending stitching on the seamlines of the small diamonds ¼″ from edge of fabric. Stitch remaining large triangles between the

**LONE STAR QUILT   QUICK-PIECING DIAGRAMS**
**DIAGRAM 1**

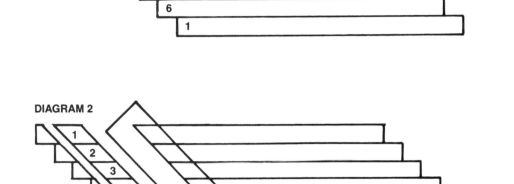

**DIAGRAM 2**

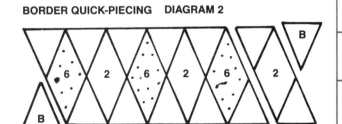

**BORDER QUICK-PIECING**
**DIAGRAM 1**

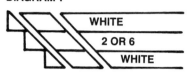

**BORDER QUICK-PIECING   DIAGRAM 2**

**BORDER QUICK-PIECING   DIAGRAM 3**

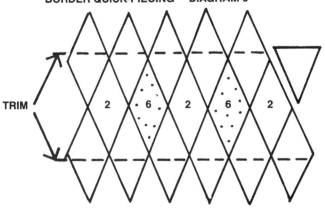

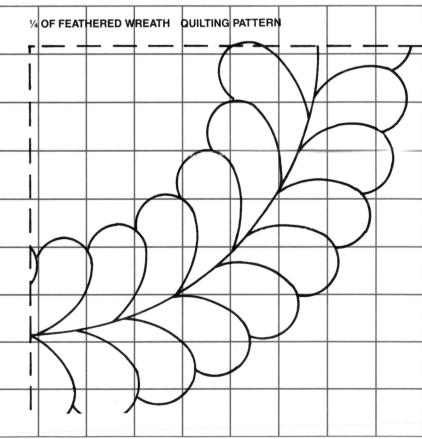

¼ OF FEATHERED WREATH   QUILTING PATTERN

**EACH SQUARE = 1″**

**LONE STAR QUILT  FLORAL BORDER MOTIF**

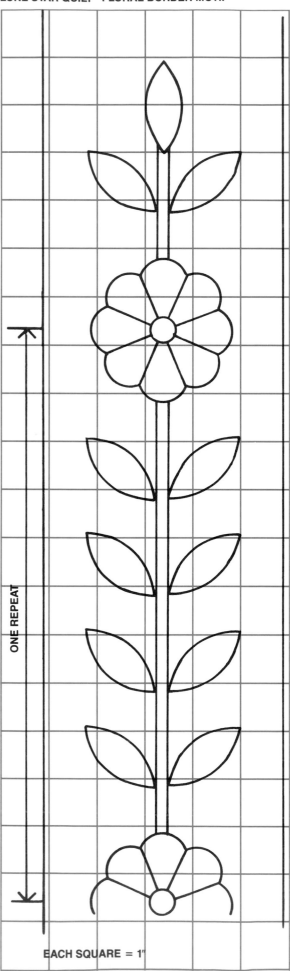

ONE REPEAT

**EACH SQUARE = 1"**

points of the diamonds. Trim outer edges of quilt top to make a square ¼" larger than points of diamonds.

*Borders*

Stitch a white border to top and bottom edges of Lone Star center. Trim ends even with side edges of center. Trim blue floral print side border strips to the length of the sides of quilt. Trim remaining border strips to the length of the top and bottom edges of the quilt. Stitch side border strips to each edge of long diamond borders. Stitch top and bottom border strips to each edge of short diamond borders. Stitch side borders to side edges of Lone Star center.

Following the 8-point star piecing diagram shown under Stars of the States Quilt on page 56, stitch dark blue print diamonds (A), small squares (C), and small triangles (D) together to form corner stars the same as large Lone Star center. Stitch a corner star to each end of top and bottom borders. Stitch these borders to top and bottom edges of quilt top.

*Quilting*

Following directions on page 15, enlarge feathered wreath and floral border motif from patterns on pages 89–90. Trace feathered wreath to four corners of a piece of tracing paper to make pattern for entire wreath. Make templates for quilting designs, following directions on page 15.

Following directions under *Quilting Basics* (page 23), mark feathered wreath centered on each large square. Mark half of feathered wreath motif on large triangles, matching center line to long outer edge of triangle. Mark floral border motif on white borders, beginning with a flower in center. Repeat motif twice, ending with three leaves along side edges. Mark a flower from border motif in center of Lone Star and in center of each corner star. Mark a small leaf in each diamond around flower.

If desired, mark quilting lines ¼" from inner edges of each diamond on Lone Star. Mark quilting lines on half diamonds ¼" from edges of diamonds. Mark quilting lines on blue print border strips ⅝" from long edges.

Cut 45" backing and seam pieces together to make backing, following directions on page 23. Place batting between backing and quilt top, right sides out. Pin, then baste, the layers together. Using matching thread, quilt by hand, along all lines just marked.

*Binding*

Following directions on page 26, cut a 36" square of dark blue print fabric and make a continuous binding 3½" wide. Trim edges of batting and backing ¼" larger than quilt top. Stitch binding around edges of quilt with a ½" seam allowance.

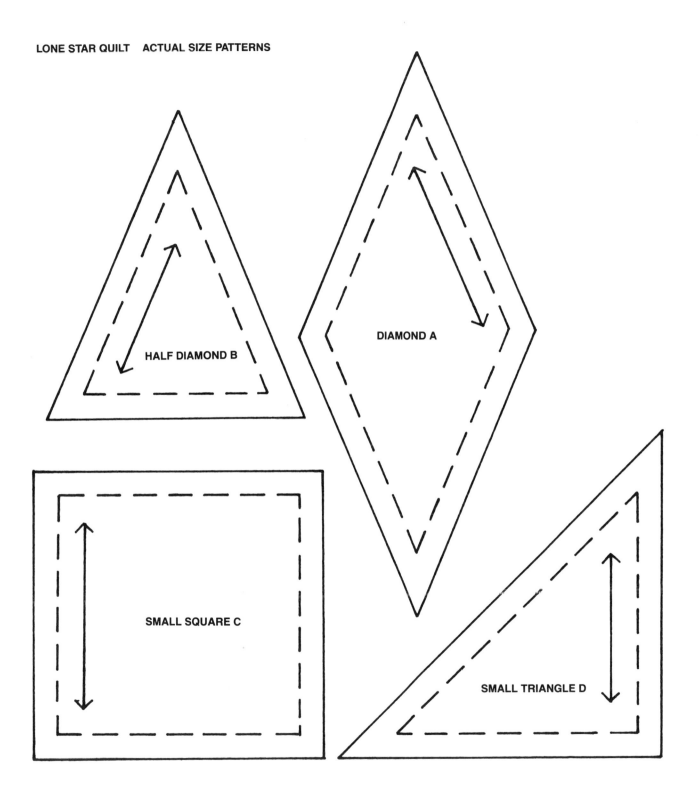

# AMISH MINI-QUILTS

he Amish first settled in Lancaster County, Pennsylvania, and later also settled in other areas in Pennsylvania and in Ohio and Indiana. They developed a unique style of quiltmaking which combined strong graphic designs with interesting color combinations, thus creating a design with the simplicity and strength comparable to that in works of modern art. Other Amish quilts were often elaborately worked with vines and flowers, cables, lattices, and feathered medallion and border patterns.

The mini-quilts shown here are a sampling of original Amish quilt patterns: the star, the diamond, bars, and sunshine and shadow. Their use of bright solid colors and black is borrowed from Amish clothing. Mini-quilts can be used alone as small wall hangings, or the designs can be made into small pillows or hot pads.

*Size: 12″ square*

**MATERIALS**

Diamond Quilt
    ⅛ yard or scraps of red, teal, and black cotton fabrics
    ⅜ yard or 13″ by 18″ piece bright blue cotton fabric
Star Quilt
    ⅛ yard or scraps black, teal, purple, and maroon cotton fabrics
    ⅜ yard or 13″ by 22″ piece rust cotton fabric
Bar Quilt
    ⅛ yard or scraps bright blue, rust, and black cotton fabrics
    ⅜ yard or 13″ by 19″ piece maroon cotton fabric
Sunshine and Shadows Quilt
    ⅛ yard or scraps bright pink, light blue, lavender, light green, green, and black cotton fabrics
    ⅜ yard or 13″ by 16″ piece purple cotton fabric
For Each Quilt
    13″-square cotton flannel for batting
    Sewing thread to match fabrics
    Black quilting thread

**DIRECTIONS**

## Diamond Quilt

*Cutting*

Following directions under *Marking and Cutting* (page 15), draw each piece on wrong side of fabric and cut out each piece. From bright blue, cut a 13″ square for backing and a 4″ square for center. From red, cut two 4¼″

squares in half diagonally to make 4 triangles. Then cut 4 inner border squares 1⅛″ by 1⅛″ and 4 border squares 2¼″ by 2¼″. From teal, for diamond borders, cut 2 strips 4″ by 1⅛″ and 2 strips 1⅛″ by 5¼″. Then cut 4 inner borders, 1⅛″ by 7¼″. Cut 4 borders 2¼″ by 8½″ from black.

## Quilt Top

Stitch all seams right sides together with ¼″ seam allowance. Stitch 4″ diamond borders to opposite sides of center. Then stitch 5¼″ diamond borders to remaining edges. Stitch a red triangle to each side of diamond borders. Stitch two inner borders to opposite edges of joined unit. Stitch inner border squares to ends of remaining inner borders. Stitch these pieces to remaining edges of top. Stitch two borders to opposite edges of top. Stitch border squares to ends of remaining borders. Stitch these pieces to remaining edges of top.

## Star Quilt

*Cutting*

Following directions under *Templates* (page 15), make a template for diamond, adding ¼″ seam allowance. Trace template or draw each piece on wrong side of fabric and cut out each piece.

From rust fabric, cut a 13″ square for backing and 8 diamonds. From black, draw two 2⅞″ squares and divide them in half to make 4 triangles. Then cut four 2½″ squares and four borders 2¼″ by 8½″. From purple, cut 4 inner borders 1⅛″ by 7¼″. From teal, cut 4 inner border squares 1⅛″ by 1⅛″. From maroon, cut 4 border squares 2¼″ by 2¼″.

## Quilt Top

Stitch all seams, right sides together, with ¼″ seam allowance. Matching edges, stitch diamonds together in pairs, ending stitching at end of seamline on side. Stitch a black square between edges of diamonds. Stitch 2 diamond pieces together, matching inner side edges. Stitch a black triangle between diamonds. Stitch halves of star together. Stitch a triangle between diamonds at sides to form a square.

Stitch 2 inner borders to opposite edges of square. Stitch inner border squares to each end of remaining inner borders. Stitch these pieces to edges of top. Stitch borders to opposite edges of top. Stitch border squares to each end of remaining borders. Stitch these pieces to edges of top.

Clockwise from top left: *Bar Quilt, Sunshine and Shadows Quilt, Star Quilt,* and *Diamond Quilt.*

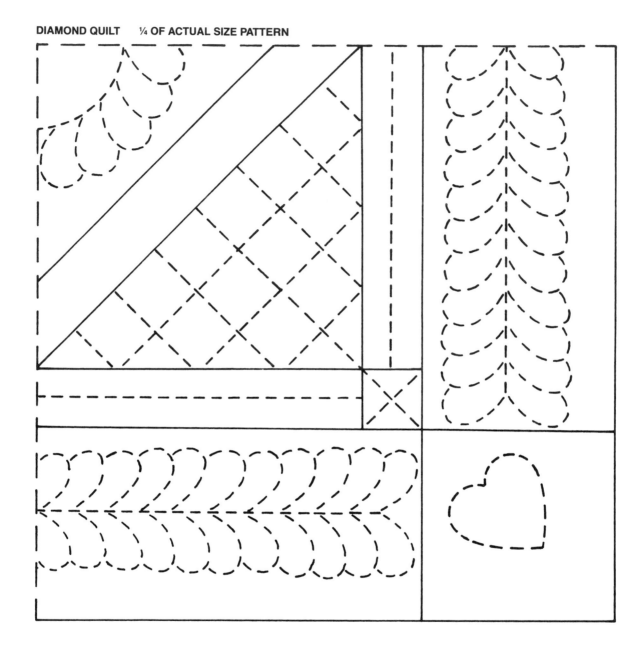

## Bar Quilt

*Cutting*

Following directions under *Marking and Cutting* (page 15), draw each piece on wrong side of fabric and cut out each piece. From maroon, cut a 13″ square for backing, 4 bars 1½″ by 7½″, and 4 inner border squares 1⅛″ by 1⅛″. From bright blue, cut 3 bars 1½″ by 7½″ and 4 border squares 2¼″ by 2¼″. From rust, cut 4 inner borders 1⅛″ by 7½″. From black, cut 4 borders 2¼″ by 8¾″.

## Quilt Top

Stitch all seams, right sides together, with ¼″ seam allowance. Alternating colors, stitch bars together along long edges to form a square. Stitch two inner borders to opposite sides of bars. Stitch inner border squares to remaining inner borders. Stitch these pieces to remaining edges of top. Stitch borders to opposite edges of top. Stitch border squares to each end of remaining borders. Stitch these pieces to edges of top.

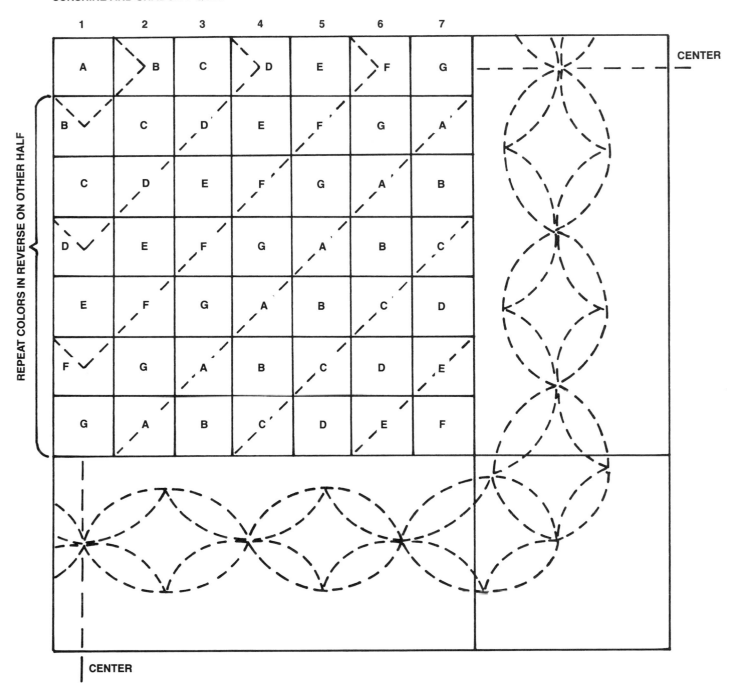

## Sunshine and Shadows Quilt

### Cutting

Following directions under *Marking and Cutting* (page 15), draw each piece on wrong side of fabric and cut out each piece. From purple, cut a 13″ square for backing. Cut the following squares 1⅛″ by 1⅛″: 25 bright pink (A), 24 light blue (B), 24 bright blue (C), 24 lavender (D), 24 purple (E), 24 light green (F), and 24 green (G). From light blue, cut 4 border squares 2¼″ by 2¼″. From black, cut 4 borders 2¼″ by 8¾″.

## Quilt Top

Stitch all seams, right sides together, with ¼″ seam allowance. Arrange squares A-G in Row 1 following Quilt Top diagram (above), and stitch them together. Then sew squares B-G together. Sew end with square B on top of center square A to form whole center strip of 13 squares. Trim seam allowance to ⅛″.

Make 2 more 13-square strips each of Rows 2 through 7 in same manner. Trim seam allowance to ⅛″, and sew

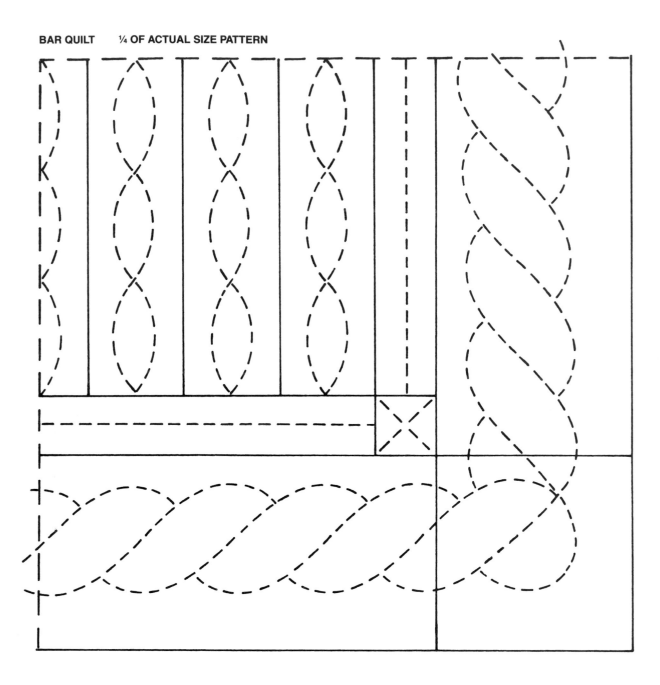

rows in order to each side of center matching seams. Stitch borders to opposite edges of top. Stitch border squares to each end of remaining borders. Stitch these pieces to edges of top.

*Quilting*

Following directions in *Quilting Basics*, (page 15), make templates for quilting designs shown in diagrams for each quilt top quarter. Mark quilting lines on quilt tops. Cut flannel the same size as quilt top. Place flannel and quilt top in center of backing square. Pin and baste the layers together. Quilt along marked lines using tiny black quilting stitches.

Trim backing ½″ larger than quilt top. Fold backing to front over edge, turning under ¼″ and mitering corners. Slipstitch edge of backing in place.

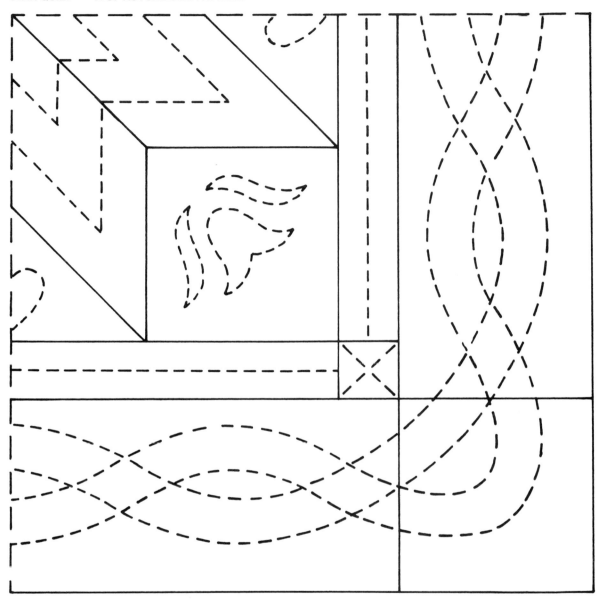

# LINCOLN'S PLATFORM PLACE MATS

Illinois is known as "the Land of Lincoln," and this place mat is based on the block called Lincoln's Platform, named for the political platform of our 16th president. Quiltmaking reached zenith proportions during the mid-19th century, and the hardships imposed by the Civil War added to its important place in history. Fairs and quilt raffles raised money for military hospitals, and quilts were made to warm and comfort soldiers far from home. Red, white, and blue was a popular color combination then, and still is: Lincoln's Platform is shown here in antique shades of those colors. These easy-to-make place mats, made from fabrics with stars and tiny prints, will complement kitchens and dining rooms of any style.

*Size: 13" by 19¼"*

## MATERIALS

For Four Place Mats
  45"-wide cotton fabrics
  ½ yard medium-scale red and blue-on-white print
  ⅜ yard blue print
  1¼ yards red print
  ⅜ yard small-scale red and blue-on-white print
  Four 14" by 20" pieces traditional-weight quilt batting
  White sewing thread; red, white, and blue quilting thread

## MATERIALS

For Four Napkins
  1 yard 45"-wide blue print cotton fabric
  Blue sewing thread

## DIRECTIONS

### Place Mats

Make templates for pieces A, B, and C and star quilting motif by tracing patterns on page 100. Cutting and sewing directions are given for one place mat; repeat directions for each additional place mat you wish to make. Stitch all seams right sides together with ¼" seam allowance. For quick-piecing triangles and squares, see *Patchwork Basics* (page 17).

### Cutting

From medium-scale red, white, and blue fabric, cut 4 triangles (A) and 12 squares (B). Do not cut triangles if you plan to quick-piece them. From blue print, cut 4 triangles (A) and 8 squares (B). Do not cut triangles if you plan to quick-piece them. From red print, cut 1 backing piece 16" by 22" and 4 rectangles (C). From small-scale red, white, and blue print, cut 2 side panels 3¾" by 13½" and center square (B).

**LINCOLN'S PLATFORM BLOCK  PIECING DIAGRAM**

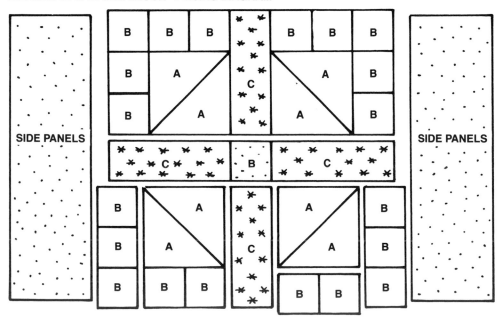

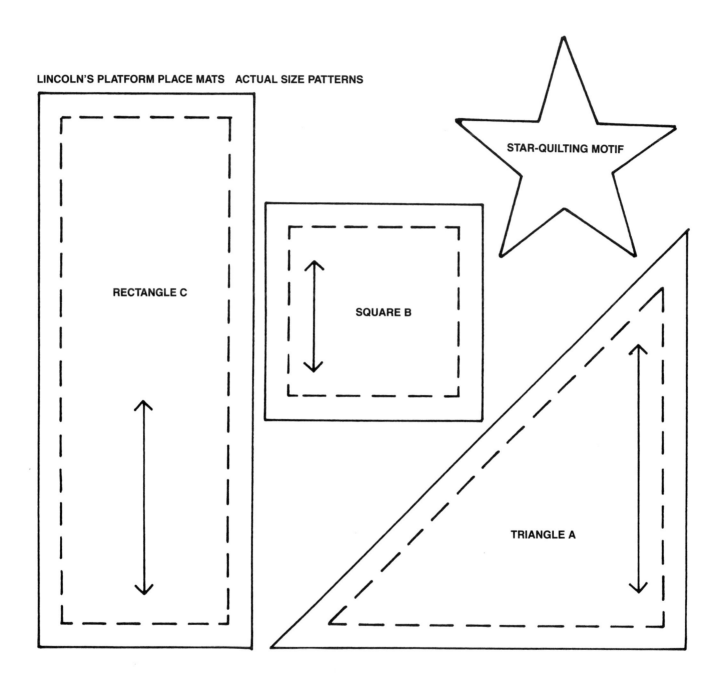

LINCOLN'S PLATFORM PLACE MATS   ACTUAL SIZE PATTERNS

STAR-QUILTING MOTIF

RECTANGLE C

SQUARE B

TRIANGLE A

100

### Piecing Place Mat

Following piecing diagram, stitch each red, white, and blue triangle (A) to a blue triangle (A) to form a square. Or quick-piece triangles. Stitch blue squares (B) to red, white, and blue squares (B). Stitch additional red, white, and blue squares to opposite sides of 4 of the blue squares. Or quick-piece squares. Stitch a strip of 2 squares to one side of blue triangles. Stitch a strip of 3 squares to remaining side of blue triangles and blue squares.

Stitch pieced sections to each long side of 2 rectangles (C). Stitch ends of remaining rectangles to opposite sides of center square (B) to make center strip of Lincoln's Platform block. Stitch pieced strips to each side of center strip, matching seams. Stitch side panels to sides of Lincoln's Platform block.

### Quilting and Finishing

Following pattern, trace star quilting motif to center of side panels ½" from inner seam. Trace star to top and bottom, 1" from edges. Trace another star centered in each space between these stars. Draw lines diagonally across center square to form an x. If desired, mark quilting lines ¼" from edges of blue, red, and red-white-and-blue areas.

Place patchwork place mat on quilt batting right side up; trim edges of batting ¼" larger than place mat. Center batting and place mat on wrong side of backing fabric. Pin, then baste, layers together. Using matching thread, hand-quilt along lines mentioned above. Trim backing fabric 1⅛" from outer edge of place mat. Fold ½" to wrong side, and pin in position on place mat top, folding fabric diagonally at corners to miter them. Slip-stitch edges to place mat top.

## Napkins

Cut a 16" square of fabric for each napkin. Turn under ¼" twice along edges, and stitch in place.

# MAP OF THE STATES WALL HANGING

istorically, maps often have been an integral part of commemorative quilts made to honor a specific town or region or to celebrate an important event, such as a centennial or bicentennial. This map, machine-appliquéd and hand-quilted in natural colors, has a red, white, and blue border. It not only will add a touch of Americana to your den or family room, but is sure to inspire anyone studying American history. A great Father's Day gift or birthday present for that special man in your life, this wall hanging could also be made for a PTA raffle or to hang in a school library.

*Size: 25½" by 31"*

## MATERIALS

45"-wide cotton fabrics
⅝ yard blue
⅝ yard gold
½ yard tan
¼ yard light green
¼ yard red
¼ yard muslin
¼ yard or 7" by 11" piece brown
⅛ yard or 3½" by 14" piece navy
28" by 35" piece backing
1 yard fusible webbing without paper
2" by 8" piece paper-backed fusible webbing
28" by 35" piece traditional-weight quilt batting
Brown, light green, and gold sewing thread
Brown, light green, blue, navy, and off-white quilting thread

## DIRECTIONS

### Map

Enlarge pattern for map on pages 104–105 by following directions under *Enlarging Patterns* (page 15). Cut a 20" by 24½" piece of light blue for background. Trace the outlines of the countries to background. Following directions under *Machine-Appliqué* (page 22), make patterns for the continental United States, Alaska, Hawaii, Canada, Mexico, and the part of Canada that adjoins Alaska. Add ⅛"–¼" seam allowance to Canada and Mexico along edges where the United States or the gold lines will overlap them. Add ¼" seam allowance to upper and side edge of Canada. Trace the United States, Alaska and Hawaii, including the state border lines, to the right side of tan fabric. Trace both Canadian pieces to light green. Trace Mexico to brown.

Place a piece of scrap paper or a Teflon sheet on your ironing board. Then place fusible webbing on paper with an appliqué piece on top. Beginning with the continental United States, work from the largest to the smallest piece. Turn off steam and, for just a few seconds, turn the very tip of your iron along the outer edges of the appliqué piece to fuse them together. Gently pull the web away from the paper or Teflon and cut out the shapes. Then cut out the center of the fusible webbing so that just about ¼" remains along the edge. Do not try to cut out center of fusible webbing on small islands.

Draw four ⅛" by 8" strips on paper-backed fusible webbing. Fuse to wrong side of gold fabric and cut out strips. Arrange appliqué pieces on the background fabric and fuse them in place. Cut the gold lines into pieces to fit along lines around Alaska and Hawaii, and fuse them in place. Using matching thread, zigzag along edges of Canada and Mexico. Zigzag around the United States, Alaska, and Hawaii with brown. Zigzag over gold fabrics strips with gold.

### Borders

Stitch all seams, right sides together, with ¼" seam allowance. Make pattern for star by tracing pattern on page 105. Cut 4 from muslin and back with fusible webbing, following directions given above. Cut four 3½" squares from navy. Fuse stars to center of squares. Zigzag stitch around stars with off-white thread. From red, cut four strips 1½" by 24½" and four strips 1½" by 20". From white, cut two strips 1½" by 24½" and 2 strips 1½" by 20". To make borders, match lengths and stitch a red strip to each side of white strips. Stitch long borders to top and bottom of map. Stitch star squares to ends of side borders. Stitch side borders to center of map and borders.

### Quilting and Finishing

Following directions under *Quilting Basics* (page 23), mark quilting lines along center of white border strips. Place batting between backing and top with right sides out. Pin, then baste, the layers together.

Using blue thread, quilt ⅛" from edges of background and edges of countries and states. Quilt along edges of Canada with light green and Mexico with brown. Quilt along the border lines of the states with brown. Quilt along the center of the white border strips and ⅛" from the edge of the stars with matching thread. Trim batting and backing ¼" larger than top. Following directions under *Binding* (page 26), make a 3½"-wide bias binding from gold fabric. Stitch binding to wall hanging ½" from edges.

MAP OF THE STATES WALL HANGING

CANADA

UNITED STATES

MEXICO

ALASKA

HAWAII

EACH SQUARE = 1"

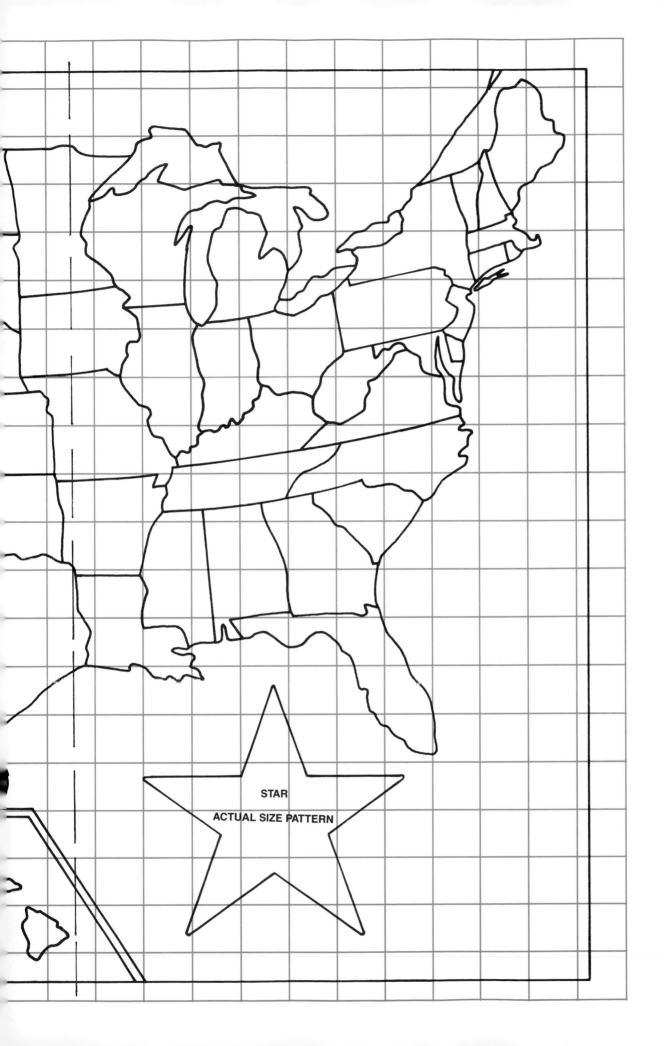

STAR

ACTUAL SIZE PATTERN

# NANTUCKET PINEAPPLE TEA COZY

 antucket schooners brought back tea from their trips to the Orient. They also brought pineapples, which New Englanders soon embraced as their own symbol of hospitality. Pineapple designs were often included in 19th-century album and appliqué quilts. This charming tea cozy will welcome friends to share a pot of tea and delicious cakes, and keep your tea warm while you enjoy a friendly chat. It is hand-appliquéd in rich, traditional shades of gold and green on a white on off-white background fabric. Hand-quilted with thick batting, its upper edges are piped and the lower edge is finished with binding.

*Size: 11¼" by 15"*

## MATERIALS

45"-wide cotton fabrics
   ½ yard white on off-white print or solid off-white
   ½ yard lining fabric
   ¼ yard gold print
   ¼ yard green-and-white print
   ⅛ yard or scraps of each sage green and olive
   Two 15" by 18" pieces quilt batting
   1⅛ yards cotton cording
   Sage green, olive, gold, and off-white sewing thread
   Quilting thread

## DIRECTIONS

### Tea Cozy Front and Back

Enlarge pattern for tea cozy onto ½ piece of tracing paper. Trace pineapple pattern (page 109) to cozy, matching center lines and keeping lower leaf 1" above lower edge. Fold paper in half along the center line of pattern, and trace onto other half to make whole pattern. Cut two 15" by 18" pieces of off-white print. Transfer cutting lines of tea cozy to center of each piece. Transfer pineapple to center of one piece for front.

Mark centers of tea cozy pieces just above and just below cutting line.

Following directions under *Hand-Appliqué* (page 19),

make patterns for pineapple and leaves. Cut pineapple from gold, leaves with dots from sage green, and the remaining leaves from olive. Beginning at the top, pin outer sage green leaves to position on front and slip-stitch them in place. Then slipstitch olive leaves in place. Slipstitch leaf to center. Slipstitch remaining leaves to position on front. Then slipstitch pineapple to position on leaves. Turn front to wrong side and trim background fabric behind appliqué to ¼" from stitching.

### Quilting

Following directions under *Quilting Basics* (page 23), mark quilting lines on pineapple, as shown on pattern. Draw vertical quilting lines on front and back 2" apart. Begin drawing lines 1" to left and right of center. Do not draw lines on top of appliqué.

Cut two 15" by 18" pieces from lining. For each front and back, place batting between lining and tea cozy pieces, right sides out. Pin, then baste, layers together. Baste along stitching line ½" in from cutting line. Hand-quilt around appliqué design, ⅛" from edge, along lines on pineapple, and along vertical lines on front and back. Do not quilt outside the cutting lines marked on front and back.

### Assembling Tea Cozy

Cut out front and back. Following directions under *Cording* (page 28), cut bias strips of green and white print fabric to cover a 34" length of cotton cording. With right sides together, match stitching lines and baste cording to upper curve of the cozy front. Cut a 5"-long bias strip 1¼" wide; fold in half lengthwise with right sides together. Stitch ¼" from fold. Trim seam allowance to ⅛" and turn right side out with a small safety pin. Insert cording into tube of fabric.

Fold covered cording in half and baste to center top of cozy front to make a 1" hanging loop. Right sides together, stitch front to back along upper curve. Zigzag-stitch or overcast edge of seam allowance. Turn right side out. Cut 3¼"-wide bias strips of gold fabric to piece a binding 33" long. Make binding and bind lower edge, following directions on page 26.

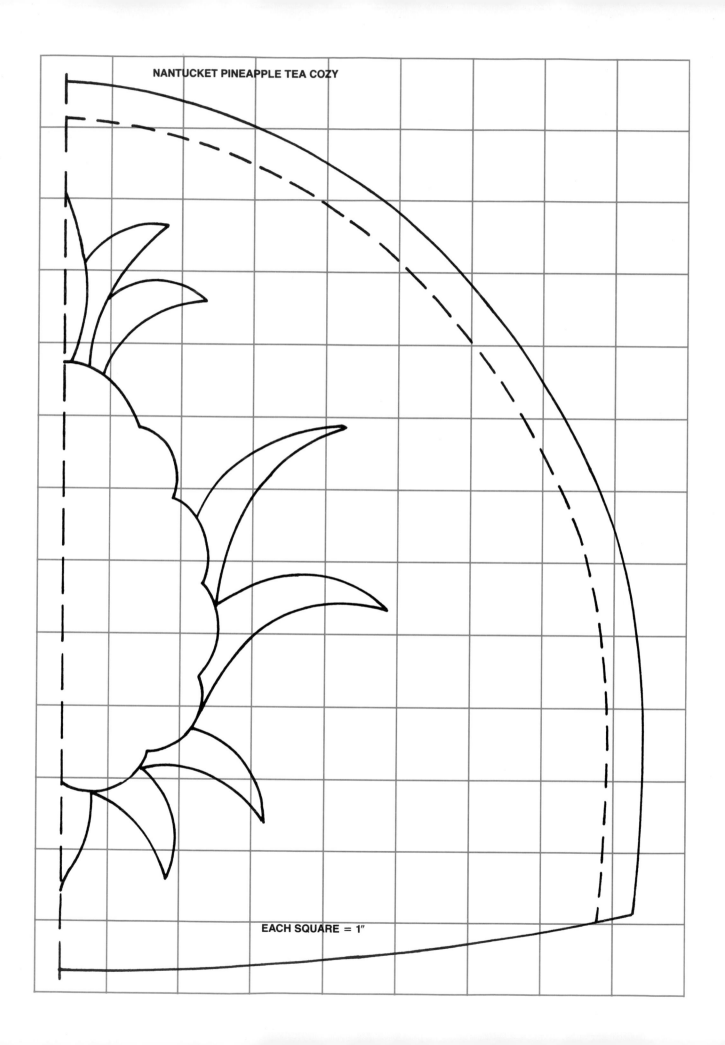

**NANTUCKET PINEAPPLE TEA COZY**

**EACH SQUARE = 1"**

QUILTING LINE

# "MOM'S APPLE PIE" KITCHEN SAMPLER

What could be more American than Mom's apple pie or the American flag? Pies made from apples grown anywhere from New York's famous Pioneer Valley to the orchards of Washington State are familiar symbols of America's bounty. This kitchen sampler would make a wonderful gift for every Mom—for Mother's Day, for a birthday, or for any day you want to say, "Thanks, Mom." You can also make this sampler for yourself, just to enjoy: it combines hand-appliqué, embroidery, and patchwork flags in a quilted tribute to this all-American dessert.

*Size: 14" by 18"*

## MATERIALS

45"-wide cotton fabrics
    ½ yard off-white muslin
    ⅛ yard or scraps of tan, rust, red, light green, red and off-white stripe and white star, or other small print on navy
    16" by 20" piece quilt batting
    Red, tan, rust, light green, and off-white sewing thread
    1 skein each navy, red, gold, and brown embroidery floss
    Off-white quilting thread
    14" by 18" picture frame

## DIRECTIONS

### Sampler Top

To make a full-size pattern, draw a 14" by 18" rectangle on tracing paper. Draw a line parallel to the top and bottom lines 2⅜" in from edges. Draw a line parallel to each side line 3½" in from edges. Mark the vertical and horizontal centers of the rectangle. Using the patterns on pages 112–113, trace "Mom's Apple Pie" and pie appliqué to upper half of center rectangle. Trace ingredients for "Crust" and "Filling" to each lower quarter. Trace four apples spaced evenly across upper and lower borders. Trace three apples to side borders. Erase lines marking centers.

Cut a 15" by 19" piece of muslin and trace pattern lightly to center. Following directions under *Hand-Appliqué* (page 19), make patterns and cut 14 apples from red, 14 leaves from green, pie crust from tan, and pie plate from rust. Pin pie plate, then pie crust, to background. Slipstitch pieces in place with matching thread. Slipstitch apples and leaves to borders.

Following directions under *Embroidery Basics* (page 32), embroider "Mom's Apple Pie" with 4 strands of navy floss and backstitches. With 3 strands of navy floss, embroider ingredients with backstitches; with 3 strands of brown floss, embroider stems on apples with stem stitch.

Make templates for flag pieces on page 113. Cut 4 rectangles from navy print and 4 striped pieces from striped fabric. Clip seam allowance at inner corner of stripes. Right sides in, stitch stars to upper left corner of stripes with ¼" seam allowance. Mark cutting lines at corners ¼" from inner lines of corner rectangles. Cut out corners. Stitch a flag to each corner of center, clipping seam allowance at inner corner.

### Quilting

Cut a 16" by 20" piece of muslin for backing. Following directions under *Quilting Basics* (page 23), place batting between backing and sampler top. Pin, then baste, the layers together. Using quilting thread or 3 strands of embroidery floss for quilting, quilt ⅛" from outer edge of pie with off-white. Quilt line on pie crust and outline of center with gold. Stitch openings in crust through all layers with Lazy Daisy stitches (see page 34). Quilt lines under words with red floss. Quilt in the ditch along seams of flags. Frame sampler.

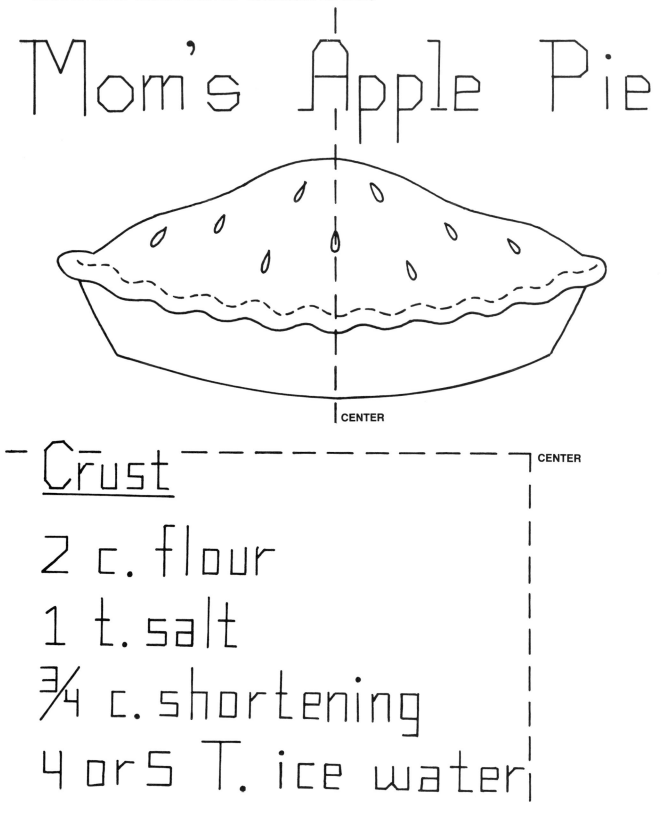

# Mom's Apple Pie

CENTER

CENTER

## Crust

2 c. flour

1 t. salt

¾ c. shortening

4 or 5 T. ice water

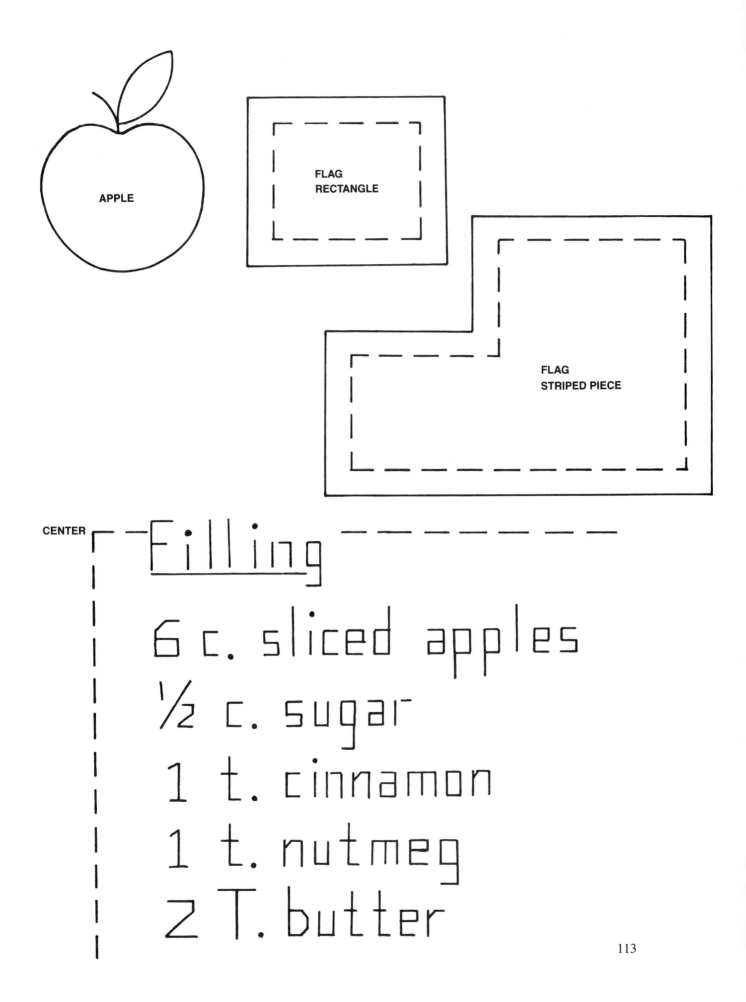

APPLE

FLAG
RECTANGLE

FLAG
STRIPED PIECE

CENTER

Filling

6 c. sliced apples

½ c. sugar

1 t. cinnamon

1 t. nutmeg

2 T. butter

# PENNSYLVANIA DUTCH CHAIR SEAT

The Pennsylvania Dutch have a rich heritage of Old World design and folk symbols. Tulips, considered a variation of the holy lily, with its three petals symbolizing the trinity, were a popular flower design. Hearts symbolized love and joy, and birds or doves were symbols of conjugal bliss. Red and yellow were the colors of the god of marriage and home. With these symbols, the Pennsylvania Dutch decorated household items such as chests, cabinets, and this chair seat. The bright colors of this attractive accessory will be a focal point when placed on your favorite rocking or straight-back chair. Machine-appliqué and quilting make this a fast and easy project.

*Size: approximately 17" by 17"*

## MATERIALS

45"-wide cotton fabrics
 1¼ yards muslin
 ⅜ yard yellow print
 ¾ yard blue micro-dot print
 ⅛ yard or scraps blue, red, green print, and red print
 2 yards cotton cording
 22" square high-loft quilt batting
 Red, yellow, green, blue, and off-white sewing thread
 Polyester stuffing
 ½ yard each, yellow and black embroidery floss

## DIRECTIONS

Following directions on page 15 and matching center lines, enlarge pattern for chair seat on page 116 on a half-sheet of tracing paper. Trace pattern onto other half of tracing paper to make entire pattern. Cut three chair seats from muslin and one from batting. Trace appliqué design to one muslin piece.

Following directions under *Machine-Appliqué* (page 22), trace patterns onto fusible webbing and cut from fabric as follows. Cut birds from blue, wings from blue micro-dot, beaks from yellow, tulip side petals from yellow print, tulip centers from red, leaves from green, and heart from red print. Draw center stems ⅛" by 7½" and two stems ⅛" by 6½". Fuse stems on the bias on the wrong side of the green print fabric.

Fuse 6½" stems in place on chair seat, stretching them to curve along curved line. Fuse long stem along center line. Fuse remaining pieces to position on chair seat. Using green thread, zigzag along stems. Using matching thread, zigzag around all other pieces. By hand, embroider bird's eyes with black satin stitch and feet with yellow backstitch.

Following directions under *Machine-Quilting* (page 24), place batting between muslin chair seat backing piece and appliquéd chair seat. Pin and baste the layers together. Machine-baste ½" from edges. Quilt along the edges of the appliqué pieces. Make 2 rows of gathering stitches between dots, ½" and ¼" from edges, on both appliquéd top and remaining chair seat piece. Gather corner edges at front of chair seat to 2½". Gather corner edges at back to 1¾". Stitch gathers in place ½" from edge.

Following directions under *Cording* (page 28), cut bias strips of yellow print fabric and cover cording. Stitch to right side of chair seat top, ½" from edges. Cut four ties 6" by 27" from blue micro-dot print. Fold in half lengthwise, right sides in, and trim one end diagonally. Stitch along long edge and diagonal end. Trim seam allowance at corners. Turn right side out. Pleat unfinished ends in thirds. Baste two ties to each side chair seat top, centered over placement mark.

Stitch top to remaining chair seat piece ½" from edges, leaving an opening in back for turning. Turn right side out. Stuff chair seat firmly with polyester stuffing. Turn under edges along opening and slipstitch them together.

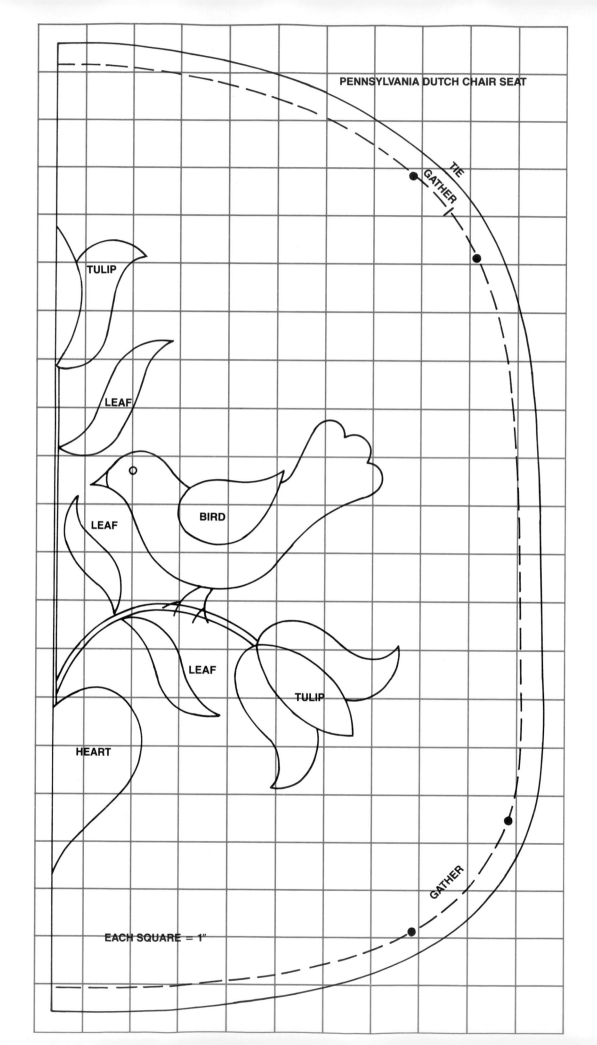

PENNSYLVANIA DUTCH CHAIR SEAT

TIE

GATHER

TULIP

LEAF

LEAF

BIRD

LEAF

TULIP

HEART

GATHER

EACH SQUARE = 1"

# UNCLE SAM DOLL

ag dolls have always been part of the American folk art tradition. Today, these historically inspired dolls add an innovative touch to a home's decor. Uncle Sam represents the United States, and here he has patchwork-striped pants, a quilted jacket, and a top hat.

*Size: 26" tall*

## MATERIALS

45"-wide cotton fabrics
  ½ yard navy
  ⅜ yard beige
  ¼ yard red
  ¼ yard off-white muslin
  18" by 24" piece lightweight quilt batting
  ½ lb. polyester stuffing
  10 yards white 3-ply Persian yarn
  Red, white, blue, and black acrylic paint
  Small artist's paintbrush
  Navy, red, off-white, and beige sewing thread
  Off-white and navy quilting thread
  2"-square fusible webbing

## DIRECTIONS

Enlarge patterns on page 121, following directions under *Enlarging Patterns* (page 15). Fold fabrics in half, matching selvages, and cut as follows: From beige, cut 2 bodies, 4 arms, 4 legs, and 1 nose. Trace markings to wrong side of fabric pieces and trace features to right side of one body piece for front. Transfer seamline of nose and ears to fabric. From navy, cut 4 shoes, 4 jacket fronts, 4 jacket backs, 4 jacket sleeves, jacket collar 3½" by 6¼", 2 hat tops, 2 hat sides, and 2 hat brims. Mark quilting lines on 2 fronts, 2 backs, 2 sleeves, and 2 hat sides.

From red, 6 stripes 1" by 33" for pants, waistband 1¾" by 11", 2 hatbands, bow tie 2½" by 5½", and bow tie center 1½" by 1½". From off-white, cut 6 stripes 1" by 33" for pants, 1 shirt back, 2 shirt fronts, shirt collar 1½" by 8¾".

## Doll

Stitch all seams, right sides together, using ¼" seam allowance. Stitch body front to back, leaving lower straightedge open. Clip seam allowance along curves. Fold shoulder to sides, matching seams, and stitch darts in shoulder (see Diagram 1). Turn right side out, stuff body, and turn under lower edge along seamline. Stitch shoes to lower edge of legs. Stitch legs together in pairs. Clip seam allowance along curves. Turn right side

out. Stuff legs using a dowel or chopstick to push stuffing in place. Fold upper edge of legs in half, matching seams in center. Baste across top edge of legs. Insert legs, feet facing forward, in lower edge of body. Slipstitch front and back to legs.

Stitch arms together in pairs, leaving straight end open for turning. Clip seam allowance along curves. Turn right side out. Stuff lower arms below broken line. Make a row of running stitches by hand across line on arm. Stuff upper arm. Turn under seam allowance on end and slipstitch edges together. Sew end of arms to sides of body along shoulder darts.

Stitch ears together in pairs along curved edge. Trim seam allowances to ⅛". Turn right side out. Turn under seam allowance along straight edge and slipstitch edges together. Paint eyes white. Paint iris (circle) of eye blue. Paint pupil of eye black with a small white dot. Paint thin line at top of eye black. Paint mouth red. Fold nose in half, matching edges, and stitch seam along lower edge. Turn under ⅛" along edges of nose, and baste them in place. Stuff nose. Pin, then slipstitch, nose to face.

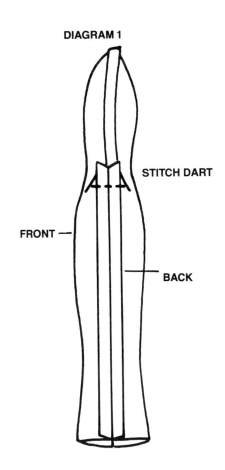

**DIAGRAM 1**

STITCH DART

FRONT —

BACK

**DIAGRAM 2**

MOUTH

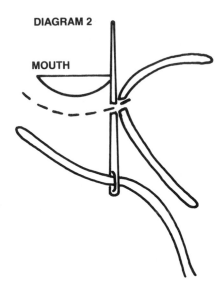

**DIAGRAM 3**

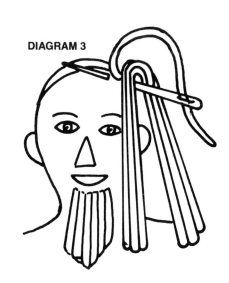

**DIAGRAM 4**

Embroider eyebrows with 1-ply of white yarn, using stem stitch. Thread a large needle with a length of 3-ply yarn. For beard, make a tiny vertical stitch across one end of line below mouth (see Diagram 2). Trim ends of yarn to about 1½". Continue making stitches along line. Trim ends into a V-shape.

Cut thirty-six 8" lengths of 3-ply yarn. Thread needle with a length of 1-ply yarn. Place hair across seam of head a few strands at a time and sew in place with back-stitches along seamline (see Diagram 3). Pin last 4 strands along seamline of head and tack strands in place about every ¾", beginning and ending above ears (see Diagram 4).

## Shirt

Turn under ¼", then ½" along center front edges. Stitch hem in place along inner edge. Stitch fronts to backs along upper arm seams. Turn under ¼", then ½", on ends of sleeves. Stitch hem in place along inner edge.

Pin, then stitch, one long edge of collar to neck edge of fronts and backs, beginning and ending ¼" from ends of collar. Press under ¼" along other long edge. Fold collar in half lengthwise, right sides in, and stitch across ends. Trim corners of seam allowance. Turn right side out. Slipstitch edge of collar along seamline of neck edge.

Stitch fronts to back along side and underarm seams. Turn under ¼" twice along lower edge and stitch hem in place. Place shirt on doll. Sew front edges together.

## Pants

Following directions under *Strip-Piecing* (page 18), stitch red and white strips together, alternating colors. Cut two 15½" lengths from this piece. Turn under ½" along one end of each piece and stitch hem in place. Fold each pants piece in half lengthwise. Beginning 3¾" from unfinished end, stitch edges together to make each leg. Clip seam allowance at top edge of stitching.

Turn leg sections right side out. Pin, then stitch, legs sections together along top edges of seam allowance, matching inside leg seams. Turn under ½" along top edge and press fold in place. Make a row of running stitches by hand ⅛" from fold. Place pants on doll. Gather waist to fit and knot thread securely.

Fold waistband in half lengthwise. Stitch long edges together. Turn right side out. Press flat with seam along one edge. Place waistband over top edge of pants, with lower edge just covering gathering stitches. Turn under ends at center back. Stitch ends together and slipstitch lower edge to pants.

## Jacket

Baste quilt batting to wrong side of backs and fronts with quilting lines. Stitch these backs together along upper edge of center back, ending at dot. Clip diagonally to dot. Stitch fronts to backs at shoulder. Stitch remaining backs and fronts together in same manner without batting for lining.

Baste batting to wrong side of one half of collar. With right sides in, fold collar in half and stitch across ends. Trim seam allowance. Turn right side out. Stitch collar to neck edge of jacket (see Diagram 5). Clip diagonally to dots. Pin, then stitch, lining to jacket along neck edge, center and lower edges of front, and center and side edges of tails (see Diagram 6). Make both tails the same as the one fully shown. Left-hand side overlaps the right-hand tail in diagram. Clip and trim seam allowances. Turn right side out. Baste batting to sleeves with quilting lines. Stitch these sleeves to remaining sleeves along straight lower edge. Turn lining to wrong side.

Baste raw edges of sleeves and fronts and backs together. Quilt lines of stars with off-white thread. Quilt ⅛" from finished edges of fronts, backs, sleeves, and collar with navy. Then quilt along remaining marked lines. Stitch sleeves to armhole edge of jacket. Stitch underarm and side seams. Slipstitch top edge of tails at center back in place.

## Hat

Fuse stars to position on hatband, and zigzag along edges with matching thread. Stitch hatband with stars to lower edge of side with quilting lines. Baste quilt batting to wrong side of this piece.

Stitch remaining hatband to side for lining. Stitch lining piece to outer piece along side edges and lower edge of hatband. Trim seam allowance. Turn right side out. Quilt hatband ⅛" from upper edge. Quilt along marked lines. Slipstitch side edges together. Place batting between hat top pieces. Baste edges together. Stitch upper edge of sides to top.

Baste batting to wrong side of one hat brim. Stitch ¼" from inner edge of remaining brim for lining. Stitch brims together along outer edge. Clip seam allowance and turn right side out. Clip seam allowance along inner edge of brim pieces and turn under along stitching. Slipstitch edges together. Slipstitch brim to lower edge of hatband. Place hat on doll.

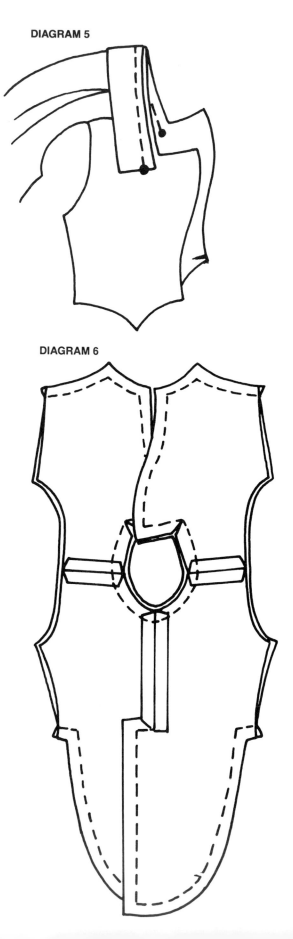

**DIAGRAM 5**

**DIAGRAM 6**

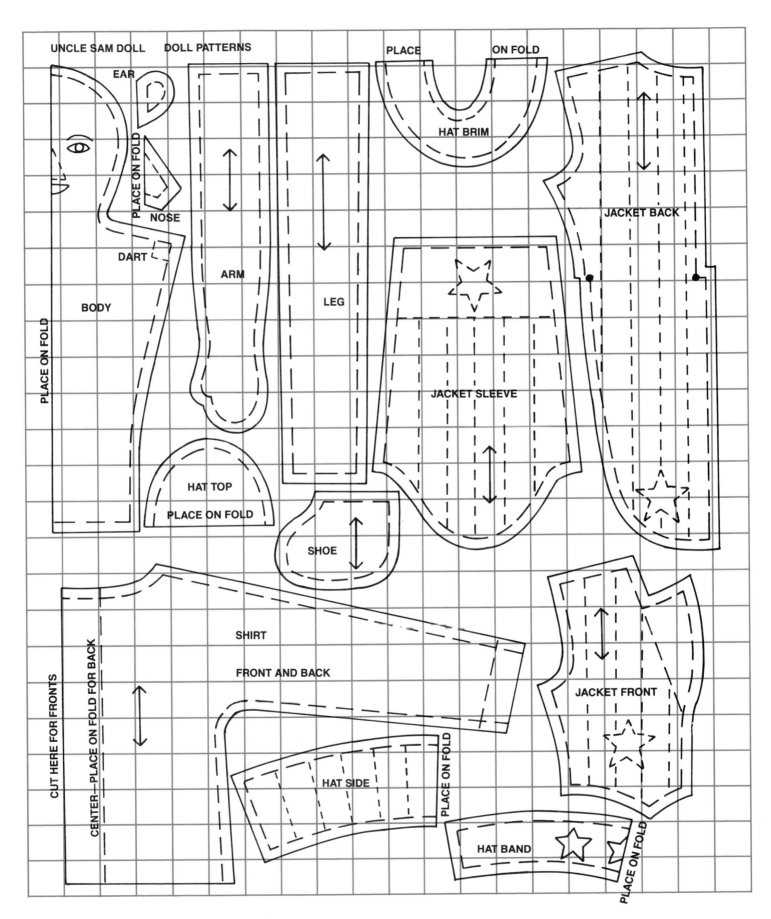

# BETSY ROSS DOLL

The woman known as Betsy Ross is credited with the creation of our first national flag. Shown here in colonial dress, she's wearing a quilted skirt that was both popular and practical in the 18th century. She stitches a miniature patchwork and appliquéd flag.

*Size: 18" high*

## MATERIALS

45"-wide cotton fabrics
  ⅜ yard beige for body
  ⅜ yard navy
  ⅜ yard off-white muslin
  ⅛ yard maroon
  13" by 26" piece lightweight quilt batting
  ½ lb. polyester stuffing

*Lace*

  10" piece ½"-wide lace edging
  6" piece ¼"-wide lace edging
  ⅝ yard 1¼"-wide lace edging
  ½ yard 2"-wide lace edging

*Ribbon*

  ¼ yard ⅛"-wide navy ribbon
  6" piece ¼"-wide maroon and off-white floral ribbon
  1 yard ⅜"-wide off-white grosgrain ribbon
  ⅝"-diameter gold button
  6"-square black felt
  2"-square fusible webbing
  1 yard each, brown and red embroidery floss
  Maroon, beige, off-white, and navy sewing thread
  Navy quilting thread

## DIRECTIONS

Enlarge patterns for Betsy Ross doll (page 125), following directions on page 15. Make pattern for shoes from leg pattern.

*Cutting*

From beige, cut 2 bodies, 4 arms, and 4 legs. Transfer features to right side of one body piece for front. Transfer lines of fingers to right side of two arm pieces for fronts. From maroon, cut 1 bodice front, 2 bodice backs, and 2 sleeves. For flag, cut 4 short stripes ⅞" by 4" and 3 long stripes ⅞" by 7½". From navy, cut a 13" by 27" piece for skirt, a 1¼" by 7" piece for waistband, and a 3¼" by 4" piece for union (upper inner corner) of flag.

From muslin, cut skirt backing 13" by 27", 2 pantelette pieces 5" by 11½", a 5" by 12½" piece for mob cap, and a 6¼" by 10¾" piece for apron. For flag, cut 3 short strips ⅞" by 4", 3 long stripes ⅞" by 7½", and flag backing 5½" by 7½". Cut 4 shoes from black felt, cutting out half circle on 2 shoes for front.

## Doll

Stitch all seams, right sides together, using ¼" seam allowance. Stitch bodies together, leaving lower straight edge open. Clip seam allowance along curves. Turn right side out. Stuff body. Baste shoes along seamline to position on leg fronts and backs. Be sure to make a right and left front and back leg. Stitch leg fronts to backs, leaving straight edge at top open. Clip seam allowance along curves. Turn right side out. Stuff legs. Baste along seamline at top edge.

Turn under ¼" along lower edge of body and insert upper edge of legs. Slipstitch front and backs to legs along seamline, with shoe front facing forward. Stitch arm fronts to backs, leaving opening at end between dots. Clip seam allowance along curves. Trim seam allowance to ⅛" along hands. Turn right side out. Stuff arms below broken lines. Quilt along lines of fingers. Fold arms in half, with seams matching in center. Stitch across arms (see Diagram 1). Stuff upper arms. Slip-

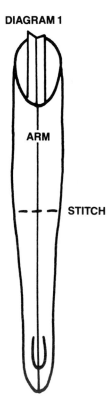

**DIAGRAM 1**

ARM

STITCH

stitch edges of opening together. Tack arms to upper side edge of body.

Using 3 strands of floss and satin stitch (see page 34), embroider eyes with brown and mouth with red. Wrap yarn around a 4¼″ piece of cardboard 15 times and slip it off. Place hair over head beginning ½″ down from seam on front. Thread a large needle with a strand of yarn. Sew hair in place along center front and back (see Diagram 2).

## Pantalettes

Turn under ¼″ along one 5″ edge of each muslin piece. Place top edge of ½″-wide lace edging over hem at lower edge, and stitch lace in place. Fold each piece in half lengthwise and stitch edges together, beginning 3¾″ from top edge for leg section. Clip seam allowance at top of stitching. Turn leg sections right side out. Pin, then stitch, leg sections together along top edges of seam allowance, matching inside leg seams. Turn under ½″ along top edge and press fold in place. Place pantalettes on doll, and make two tucks in front and back of top edge to fit waist. Sew tucks in place.

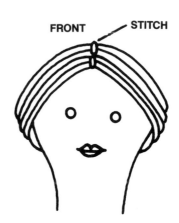

FRONT — STITCH

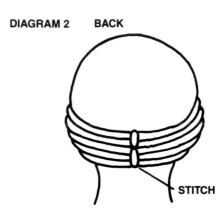

DIAGRAM 2    BACK

STITCH

QUILTING MOTIF FOR SKIRT    ACTUAL SIZE PATTERN

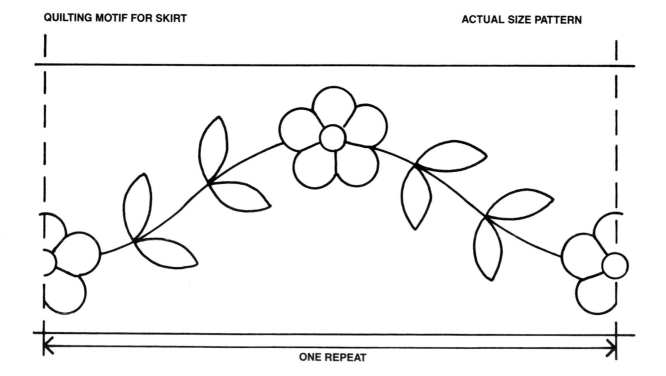

ONE REPEAT

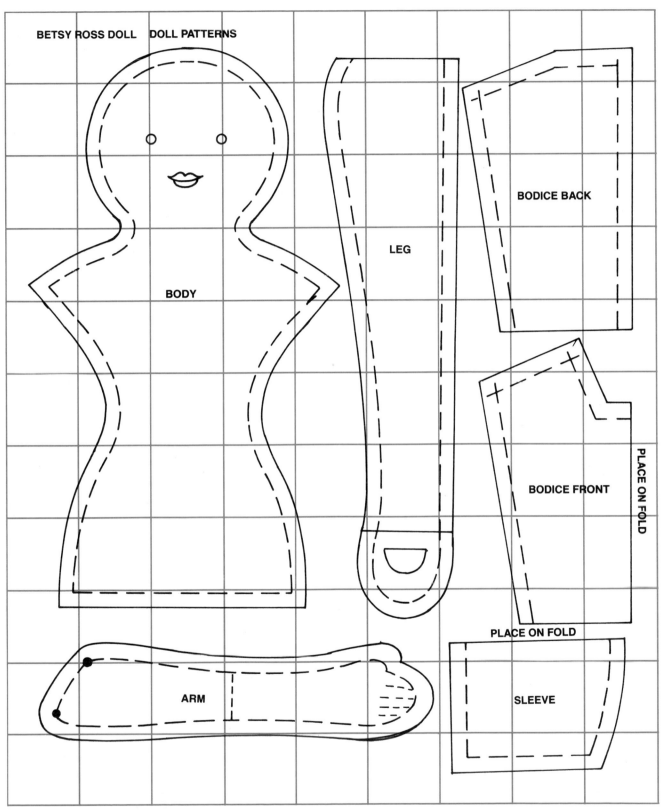

BETSY ROSS DOLL   DOLL PATTERNS

BODY

LEG

BODICE BACK

BODICE FRONT

PLACE ON FOLD

ARM

PLACE ON FOLD

SLEEVE

EACH SQUARE = 1"

## Bodice

Stitch backs to front along shoulder seams. Press seams open. Stitch along seamline of neck edge. Clip seam allowance at corners on fronts. Turn under seam allowance on neck edge, and stitch it in place ⅛″ from edge. Turn under ¼″ along lower edge of sleeve. Cut two 11″ pieces of 1¼″-wide lace edging. Make a row of gathering stitches along top edge of each piece. Gather lace to fit along lower edge of sleeve. Place sleeve over top edge of lace and stitch ⅛″ from the edge.

Stitch sleeves to front and backs between dots. Stitch front and backs together along side and underarm seams. Place bodice on doll. Turn under seam allowance on one back edge. Slipstitch edges together. Make 2 small bows of ⅛″-wide navy ribbon. Stitch bows to sides of lower edge of sleeves.

## Skirt

Following directions under *Quilting Basics* (page 23), mark a 11¼″ by 24″ rectangle in center of navy skirt piece. Trace floral quilting motif to skirt rectangle ½″ from one long edge, repeating motif 4 times. Draw diagonal lines 1″ apart to form diamonds above floral border. Place batting between backing and skirt, right sides out. Pin, then baste, the layers together. Quilt along all marked lines, stopping 1″ from center back edges.

Trim fabric and batting ¼″ from rectangle. Beginning 2″ from upper edge, stitch skirt and batting together along center back edge, keeping backing fabric free. Trim batting close to stitching and press seam open. Turn under edges of backing along center back seam and slipstitch them together. Finish quilting center back of skirt. Trim ¼″ from lower edge of batting. Turn under ¼″ along lower edge of skirt and backing, and slipstitch edges together.

Make a row of gathering stitches, by hand, along upper seamline of skirt. Gather upper edge to fit waistband with ¼″ seam allowance left on each end of waistband. Press under ¼″ on other long edge of waistband. Fold waistband in half lengthwise. Stitch ¼″ from ends. Trim seam allowance. Turn waistband right side out. Slipstitch edge to seamline. Place skirt on doll over lower edge of bodice. Sew ends of waistband together in back.

## Apron

Press up ¼″ on one short end of apron piece. Stitch hem in place. Then press up 3¼″ on this same end to form a pocket. Baste side edges together. Sew ¼″-wide lace

**DIAGRAM 3**

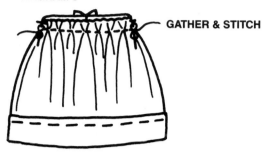

**GATHER & STITCH**

edging to lower edge of pocket. Mark lines on pocket parallel to sides 2¼″ in, and stitch along these lines. Turn under ¼″ twice along sides of apron and stitch hem in place.

Make 2 rows of machine-gathering stitches ⅛″ and ¼″ from top edge of apron. Gather top edge to 2¼″. Place center of a 30″-length of off-white grosgrain over top edge. Stitch ribbon to apron. Place apron on doll, and tie ribbon in a bow in back. Tack ribbon to waistband of skirt if desired.

## Mob Cap

Stitch short edges of mob cap together. Turn under ¾″ along lower edge and make a row of gathering stitches ⅝″ from fold. Make a row of gathering stitches along top edge, beginning and ending 1″ from center back seam. Gather this row of stitching to 2″. With right sides together, stitch the gathered edge to the back, using ¼″ seam allowance (see Diagram 3). Turn cap right side out.

Place cap on doll and gather lower edge around head. Knot ends of thread securely. Tack cap to head along lower row of gathers. Make a small bow from maroon and white ribbon and sew it on cap.

## Fichu

Fold 2″-wide lace in half and make a ¾″-wide dart at center (see Diagram 4). Trim lace ¼″ from stitching and zigzag-finish edges. Trim ends of lace diagonally and finish edges with a narrow hem. Make a 4″-long row of gathering stitches along straight edge at center. Place fichu on doll and gather stitches to fit around neck. Knot thread. Make a gathering row across lace 2″ from points (see Diagram 5). Gather fronts together and knot ends of thread. Sew button to center of gathers.

**DIAGRAM 4**

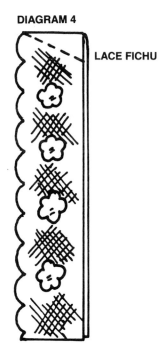

LACE FICHU

**DIAGRAM 5**

FICHU

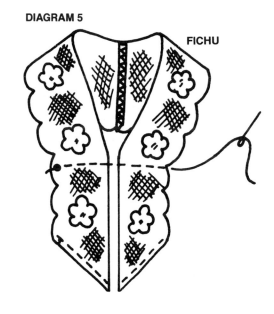

## *Flag*

Fuse stars to navy union as indicated on pattern. Whipstitch around edges of stars, if desired. Alternating maroon and muslin stripes, stitch short stripes together. Stitch short stripes to side of union. Stitch long stripes together, alternating colors. Stitch muslin edge of long stripe piece to lower edge of union and short stripes.

Right sides in, stitch flag to lining piece, leaving an opening for turning. Clip corners of seam allowance. Turn flag right side out. Turn under edges of opening and slipstitch them together. Place flag across doll's lap.

**UNION PATTERN    ACTUAL SIZE PATTERN**

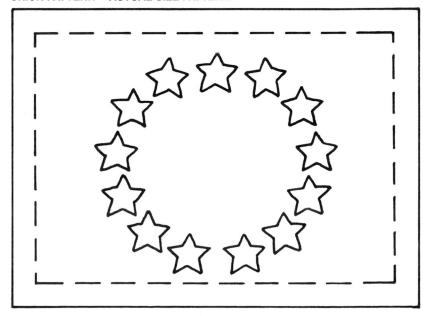

# BALTIMORE ALBUM WREATH

The art of fine floral appliqué flourished in the city of Baltimore, Maryland, in the mid-19th century. A designer named Mary Ann Evans, who had a very distinctive style, is thought to have designed symbolic blocks of wreaths, urns, flowers, and other designs which were stitched by many different needlewomen and incorporated with other appliqué blocks into elaborate album quilts made for presentation to an honored person—a minister perhaps, or a schoolteacher. Celebrate a very special friendship by making this wreath.

*Size: 18" in diameter*

## MATERIALS

45"-wide cotton fabrics
   1½ yards muslin
   ⅜ yard olive green
   ⅜ yard red
   ⅛ yard or scraps dark green, green print, blue, pink, gold, and yellow print
   1 yard paper-backed fusible webbing
   25"-square traditional-weight quilt batting
   3 yards cotton cording
   Sewing thread to match fabrics
   Off-white quilting thread for hand-quilting
   24 oz. polyester stuffing
   12" piece ¼"-wide off-white grosgrain ribbon

## DIRECTIONS

### Wreath Front

Following directions for enlarging (see page 15), enlarge wreath front pattern on page 130 on one half of a sheet of tracing paper, matching centers. Trace wreath pattern onto other half of paper to make entire pattern. Trace outline of stems, flowers, leaves, and cutting line to a 26" square of muslin.

Following directions under *Stems* (page 21), cut six ⅞" by 6" bias strips of dark green fabric and make ¼"-wide seams. Pin stems to position on wreath front, trimming ends ¼" inside appliqué shapes. Slipstitch edges of stems in place.

Following directions under *Machine-Appliqué* (page 22) make patterns for leaves 1–22 for each side of wreath. Label each piece. Cut leaves marked with dots from olive green. Cut leaves marked with small triangles from dark green. Cut remaining leaves from green print. Fuse leaves to background fabric.

In same manner, make patterns for flowers and centers, A-P for each side of the wreath. Label each piece.

From pink, cut pieces A, H, and P. From red, cut B, G, and O. From gold, cut C, E, I, M, and Q. From blue, cut D and K. Cut J from light blue. From yellow print, cut F, L, and R. Fuse flowers in place, except for gold flower at lower center seam. Zigzag-stitch around leaves and flowers with matching thread.

### Quilting

Cut a 26" square from muslin for backing. Following directions in *Quilting Basics* (page 23), place batting between backing and wreath top, right side up. Pin and baste the layers together. Baste along stitching line, ½" in from cutting line.

For hand-quilting, quilt ⅛" from outer edges of appliqué shapes with off-white quilting thread. For machine-quilting, quilt along outer edge of zigzag-stitching and stems with off-white sewing thread. Cut out wreath along cutting lines.

### Finishing

Following directions under *Cording* (page 28), cover cording with olive green fabric. Baste cording to inner and outer curved edges of wreath front along stitching lines. Finish edges of cording even with stitching line on straight lower edges.

Cut wreath back from muslin, using wreath front pattern. Stitch front to back along curved edges ½" from edge, starting and stopping even with stitching line on straight lower edge. Clip seam allowance along curves. Turn wreath right side out. Stitch straight edges of lower front together. Fuse remaining flower and center to lower front over seam. Stitch around edges with buttonhole stitch (see *Embroidery Basics*, page 32.) Stuff wreath firmly. Turn under seam allowance on lower edge of back. Slipstitch edges together.

From red, cut bow 6" by 22", tie 6" by 28", and center 6" by 6". Right sides in, fold bow and center pieces in half lengthwise and stitch long edges together. Turn right side out and press with seam along one edge. Fold tie in half lengthwise and trim ends diagonally. Stitch along ends and long edges, leaving an opening in center for turning. Clip seam allowance at corners. Turn right side out.

Fold ends of bow to center back, overlapping them 1". Place bow at center of ties. Make pleats in center of bow and stitch in place by hand. Wrap center around center of bow, with ends overlapping in back. Turn under ends and slipstitch them together. Sew bow to wreath at lower center. For hanger, turn under ends of ribbon. Place across back, just above center hole. Stitch ends in place securely.

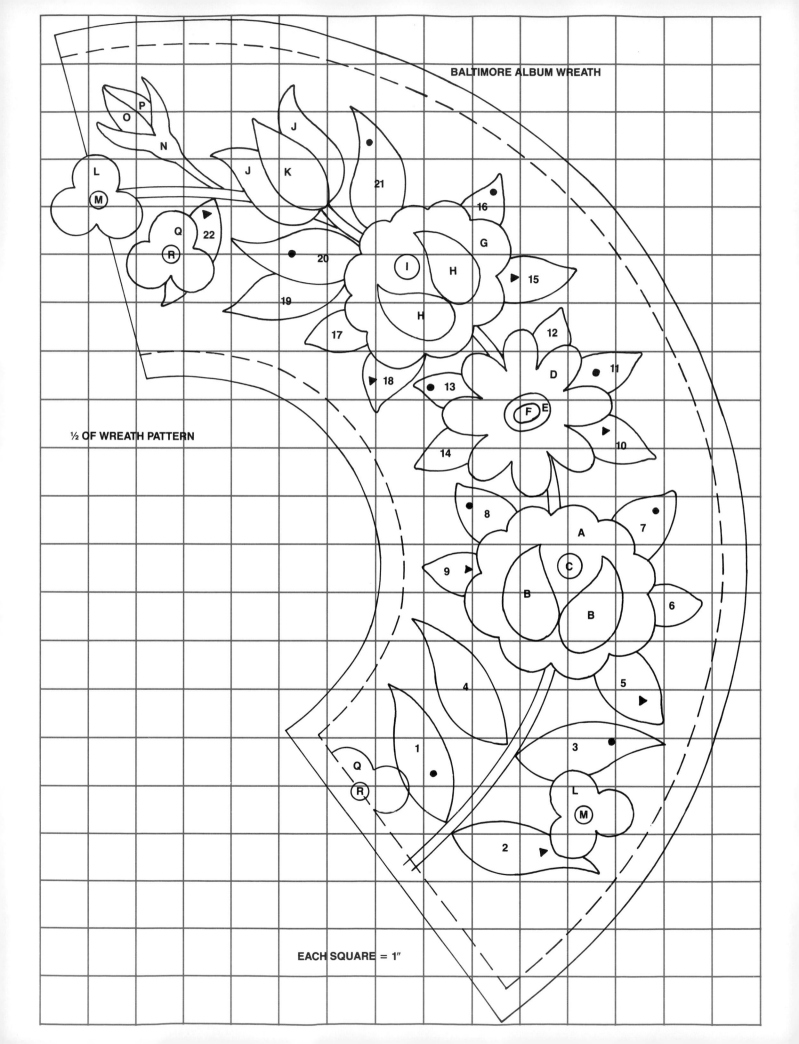

BALTIMORE ALBUM WREATH

½ OF WREATH PATTERN

EACH SQUARE = 1"

# CAROLINA LILY PILLOW

T his elegant version of the lily pattern is another beautiful flower design that can be pieced instead of appliquéd. Its intricacy was most likely developed in a setting that allowed many hours of quiet leisure time for decorative sewing. Here, the lily pattern is stitched into a pillow trimmed with a 3″ ruffle. The soft pastel colors were frequently used on quilts made in the South. A beautiful quilt top could be made by alternating this quilt block with 10″ squares of print or solid fabrics set on the diagonal.

*Size: 14″ square, plus 3″ ruffle*

## MATERIALS

45″-wide cotton fabrics
  ½ yard muslin
  ½ yard off-white floral print
  ⅝ yard green print
  ⅛ yard salmon
  ¼ yard green
  17″-square batting
  Salmon and off-white sewing thread
  Off white, green, and salmon quilting thread
  14″ pillow form or polyester stuffing

## DIRECTIONS

Make templates for pattern pieces A–G (see page 132), following directions under *Templates* (page 15).

### Cutting

Trace around the templates on the wrong side of the fabric, and cut out each piece. From salmon fabric, cut 12 diamonds (A). From muslin, cut 5 small triangles (B), 3 squares (C), 1 medium triangle (D), 12 large triangles (E), 1 rectangle (F), and 1 strip (G). From green, cut 2 diamonds (A) and 3 medium triangles (D). Draw two 9⅝″ squares on wrong side of off-white floral print. Divide them in half diagonally to make four corner triangles. Cut out triangles.

## Pillow Top

Stitch all seams, right sides together, using ¼″ seam allowance. Following piecing diagram for Carolina Lily, stitch diamonds (A) together in pairs along one side, ending stitching at dot on seamline. Join all diamonds in this manner. Stitch a small triangle (B) between four pairs of diamonds. For lily in upper corner, stitch diamonds with triangles together. Stitch a square between them.

Stitch a square between remaining pairs of diamonds. For remaining lilies, stitch diamonds with triangles to diamonds with squares. Be sure to make a right and a left lily. Stitch a triangle between them. Stitch green medium triangles (D) to corner of lilies. Stitch large triangles (E) to two sides of lily for upper corner. Stitch remaining lilies to opposite sides of rectangle (F) for center of block.

Stitch green diamonds to remaining small triangle. Stitch strip (G) to long side of this piece and stitch off-white medium triangle to short side to make lower corner. Stitch upper and lower corners to center of block.

Make one 8½″ stem and two 7″ stems from green fabric, following directions under *Stems* (page 21). Pin 7″ stems to block along curved broken lines indicated on piecing diagram. Slipstitch them in place. Place 8″ stem along straight broken lines indicated on piecing diagram. Slipstitch stem in place. Stitch off-white floral triangles to each side of block.

### Assembling Pillow Top

Mark quilting lines ¼″ from edges of salmon green and muslin sections on Carolina Lily block, if desired. Mark quilting lines on corner triangles ¼″ from seam and at 1¾″ intervals parallel to seam.

Cut a 17″ square of muslin for backing. Following directions in *Quilting Basics* (page 23), place batting between backing and pillow top. Pin and baste the layers

**CAROLINA LILY BLOCK   PIECING DIAGRAM**

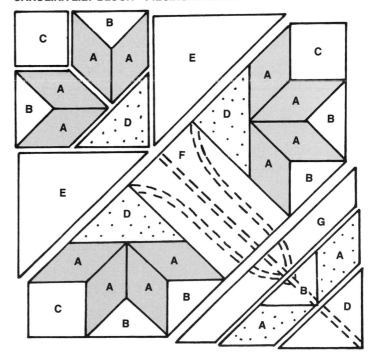

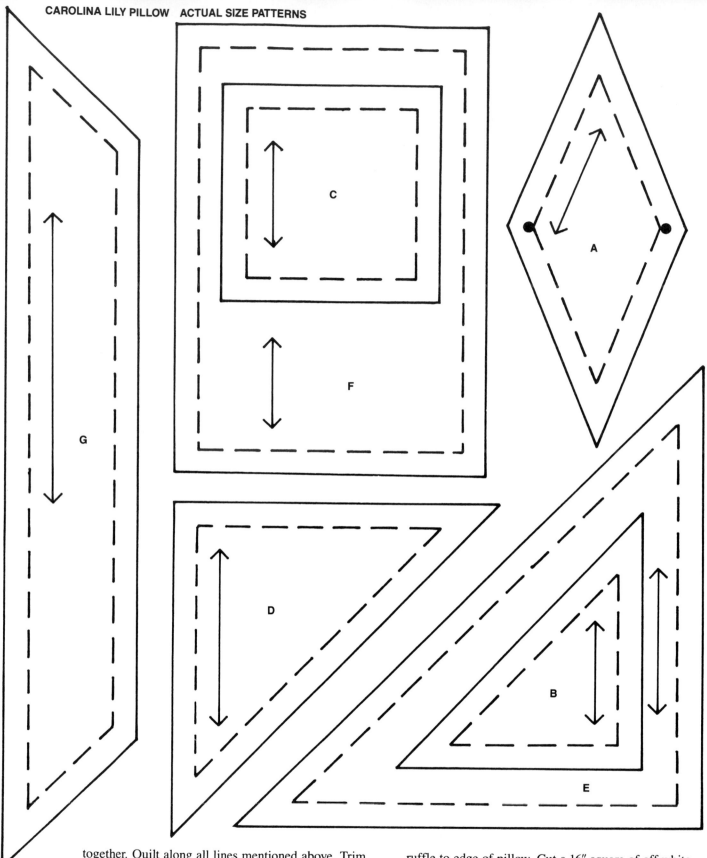

together. Quilt along all lines mentioned above. Trim backing and batting even with pillow top.

*Finishing*

Cut three 6″ by 40½″ strips of green print fabric and make a ruffle, following directions on page 28. Baste ruffle to edge of pillow. Cut a 16″ square of off-white floral print for pillow back, or make pillow back as desired following directions on page 30. Stitch pillow front to pillow back, leaving an opening if necessary. Turn right side out. Insert pillow form or stuffing. If necessary, slipstitch edges of opening closed.

# KANSAS SUNFLOWER PILLOW

**S**unflower quilt blocks were, and probably still are, favored by quilters in Kansas because they feature the Kansas state flower. They are often stitched like the Kansas Sunflower pillow, in shades of yellow and brown, both natural sunflower colors. This simplified version of the sunflower pattern offers a great way to practice both curved piecing and making neat points at the corners of your petals. The 10½″ sunflower block is sashed with a coordinating floral print and quilted with heart motifs in the corners. The Kansas Sunflower Pillow will brighten your sunroom, even on rainy days. You can also use this block to make a sunny quilt.

*Size: 14″ square*

## MATERIALS

45″-wide cotton fabrics
   ½ yard brown floral print
   ⅜ yard yellow print
   ½ yard muslin
   ⅛ yard or scraps of each green, gold, and brown print
   17″-square quilt batting
   2 yards cotton cording
   Sewing thread to match fabrics
   Gold, brown, yellow, green, and off-white quilting
     thread
   14″ pillow form or stuffing

## DIRECTIONS

Following directions under *Templates* (page 15), make templates for pattern pieces A-E on pages 136 and 137.

### Cutting

Cut 8 petals (A) from gold; 8 diamonds (B) from yellow print; 8 wedges (C) from green. Cut center from brown print. Trace inner border (E) to muslin four times, matching ends to make a square with a circle inside. Cut out shape as one piece, then cut out center. Cut two border strips 3″ by 10½″ and two border strips 4″ by 15½″ from brown floral print.

### Pillow Top

Stitch all seams, right sides together, with ¼″ seams. It's best to piece this block by hand. Following Diagram 1, stitch 2 petals (A) to short edges of 4 diamonds (B). Stitch the other long edge of petals to short edges of remaining 4 diamonds, alternating petals and diamond (see Diagram 2). Continue until all pieces have been joined around flower. Then stitch a wedge (C) between outer edges of diamonds (see Diagram 3).

**DIAGRAM 3**

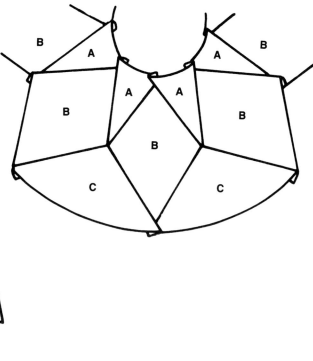

**DIAGRAM 1**

**KANSAS SUNFLOWER PILLOW**

**DIAGRAM 2**

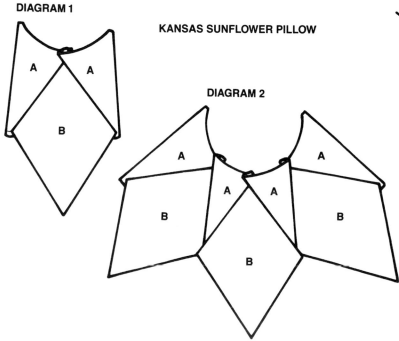

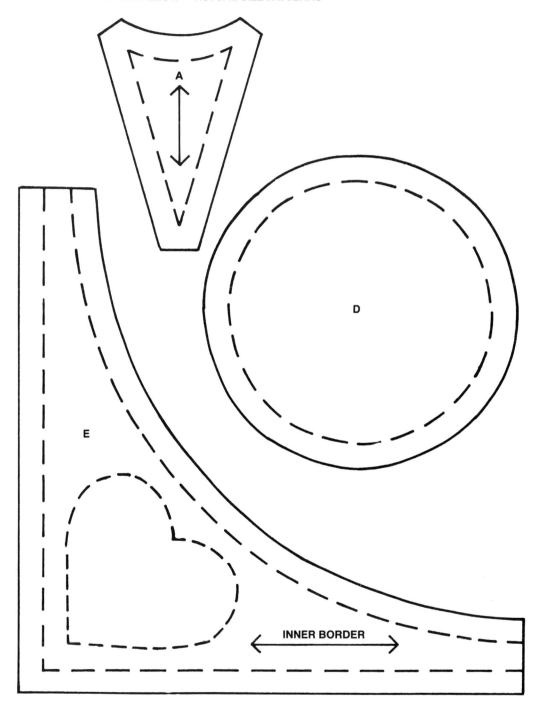

A

D

E

INNER BORDER

Stitch center (D) to center of petals, or turn under ¼" around edges and slipstitch center in place. Matching curves, stitch inner border around flower. Clip inner edge of inner border if necessary. Stitch 10½" border strips to opposite sides of inner border. Stitch 15½" border strips to remaining edges.

*Quilting Pillow Top*

Trace heart quilting motif to corners of inner border, as indicated on pattern. If necessary, mark quilting lines ¼" from edges of patchwork pieces A-D and along inner edge of border strips.

Cut a 17" square of muslin for backing. Following directions in *Quilting Basics* (page 23), place batting between backing and pillow top, right sides out. Pin, then baste, the layers together. Quilt along lines mentioned above. Trim batting and backing even with pillow top.

*Finishing*

Following directions under *Cording* (page 28), cut bias strips from yellow print to cover cotton cording. Stitch cording to edge of pillow top. Cut a 16" square for pillow back, or make pillow back as desired, following directions on page 30. Stitch pillow top to back, leaving opening for turning if necessary. Turn right side out. Insert pillow form or stuff pillow. Turn under edges of opening and slipstitch them together if necessary.

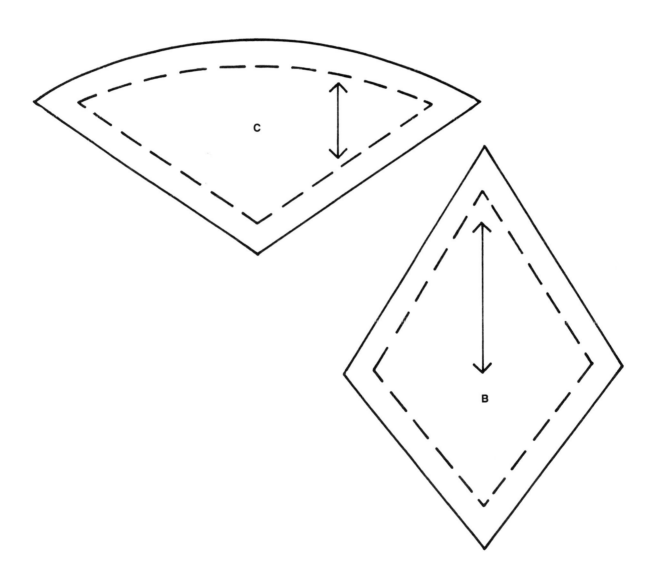

# KENTUCKY ROSE PILLOW

and-appliqué was first used to attach flowers cut from imported chintz fabrics to plain colored backgrounds. Early in the 19th century, American needlewomen who could not obtain or afford the expensive fabrics began to cut flowers from the solid fabrics that they had on hand. The flowers were often simplified and stylized. Many patterns featured the rose, and this one, featuring a wreath of roses, is named for the state of Kentucky. This is a very portable hand-appliqué project and a good way for the beginner to practice her skills. You can also make several blocks, joining them to make the center of a quilt top.

*Size: 14" square*

## MATERIALS

45"-wide cotton fabrics
  1 yard muslin
  ⅜ yard salmon pink
  ⅛ yard or scraps of each red, green, and gold
  17"-square quilt batting
  2 yards cotton cording
  Red, green, salmon pink, and gold sewing thread
  Off-white quilting thread
  14" pillow form or stuffing

## DIRECTIONS

*Kentucky Rose Appliqué*

Trace pattern for Kentucky Rose design (page 140) to tracing paper. Cut a 16" square of muslin. Fold it into quarters and finger-press folds. Matching centers, place broken lines along the folds and place placement lines onto each quarter. Follow directions under *Appliqué*

*Basics* (page 19) to make patterns for appliqué pieces. Make patterns for large rose, small rose, center, leaf, bud, and bud center. From red fabric, cut 4 large roses and 4 bud centers. Cut 4 small roses from salmon pink. Cut 4 centers from gold. From green, cut 4 buds and 16 leaves. From green make four 5" stems (see *Stems*, page 21). Make stems ¼" wide. Pin stems along placement lines, trimming ends ¼" inside outer edge of large roses. To make roses, slipstitch large rose, small rose, and then center in place on pillow top. To make bud, slipstitch center, then bud piece, in place. Then slipstitch leaves in place. From wrong side, trim background fabric from inside of appliqué pieces and remove paper patterns.

## Pillow Top

Trace heart motifs to pillow top as indicated on pattern. Cut a 17" piece of muslin for backing. Following directions in *Quilting Basics* (page 23), place batting between backing and pillow top. Pin, then baste the layers together. Using off-white thread, quilt ⅛" from edges of appliqué design and along lines of heart. Using salmon pink thread, quilt ⅛" from inner edge of small rose. Trim edges of backing and batting even with pillow top.

*Assembling Pillow*

Following directions under *Cording* (page 28), cut bias strips from salmon pink fabric and cover cording. Baste to edges of pillow top. Cut a 16" square of muslin for pillow back, or make pillow back as desired following directions under *Pillow Backs* (page 30). With right sides in, stitch top to back, leaving an opening for turning if necessary. Insert pillow form or stuff pillow. Slipstitch edges of opening closed if necessary.

CENTER

CENTER

SMALL ROSE

LARGE ROSE

STEM

LEAF

BUD

CENTER

HEARTS

# IOWA HARVEST APRON

I n Iowa, famous for its cornfields, traditional aprons of this type have been worn for generations by farm women. The appliquéd ear of corn with kernels made from tiny squares of fabric can be assembled quickly and easily by strip-piecing. Blue and white fabrics and a solid yellow trim give the apron a crisp look. Learn to quick-piece triangles for the saw-tooth border on the skirt and pockets.

*Size: Medium (10–12)*

## MATERIALS

45"-wide cotton fabrics
  3½ yards muslin
  1 yard blue on off-white print
  ½ yard off-white on blue print
  ¼ yard bright yellow
  ⅛ yard or scraps of green, sage green, gold, light yellow, yellow print, gold print, gold micro-dot, and rust micro-dot
  8" by 10" piece low-loft quilt batting
  Strip of stiff interfacing 2¼" by 25" (or waist measurement minus 3")
  Off-white, blue, yellow, green, and sage green sewing thread
  Off-white and green quilting thread

## DIRECTIONS

Seam allowance is included in all measurements. With right sides together, stitch all seams with ¼" seam allowance unless otherwise indicated.

### Cutting

From muslin, cut upper front of skirt 27" wide by 44" long (or desired skirt length minus 5¾"), 2 upper backs 11" wide by 27" long (or same length as skirt front), lower front 9" by 44" and 2 lower backs 9" by 11". Then cut an 8" square for bib, an 8" by 9¼" bib facing, and two pocket facings 3¼" by 7". From remaining fabric, cut 50 triangles if you do not plan to quick-piece triangles.

From blue on off-white print, cut shoulder straps 3½" by 32" (or length from front waist over shoulder to back waist plus 1"), 2 ties 4½" by 38", 2 front borders 1½" by 43½", and 4 back borders 1½" by 12", 2 pockets 3¾" by 7", and 2 pocket borders 1½" by 7". From off-white on

blue, cut 2 waistbands 2¼" by 25" (or waist measurement minus 3"), bib border 1¾" by 8". Then cut 50 triangles, or quick-piece triangles later. From yellow, cut 2 front borders 1" by 43½", 4 back borders 1" by 12", and 4 pocket borders 1" by 7".

### Bib

Trace pattern for ear of corn (page 142) diagonally across bib. Allow at least ½" around edges for border and seam allowance. Following directions under *Appliqué Basics* (page 19), make patterns for corn husks and stems. Cut pieces A, B, E, and F from green. Cut pieces C, D, and stem from sage green.

Cut a strip approximately 15" long and ¾" or ⅞" wide from all yellow, gold, and rust fabrics. Cut each strip into thirds. Following instructions under *Strip-Piecing* (page 18), stitch strips together with varying color order to make about 3 lengths of 10 strips each. Cut strips into lengths ¾"–1" wide. Stitch 3 strips together with varying color order to make lengths of 7" or more. Trim seam allowances to ⅛". Stitch lengths together to make one piece 3" wide. Trim seams to ⅛". Make a pattern for corn from plain paper, adding ¼" seam allowance. Cut out corn from patchwork piece. Turn under seam allowance and hand-baste edges in place.

**TRIANGLE FOR BORDERS   ACTUAL SIZE PATTERN**

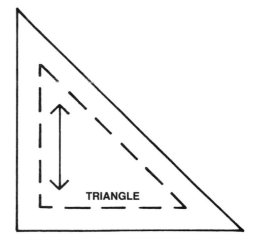

TRIANGLE

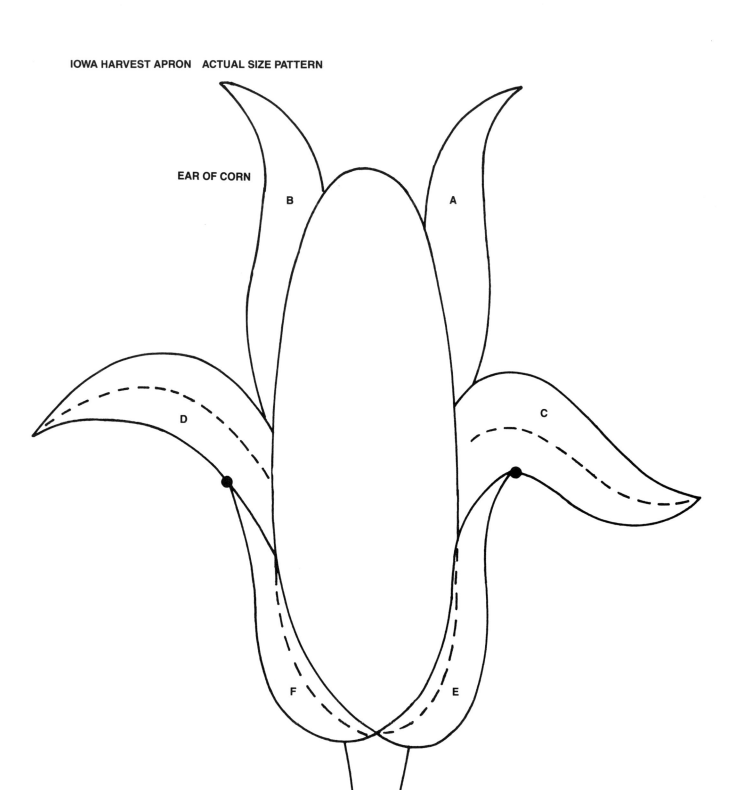

IOWA HARVEST APRON   ACTUAL SIZE PATTERN

EAR OF CORN

B

A

D

C

F

E

## IOWA HARVEST APRON

### DIAGRAM 1

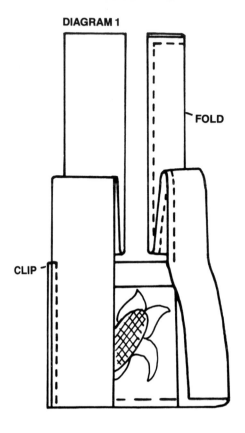

FOLD

CLIP

### DIAGRAM 2

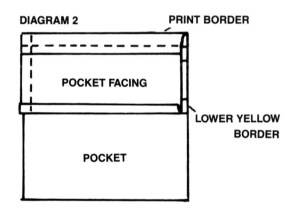

PRINT BORDER

POCKET FACING

LOWER YELLOW BORDER

POCKET

### DIAGRAM 3

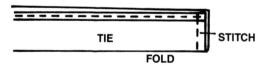

TIE

STITCH

FOLD

### DIAGRAM 4

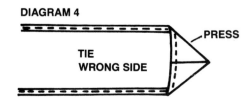

PRESS

TIE
WRONG SIDE

Place pieces A and B and stem on bib; slipstitch edges in place. Pin pieces C and D on bib. Slipstitch edges in place, stopping at small dots on lower edge of pattern. Slipstitch corn to bib. Pin, then slipstitch, pieces E and F in place, slipping upper edges under pieces C and D. For bib front, stitch bib border to top edge of bib. Baste quilt batting to wrong side of bib front. Right sides together, stitch bib facing to top edge of bib front. Press seam allowance toward facing without pressing front. Fold facing over batting and baste the remaining edges together.

Following directions in *Quilting Basics* (page 23), mark quilting lines along center of pieces C and D. Quilt ⅛″ from outer edge of ear of corn with off-white thread, and along lines on leaves with green thread.

## Apron

With right sides together, stitch one edge of each strap to each side of bib, keeping lower edges even (see Diagram 1). Clip seam allowance to stitching at top of bib seams. With right sides together, fold straps in half lengthwise and stitch free edges of each strap together across end and long edge to top edge of bib. Trim seam allowance; turn straps right side out. Turn under seam allowance on lower edge of strap. Slipstitch edge in place along seamline of bib facing. Stitch each blue print triangle to a muslin triangle, or quick-piece triangles following directions on page 17.

For skirt, stitch upper backs to upper front along side seams, using ½″ seam allowance. Make a French seam or zigzag-finish seam allowance. Stitch lower backs to front along side seams, using ½″ seam allowance. Trim seam allowance to ¼″. On both pieces, turn under ½″ twice on center back edges and stitch hem in place.

For border, stitch 42 pairs of triangles together in a row, joining blue edge to white edge of adjacent triangle. Make two yellow borders and two blue on off-white print borders by stitching backs to fronts and using ¼″ seams. Stitch yellow borders to upper and lower edge of triangles. Stitch remaining borders to outer edges of yellow borders. Matching side seams, stitch border to lower edge of upper skirt. Press seam toward border. Stitch lower skirt to border. Turn under border even

with center back edge of skirt. Turn under hem 2″ below border, turning under edge of lower skirt along upper seamline of border to face wrong side of patchwork. Slipstitch upper edge of hem in place; slipstitch center back edges together.

Stitch four pairs of triangles together in a row. Stitch yellow pocket borders to edges of each piece. Stitch pocket to lower edge of one yellow border and, blue on off-white print border to other yellow border. Stitch pocket facing to print border. Trim edges of fabric pieces even with rows of triangles. With right sides in, fold facing to right side along center of print border strip. (Only ½″ of print border shows on right side of pocket.) Turn up lower edge of facing even with lower edge of yellow pocket border (see Diagram 2). Stitch along side edges, using ¼″ seam allowance. Turn facing to wrong side. Slipstitch lower edge of facing to wrong side. Press under ¼″ around remaining edge of pockets.

Place pockets on skirt front 8″ from center and 6″ below upper edge. Stitch sides and lower edge in place. Fuse or baste interfacing to wrong side of one waistband piece. Make a row of gathering stitches along top edge of skirt, ¼″ and ½″ from edge. Gather skirt evenly to interfaced waistband, beginning and finishing ½″ from ends. Stitch bib to other edge of waistband, matching centers and using a ¼″ seam allowance.

Press under ¼″ twice on long edges of ties, and stitch hems in place. Fold ties in half lengthwise, right sides in. On one end of each tie, stitch across end ¼″ from edge (see Diagram 3). Turn right side out to form a point (see Diagram 4). Pleat other end of tie so it is about 1⅜″ wide. Baste this end to ends of waistband, using a ½″ seam.

Fold bib forward, down along apron front from top of waistband. Pin waistbands together along ends and top edge with bib and ties between them. Stitch along ends ½″ from edge and along top edge ¼″ from edge. Trim seam allowance. Turn waistband to wrong side. Turn under lower edge along seamline and slipstitch edge in place. Pin ends of shoulder straps to wrong side of waistband and stitch them in place along top and bottom edges of waistband.

# AMBER WAVES OF GRAIN WALL HANGING

he words to "America, the Beautiful" were the inspiration for this modernistic wall hanging. Spacious skies, fruited plains, and purple mountains are depicted in a variety of fabrics. The amber waves of grain in our country's Midwest is truly America's patchwork. This wall hanging is made with patchwork and appliqué techniques utilizing both hand and machine. The border features an ocean wave quilting pattern representing the shining seas on either side of our country. It is stitched with free-motion machine quilting techniques. This wall hanging would look superb in an entryway or near a living room window.

*Size: 24" by 48"*

**MATERIALS**

45"-wide cotton fabrics

¾ yard amber
⅛ yard white, light blue, light blue print, and blue
¼ yard purple and light purple
⅛ yard or scraps of 7 different solid greens and green prints
⅛ yard or scraps of rust, gold, gold prints, tan, brown, green, and light green solids and prints
1½ yard light teal blue for borders and backing
28" by 52" piece quilt batting
Blue, white, green, purple, light purple, gold, and teal sewing thread

**DIRECTIONS**

Following *Enlarging Patterns* on page 15, enlarge each half of patterns for wall hanging on pages 148 and 149.

## Sky

To make patterns for two clouds and sky pieces 1–7, trace shapes from enlarged pattern, adding ¼" seam allowance to top and bottom edges. Make a notch on each pattern at marks on lines shown in pattern. For sky piece 9, trace lower edge of shape along broken line on pattern and add ¼" seam allowance to top edge. Cut clouds from white. Cut sky pieces 5 and 8 from blue print. Cut sky pieces 3, 4, and 7 from light blue. Cut sky pieces 1, 2, 6, and 9 from blue. Follow pattern, placing right sides together and matching notches, then pin, and stitch sky pieces and clouds together in numerical order. Clip seam allowance of inner curves to fit pieces together.

## Mountains

Make patterns for mountains following directions under *Hand-Appliqué* (page 19). Trace lower edge of mountain shapes along second broken line shown on pattern. Cut large mountain from purple and small mountain from light purple. Pin small mountain to lower edge of sky as indicated on pattern, and slipstitch it in place. Pin, then slipstitch, large mountain to lower edge of sky and small mountain.

## Fruited Plain

Following directions under *Hand-Appliqué* (page 19), make pattern pieces for pieces 1–10. Add ¼" seam allowance to lower edge of shapes. Cut shapes from solid green and green print pieces. Following numerical order, place pieces on lower edge of mountains as indicated on pattern and slipstitch them in place.

## Waves of Grain

To make a pattern for each patchwork piece, trace the shape on the pattern and add ¼" seam allowance to each edge. Be sure to label pieces with their row numbers and letters as indicated on pattern for lower half of project.

Cut pieces from amber, gold, tan, brown, rust, greens, light greens, and yellow fabrics. Stitch together pieces in each row, working in alphabetical order and from left to right, as indicated on pattern. Then, matching seams, stitch all rows together following numerical order and working from top to bottom. Clip seam allowance along inner curves to ease rows together. Stitch top edge to lower edge of fruited plain in same manner.

### Borders

From light teal, cut two side borders 4¼" by 49" and two top and bottom borders 4¼" by 25". Stitch side borders to sides of wall hanging, using ¼" seam allowance. Trim ends even with top and bottom edge. Stitch top and bottom borders to edges of wall hanging. Trim ends of borders even with side edges.

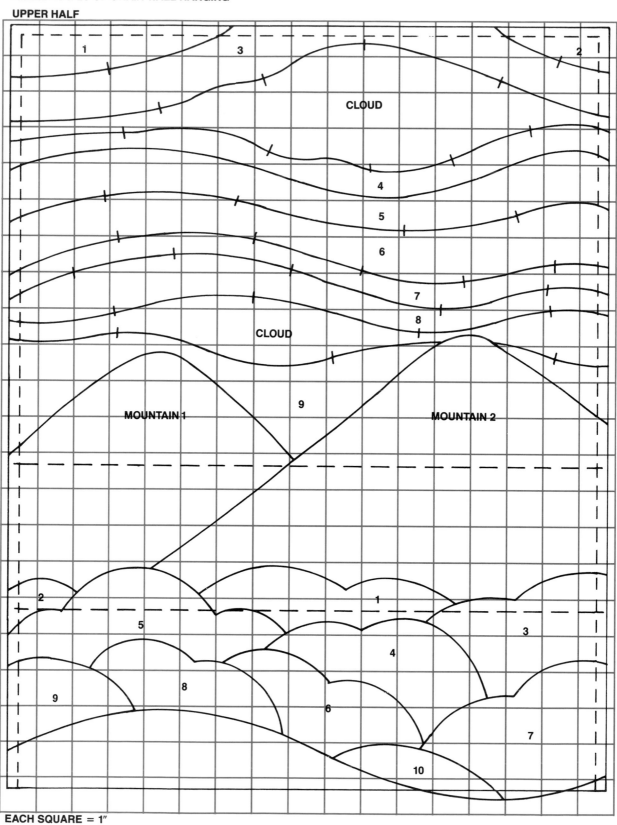

**EACH SQUARE = 1"**

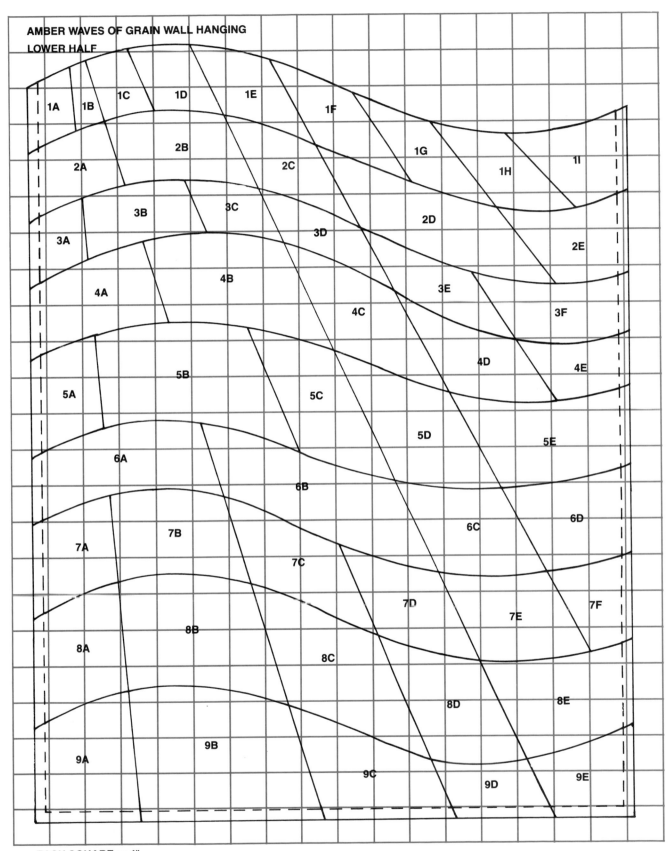

AMBER WAVES OF GRAIN WALL HANGING
LOWER HALF

EACH SQUARE = 1"

149

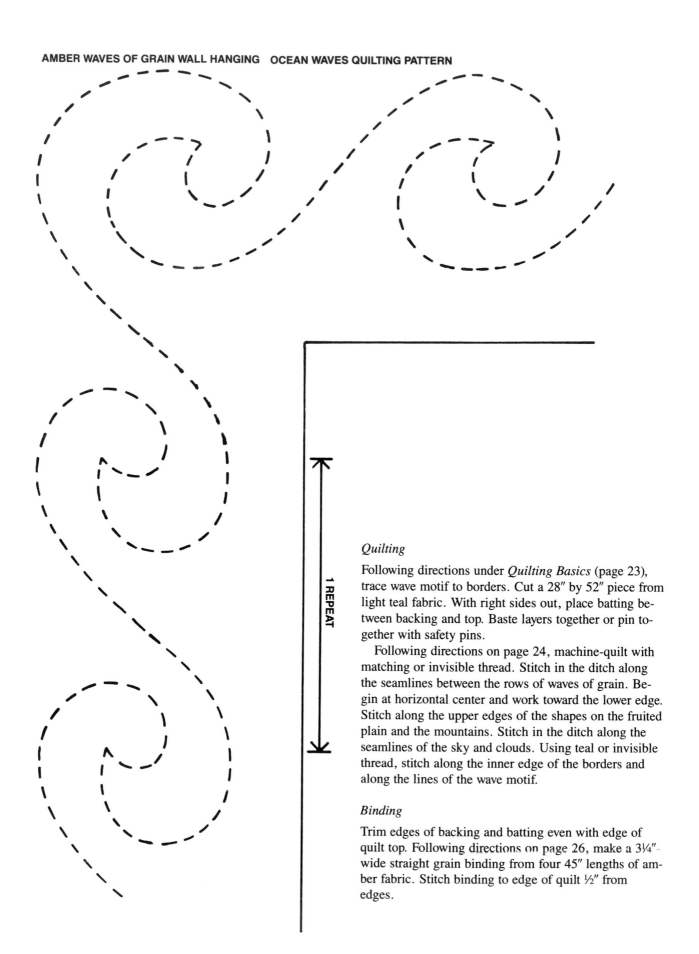

1 REPEAT

### Quilting

Following directions under *Quilting Basics* (page 23), trace wave motif to borders. Cut a 28″ by 52″ piece from light teal fabric. With right sides out, place batting between backing and top. Baste layers together or pin together with safety pins.

Following directions on page 24, machine-quilt with matching or invisible thread. Stitch in the ditch along the seamlines between the rows of waves of grain. Begin at horizontal center and work toward the lower edge. Stitch along the upper edges of the shapes on the fruited plain and the mountains. Stitch in the ditch along the seamlines of the sky and clouds. Using teal or invisible thread, stitch along the inner edge of the borders and along the lines of the wave motif.

### Binding

Trim edges of backing and batting even with edge of quilt top. Following directions on page 26, make a 3¼″-wide straight grain binding from four 45″ lengths of amber fabric. Stitch binding to edge of quilt ½″ from edges.

EACH SQUARE = 1″

# PACIFIC NORTHWEST PINE TREE TOTE

he traditional pine tree block, one of America's oldest pictorial patchwork patterns, originated in colonial Massachusetts and is now a fitting symbol of our Northwestern states. In the machine-quilted tote bag, the pine tree forms the patchwork center and the appliqué scene depicting the pine-covered mountains of the Northwest. Carry your quilting in the handsome bag or take it shopping. Using totes instead of disposable bags does help protect our environment!

*Size: 14″ by 16″*

## MATERIALS

45″-wide cotton fabrics
   1½ yards floral print
   1½ yards backing
   ¼ yard light blue
   ⅛ yard green micro-dot
   ⅛ yard green leaf print
Cotton fabrics
   7″ square each, white solid and purple print
   Small scraps of gold and brown
   3″ by 12″ piece small green floral print
   36″ by 45″ piece of traditional-weight quilt batting
   Sewing thread to match fabrics

## DIRECTIONS

Following directions under *Templates* (page 15), make templates for patchwork patterns A–F.

*Cutting*

Trace templates to wrong side of fabrics and cut out each piece. From green micro-dot, cut tree triangle (C) and 14 small triangles (A). Do not cut small triangles if you plan to quick-piece triangles. From light blue, cut 1 square (B), 2 lower sides (F), and 8 small triangles (A). If quick-piecing, do not cut triangles. Draw a 6″ square on wrong side of fabric, and divide it in half diagonally to make corner triangles. Cut upper strip 2½″ by 11″.

From green leaf print, cut 1 square (B) and 7 small triangles (A). If quick-piecing, cut only 1 small triangle. From brown, cut upper trunk (D) and lower trunk (E). Draw a 6″ square on purple print, and divide it in half diagonally to make corner triangles. Cut lower strip 2½″ by 11″ from green floral print.

From floral print, cut two 16″ by 22″ pieces for sides and back and a 8″ by 20″ piece for handles. Cut 2 side borders 3″ by 15″, upper border 4″ by 15½″, and lower border 4″ by 15½″. From lining and quilt batting, cut three 16″ by 22″ pieces and one 8″ by 20″ piece.

## Tote Front

Using ¼″ seam allowance, stitch all seams right sides in. Stitch each green micro-dot small triangle (A) to either a light blue or a green leaf print small triangle (A) to form a square, or quick-piece triangles following directions on page 17. There will be one green print triangle left over. Following diagram for Pine Tree block, stitch squares of green micro-dot and green print together in groups of three. Be sure to make a right and a left side. Stitch small green print square (B) to top end of one strip. Stitch strip without green print square to side of tree triangle (C). Stitch remaining strip to other side of tree.

Stitch squares of green micro-dot and light blue triangles together in groups of four. Be sure to make a right and left side. Stitch small light blue square (B) to top end of one strip. Stitch strip without square to side of tree. Stitch remaining strip to other side of tree. Stitch upper trunk (D) to lower trunk (E), beginning and ending stitching ¼″ from edges of upper trunk. Stitch lower sides (F) to sides of trunk. Stitch small green print triangle (A) to lower trunk. Stitch this section to tree triangle (C).

Stitch light blue corner triangles to upper edges of Pine Tree block. Stitch purple triangles to lower edges. Trim outer edges of triangles to form a square ¼″ larger

**PINE TREE BLOCK**
**PIECING DIAGRAM**

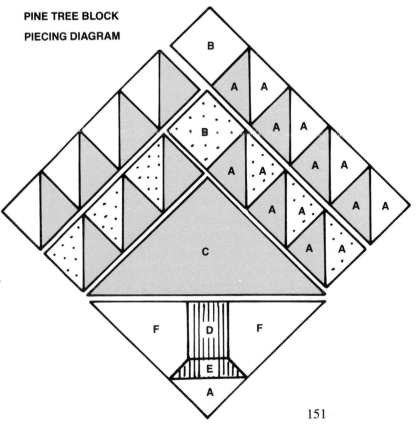

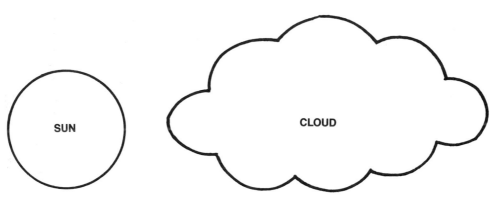

than corners of Pine Tree block. Stitch upper and lower strips to corner triangle. Trim ends even with edge of triangles. Stitch side borders to side edges. Stitch upper border to upper edge, and lower border to lower edge. Following directions under *Hand-Appliqué* (page 19), make patterns for 2 clouds and a sun. Cut clouds from white and sun from gold. Position sun in upper left corner of light blue sky and slipstitch in place. Position clouds in sky and slipstitch them in place.

### Quilting

Mark diagonal quilting lines 2″ apart on floral print back, side, and handle pieces. Then mark diagonal quilting lines 2″ apart on borders of front. Following instructions under *Machine-Quilting* (page 24), place batting between backing and tote front. Place a piece of batting between each backing piece and back, sides, and handles. Pin, then baste, the layers together. Using matching thread, machine-quilt along seams of Pine Tree block as follows: around outer edge, along lines between strips of triangles, and around tree triangle and trunk. Quilt along inner edges of borders, along upper edge of lower strip, and around clouds and sun. Then quilt diagonal lines on all pieces.

### Making Tote

Stitch tote pieces together, with right sides in, using ½″ seams unless otherwise indicated. Trim batting and backing even with tote front. Cut tote back same size as front. From 16″ by 22″ quilted piece, cut 2 sides the length of front by 4½″. Cut bottom the width of front by 4½″. From 8″ by 20″ quilted piece, cut two handles 3½″ by 19″.

Stitch sides to ends of bottom, beginning and ending ½″ from edges. Stitch this strip to front, matching seams to corners. Stitch remaining side of strip to back, matching seams to corners. Zigzag-finish seam allowance. Turn under ½″, then 1″, along top edge of tote. Stitch hem in place. With right sides out, fold front to strip along seam. Topstitch ⅛″ from seam. Repeat along back seam.

Fold handles in half, right sides in, and stitch edges together using ¼″ seam allowance. Turn right side out. Press lightly so seam is along one side edge. Zigzag-finish ends. Pin ends of one handle under top edge of front hem 2½″ from center. Stitch front to handle along top and bottom of front hem. Attach other handle to back in same manner.

PACIFIC NORTHWEST PINE TREE TOTE

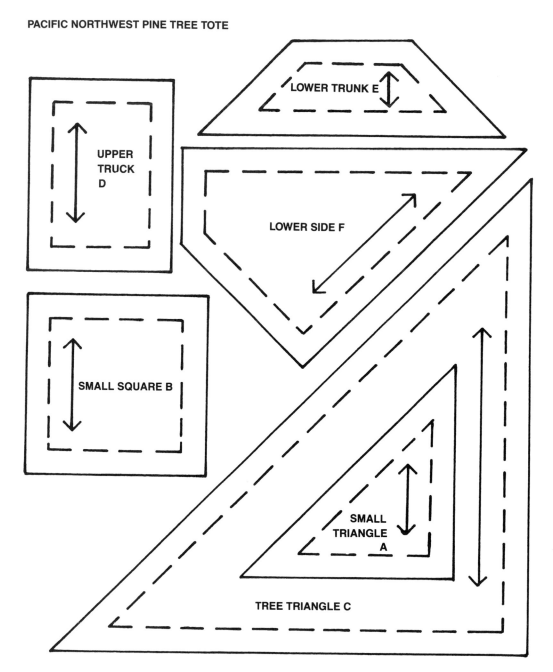

LOWER TRUNK E

UPPER
TRUCK
D

LOWER SIDE F

SMALL SQUARE B

SMALL
TRIANGLE
A

TREE TRIANGLE C

ACTUAL SIZE PATTERNS

# POLITICAL PINCUSHIONS

I n the 18th and early 19th centuries, politics were left primarily to men, but that didn't mean that women had no opinion about political events. Perhaps they discussed the issues of the day as they stitched quilts at quilting bees, for quite a number of quilt blocks are named for politicians, presidents, political events, and slogans. The blocks shown here are Martha Washington's Star, named for the wife of our first president; Clay's Choice, named for Henry Clay, the Virginia senator known as the "great compromiser," who devoted 50 years of his life to abolishing slavery; and Old Tippecanoe, the nickname of William Henry Harrison, our ninth president who, as a soldier, led a military campaign at the Tippecanoe River. His political slogan was "Tippecanoe and Tyler Too."

*Size: 4" square*

## MATERIALS

For Each Pincushion
Scraps of red, white, and blue print or solid cotton fabrics (see photograph)
   5"-square muslin for backing
   5"-square fabric for pincushion back
   5"-square low-loft quilt backing
   ½ yard narrow cotton cording, or ½ yard ¼" lace
   Red, white, and blue sewing and quilting thread
   Polyester stuffing

## DIRECTIONS

### Old Tippecanoe

Follow directions for making templates (page 15), make template for triangle (A) on page 156. Trace template to wrong side of fabric adding ¼" seam allowance to each piece, and leaving at least ¼" around each piece. Then cut 12 from blue on white print fabric and 12 from white on blue print fabric, and 8 from red fabric.

Following directions under *Hand-Piecing* (page 17), stitch each of 8 blue on white print triangles (1) to a white on blue print triangle (2) to form a square. Stitch each of 4 blue on white print triangles (1) to a red triangle (3) to form a square. Stitch remaining white on blue print (2) and red (3) triangles together in the same manner. Trim seam allowance along stitched seams to ⅛".

### Clay's Choice

Following directions for making templates (page 15),

making templates for pieces A, B, and C on page 156. Trace each template to wrong side of fabric, adding ¼" seam allowance to each piece and leaving at least ¼" around each piece. Then cut out 8 triangles (A) from blue fabric, 4 triangles (A) from red colored fabric, and 4 squares (B). Cut 4 trapezoids (C) from muslin. Following directions under *Hand-Piecing* (page 17), stitch each of 4 blue triangles to a red triangle to form a square. Trim seam allowance on seams to ⅛" after stitching. Following piecing diagram, stitch squares together in pairs. Then join pairs to form center. Stitch each remaining blue triangle to a muslin trapezoid (C) to form a rectangle. Stitch a rectangle to top and bottom of center. Stitch red squares (B) to top and bottom of rectangles to form side strips. Join side strips to center strips, matching seams.

**OLD TIPPECANOE BLOCK   PIECING DIAGRAM**

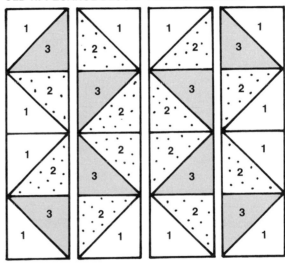

**CLAY'S CHOICE BLOCK   PIECING DIAGRAM**

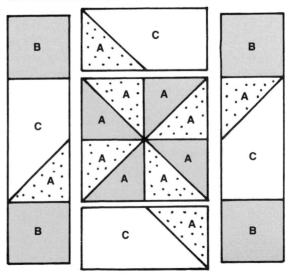

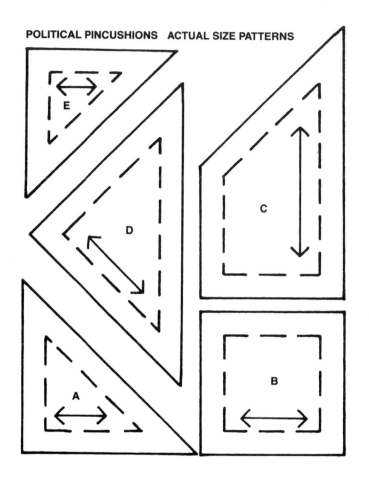

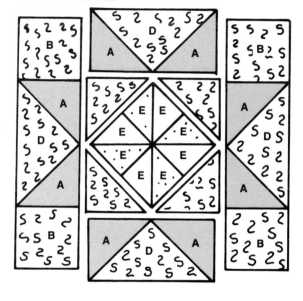

**MARTHA WASHINGTON'S STAR BLOCK**

**PIECING DIAGRAM**

## *Martha Washington's Star*

Following directions for templates (page 15), make templates for pattern pieces A, B, and E. Trace each template to wrong side of fabric adding ¼″ seam allowance to each piece and leaving at least ¼″ around each piece. Then cut out 4 small triangles (E) from each white-on-blue print fabric and muslin. From red-on-white print fabric, cut 4 medium triangles (A), 4 squares (B), and 4 large triangles (D). Cut 8 triangles (A) from white-on-red print fabric.

Following directions under *Hand-Piecing* (page 17), stitch each small blue triangle (E) to a muslin triangle to form a square. Trim seam allowances to ⅛″ after stitching seams. Stitch pieced square together in pairs. Then stitch pairs together to form center.

Stitch a red-on-white print medium triangle (A) to edges of center. Stitch white-on-red print triangle (A) to

sides of a large triangle to form a rectangle. Stitch a rectangle to two opposite edges of center. Stitch square (B) to each end of remaining rectangles to make side strips. Stitch side strips to center matching seams.

### *Quilting and Finishing*

Place batting between backing and pincushion top, right sides out. Pin and baste the layers together. Hold pieces in your hand and quilt ⅛″ from edges of patchwork pieces, as desired. Use matching or contrasting color quilting thread. Make cording, if desired, following directions on page 28. Sew cording around pincushion, ¼″ from edge. Stitch pincushion top to back ¼″ from edge, leaving an opening for turning. Turn right side out. Stuff pincushion. Slipstitch edges of opening together. If desired, stitch lace around pincushion, mitering corners.

# NAVAHO PATCHWORK VEST

**T**he Navaho Indians of the southwestern United States have a rich tradition of weaving blankets, rugs, and other textiles. Although the earliest Navahos made their textiles from locally grown cotton, contemporary Navahos use wool from their flocks of sheep. The beauty and color of Navaho geometric designs are the inspiration for this patchwork vest made from wool fabrics. The vest is lined with satin and finished with a bound edge.

*Size: Medium (10–12)*

## MATERIALS

60"-wide wool fabrics
  ½ yard red
  ⅝ yard black
  ¼ yard white
  ⅛ yard taupe
  ⅝ yard red taffeta
  Red, white, and black sewing thread

## DIRECTIONS

Cut a 2" by 60" strip from each white, red, and black fabric. Following directions under *Strip-Piecing* (page 18), stitch white and black strips to edges of red strip. Cut the pieced strip into strips 1¾" wide. Use this quick-pieced section near the lower edge of each row, (see Row 1, piecing diagram). Cut a strip 1¾" wide each of the red, white, black, and taupe fabric. Cut a 1½"-length of taupe strip and stitch to lower edge of quick-pieced section. Stitch all seams, right sides together, using ¼" seam allowance and 12–15 stitches per inch (2.0 on European machines). Press seams toward lower edge. Then cut a 4" length from red strip and stitch it to the top of a quick-pieced section. In this manner, cut each length from the color strip indicated, following measurements given on piecing diagram (page 160). Stitch lengths together to form Row 1.

Following vest piecing diagram, make two of Row 2 in the same manner. Remember that the measurements given are the cut size of each length and that they include ¼" seam allowance on each end. Press seams on each row toward lower edge. Stitch a Row 2 to each side of Row 1. Using a damp pressing cloth, steam press vertical seams open. Make two of each Row 3–17, and stitch one to each side of center back. Cut more strips of fabric as you need them.

For front yokes, cut one 1¾" by 16" strip and five 1" by 16" strips of red, three 1" by 16" strips of white, and three ¾" by 16" strips of black. Stitch strips together following front yoke section of vest piecing diagram. Steam press seams open using a damp pressing cloth. Cut yoke piece in half to make two 8"-wide pieces. Stitch yokes to upper edge of front. Following cutting line on diagram, draw outline of neck edge, shoulder, and armhole edge on vest. Cut along this line. Pin vest, right side up, on wrong side of red taffeta. Cut the lining out around the edges of the vest.

With right sides together, stitch back to fronts along shoulder seams, using ½" seam allowance. Right sides in, pin, then baste, vest to lining ⅜" from edges of armholes, neck, front, and lower edges. Pin vest to lining along one side of Row 1 at center back. Using red thread, machine-quilt along the seamline (in the ditch). Repeat along seam between Rows 9–10 and along seam between Rows 13–14.

Following directions under *Binding* (page 26), cut 1¾"-wide bias strips of black wool to piece a binding that is 150" long. Do not fold binding in half. Right sides together, beginning at side of lower edge, stitch binding along lower edge, center front, and neck edges. Miter binding at lower corners. Join ends of binding on the straight grain. Fold binding to lining side over edge of vest. Turn under raw edge of binding along stitching line and slipstitch edge in place. Bind edges of armholes in the same manner.

**NAVAHO PATCHWORK VEST PIECING DIAGRAM**

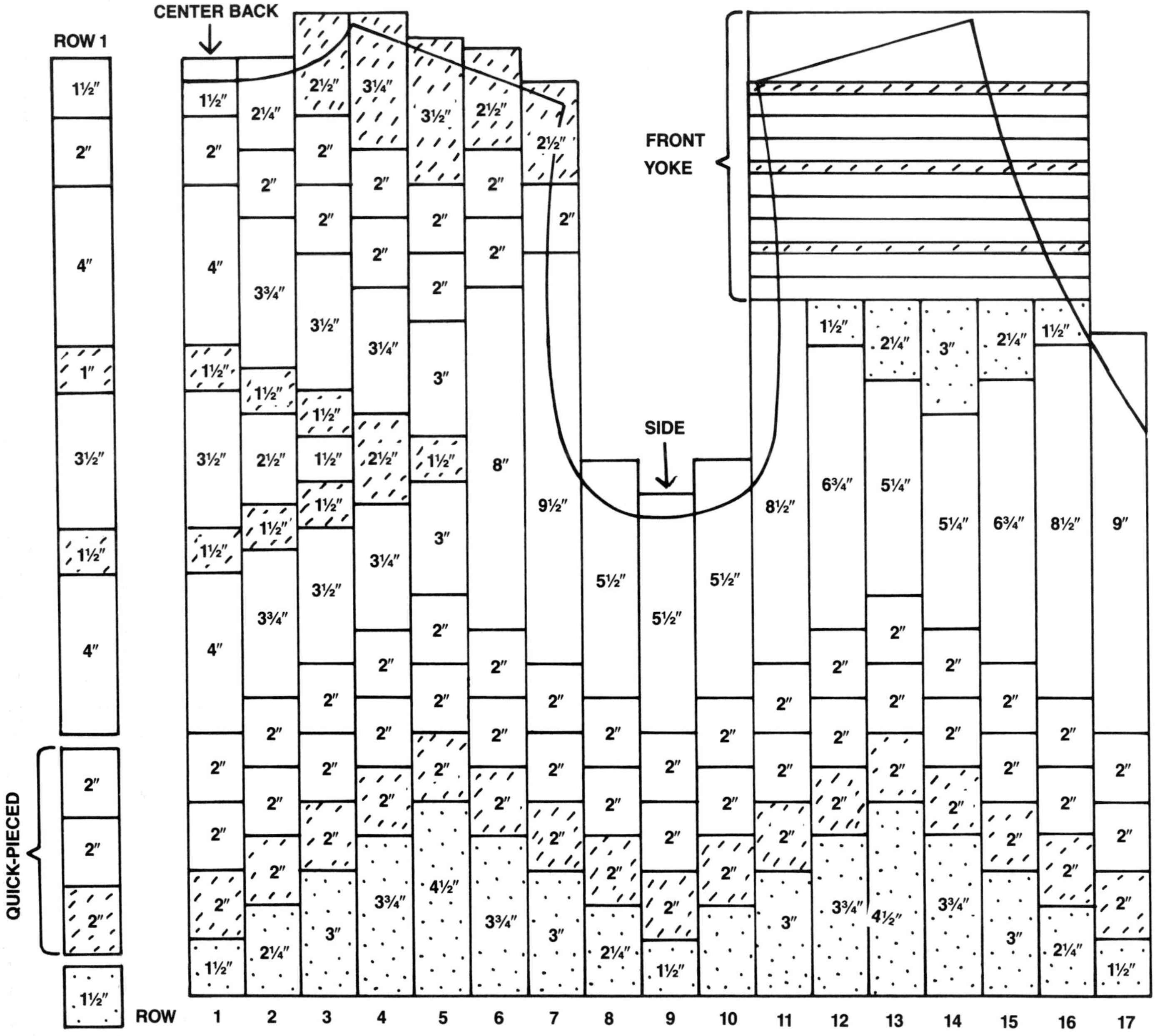
CENTER BACK
ROW 1
1½″ 2″ 4″ 1″ 3½″ 1½″ 4″
QUICK-PIECED
2″ 2″ 2″ 1½″
1½″ 2″ 4″ 1½″ 3½″ 1½″ 4″ 2″ 2″ 2″ 1½″
2¼″ 2″ 3¾″ 1½″ 2½″ 1½″ 3¾″ 2″ 2″ 2″ 2¼″
2½″ 2″ 2″ 3½″ 1½″ 1½″ 1½″ 3½″ 2″ 2″ 2″ 3″
3¼″ 2″ 2″ 3¼″ 2½″ 3¼″ 2″ 2″ 2″ 3¾″
3½″ 2″ 2″ 3″ 1½″ 3″ 2″ 2″ 2″ 4½″
2½″ 2″ 2″ 8″ 2″ 2″ 2″ 3¾″
2½″ 2″ 9½″ 2″ 2″ 2″ 3″
5½″ 2″ 2″ 2″ 2¼″
SIDE
5½″ 2″ 2″ 2″ 1½″
5½″ 2″ 2″ 2″
FRONT
YOKE
8½″ 2″ 2″ 2″ 3″
1½″ 6¾″ 2″ 2″ 2″ 3¾″
2¼″ 5¼″ 2″ 2″ 2″ 4½″
3″ 5¼″ 2″ 2″ 2″ 3¾″
2¼″ 6¾″ 2″ 2″ 2″ 3″
1½″ 8½″ 2″ 2″ 2″ 2¼″
9″ 2″ 2″ 2″ 1½″
ROW 1 2 3 4 5 6 7 8 9 10 11 12 13 14 15 16 17

# ROSE APPLIQUÉ BOX

ecause roses have always been a favorite flower, it is not surprising that they appear in many forms and in a variety of quilting projects. This realistic but simplified version of the American Beauty rose, our national flower, is hand-appliquéd on off-white fabric and decorates a heart-shaped box. Make an appliqué box for someone you care about, and enclose a string of pearls, potpourri, or a silk scarf.

*Size: 9"*

## MATERIALS

9" heart-shaped bandbox (or 10" by 20" piece corrugated cardboard and 6" by 30" piece railroad board or poster board)
45"-wide cotton fabrics
⅜ yard dusty rose and off-white print
⅛ yard dusty rose
⅝ yard lining fabric
⅜ yard or 11" square off-white
Scraps of red, maroon, red print, maroon micro-dot, green, and light green cotton fabrics
10" by 20" piece quilt batting
1 yard 18"-wide paper-backed fusible webbing
1 yard ⅜"-wide off-white feather-edged satin ribbon
Red and maroon sewing thread
Green and light green embroidery floss

## DIRECTIONS

To draw a heart for box top, fold a 9" piece of paper in half and draw half a heart; cut out shape along line. Draw a heart ⅛" smaller all around for bottom of box. Trace top and bottom to corrugated cardboard. Draw a 1¼" by 30" piece for rim and a 4" by 29" piece for sides on railroad or poster board. Cut out pieces. Alternatively, pieces from a bandbox kit can be used. Add 1" to edges of heart pattern for box top and trace American Beauty rose onto center of heart. Trace pattern to center of an 11" square of off-white fabric. Following directions under *Hand-Appliqué* (page 19), make patterns for leaves and petals and cut as follows: Cut leaf 1 and bud piece 4 from light green; cut remaining leaves and bud pieces 5–7 from green. Cut petals, 1, 3, and 7 from red print; petals 2, 4, 12 and 13 from red; petals 5, 8 and 9 from maroon; and petals 6, 10 and 11 from maroon

micro-dot. Cut bud piece 1 from maroon and bud pieces 2 and 3 from maroon micro-dot. Following directions under *Stems* (page 21), make a 4"-long stem ⅛" wide from light green. Slipstitch stems to position on off-white fabric. Slipstitch light green leave in place. Then slipstitch green leaves in place. Slipstitch bud pieces to position in numerical order. Matching thread to fabrics, slipstitch petals in place in numerical order.

With 2 strands of embroidery floss, make a row of running stitches along centers of leaves. (See *Embroidery Basics*, page 32.)

### Covering Box

Cut a piece of fusible webbing 1" longer and 1" wider than sides of box. Trace box bottom onto fusible webbing and add ½" around edges. Fuse these pieces to wrong side of print fabric. Place cardboard piece in center of wrong side of fabric pieces and fuse them in place. Clip edge of fabric on bottom to position ¼" from edge of cardboard. Fold edges of fabric over edges of cardboard and fuse them in place. Glue sides to box bottom using tacky glue or hot glue gun. Glue ends of sides together. Glue uncovered cardboard rim to box top in same manner.

Cut two pieces of quilt batting using box top as pattern. Place batting on top. Cut out appliquéd fabric pieces along outer line. Using tacky glue, glue fabric piece on top over batting, clipping edge of fabric about ½" deep. Cut a piece of solid fabric ¾" wider and 1" longer than circumference of rim. Press under ¼" on one long edge. Using tacky glue, glue finished edge around top edge of rim. Turn under ¼" on one end and glue it over other edge of strip. Fold lower edge to inside of rim and glue it in place. Glue lace and ribbon to rim with tacky glue.

### Lining

Trace top and bottom patterns to lining fabric. Cut out shapes, adding ½" to edges. Clip edges to drawn lines. Using tacky glue, glue lining pieces in place, centered inside top of lid and bottom of box. To line box sides and rim, cut lining fabric 1" longer and ¼" wider than measurements of box and rim. Press under ¼" on each long edge and ½" on one end. Apply glue to wrong side of hems of lining, and place inside along sides of box and rim of lid.

ROSE APPLIQUÉ BOX   ACTUAL SIZE PATTERN

LEAVES

STEM

PETALS

# YANKEE PUZZLE HOT PAD

he name "Yankee" was given during the War of Independence to those who supported the American Revolution. Later, during the Civil War, it was used to refer to someone who came from the North. During wartime, it was necessary to economize and use every scrap of fabric—and these puzzle patterns, made of tiny triangles sewn together, are the perfect way to use every scrap. Quick-piecing techniques make joining these tiny pieces fast and easy. An excellent bazaar best-seller, this hot pad can be used under teapots or casseroles to protect countertops and tables.

*Finished size: 9½" square*

## MATERIALS

45"-wide cotton fabrics
⅜ yard blue-on-white print
⅛ yard or scraps of blue print
¼ yard or scraps of muslin, including an 11" square
   for backing piece
Four 11" squares cotton quilt batting
Off-white sewing and quilting thread

## DIRECTIONS

Stitch all seams, right sides together, using ¼" seam allowance.

*Cutting*
*For Traditional Piecing*

Make template for small triangle (A) by tracing pattern on page 166. Trace template to wrong side of each muslin and blue print fabric, and cut 16 triangles from each. Stitch blue triangles to white triangles to form squares.

*For Quick-Piecing*

Following directions under *Quick-Piecing Triangles* (page 17), cut a 6" by 11½" piece of each muslin and blue print fabric. Draw eight 2⅝" squares (2 rows of 4 squares). Divide them in half diagonally to form 16 triangles. Right sides in, stitch to blue fabric.

## Hot Pad Top

Following piecing diagram, arrange squares and stitch them together in pairs. Stitch pairs together to make each quarter of Yankee Puzzle block. Stitch quarters together, then stitch halves together. Make a template for corner triangle (B) by tracing pattern on page 166. Trace template to wrong side of blue-on-white print fabric and cut 4 corner triangles. Stitch a corner triangle to each side of Yankee Puzzle block. Press seams toward triangles.

   Mark quilting lines on large triangles as indicated on the pattern. If desired, mark quilting lines on muslin triangles ¼" from edges. Cut an 11" square of muslin. Following directions in *Quilting Basics* (page 23), place 2 pieces of batting between the muslin and the top, keeping right sides out. Pin and baste the layers together. Quilt along the lines just marked.

## *Assembling Hot Pad*

Cut an 11" piece of blue-on-white print fabric for back. Place it, right side up, on top of remaining two quilt batting squares. Pin, then baste, the edges together. With right sides together, pin, then stitch, top to back ¼" from edge, leaving an opening for turning. Trim corners and turn right side out. Turn under edges of opening and slipstitch them together. Lightly steam-press edges in place.

**YANKEE PUZZLE BLOCK   PIECING DIAGRAM**

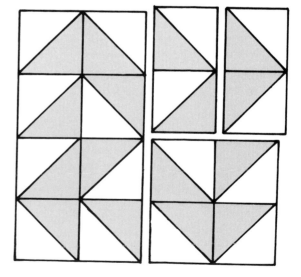

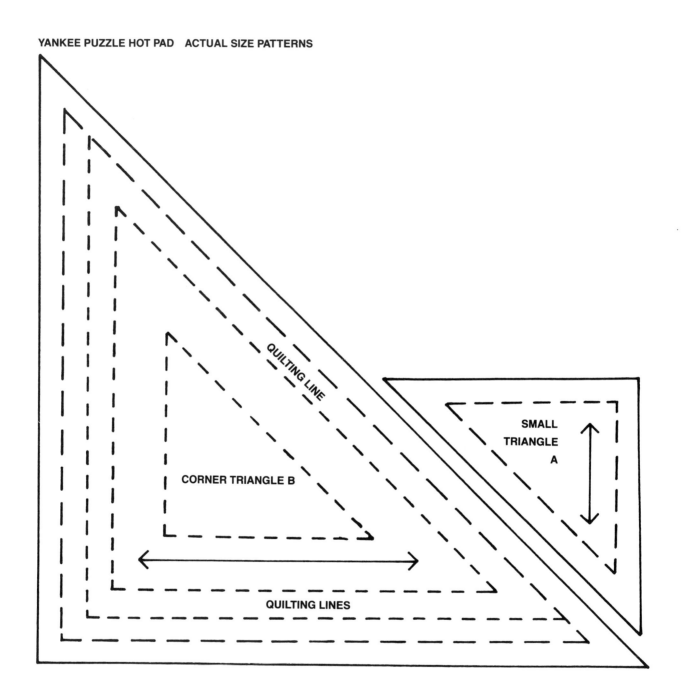

QUILTING LINE

CORNER TRIANGLE B

QUILTING LINES

SMALL
TRIANGLE
A

# INDIANA PUZZLE POT HOLDERS

hese pot holders are made from a pattern created during the pioneer days in Indiana. Patterns named "puzzle" are usually blocks made of small triangles and squares that create an intricate and striking geometric effect when placed side by side. Used separately, they fashion bold red-and-white pot holders. Quick-piecing techniques make joining the small pieces both fast and easy.

*Size: 8″ square*

## MATERIALS

45″-wide cotton fabric
  For one pot holder: ¼ yard main color and ⅛ yard
    second color
  For both pot holders: ¼ yard of each color
  Sewing thread to match main color
  Quilting thread to match second color of each pot
    holder
  9″-square cotton quilt batting

## DIRECTIONS

Right sides together, stitch all seams using ¼″ seam allowances.

### For Traditional Piecing

Make templates for triangle (A), small square (B), and large square (C) by tracing patterns on page 168. From main fabric, cut 1 large square, 4 triangles, and 8 small squares. From other fabric, cut 4 triangles and 8 small squares. Following piecing diagram, stitch each triangle to a triangle of the other color to form a square. Stitch each small square to a small square of the other color.

### For Quick-Piecing

Following directions under *Quick-Piecing Triangles* (page 17), draw two 3⅜″ squares; divide in half diagonally to form triangles. Stitch triangles. Following directions under *Quick-Piecing Squares* (page 19), cut a 2½″ by 15″ strip of each fabric and stitch them together. Cut strips into 2¼″ pieces perpendicular to seamline.

### Assembling Puzzle Block

Alternating colors, stitch pairs of squares together to form a four-patch section. Stitch triangle pieces to opposite sides of the large square, matching colors. Stitch four-patch sections to opposite sides of triangle pieces, with colors arranged as shown in piecing diagram. Matching seams, stitch three strips together, with inner edges of triangles matching color of center square.

### Quilting and Finishing

Mark heart in center square. If desired, mark quilting lines ¼″ from edges of main color sections. Cut a 9″ square of batting and a 9″ square of second fabric for backing. Place batting between backing and pot holder top, keeping right sides out. Pin and baste the layers together. Quilt along the lines as marked, using contrasting thread. Trim edges of batting and backing ⅛″ bigger than top. Cut bias strips 3¼″ wide to form a binding 36″ long. Beginning at top corner, bind edges of pot holder, making a loop for hanging with end of binding.

**INDIANA PUZZLE BLOCK    PIECING DIAGRAM**

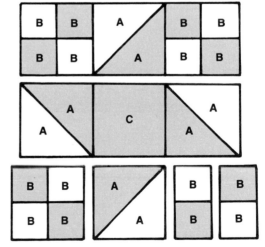

MAIN COLOR

**INDIANA PUZZLE POT HOLDERS   ACTUAL SIZE PATTERNS**

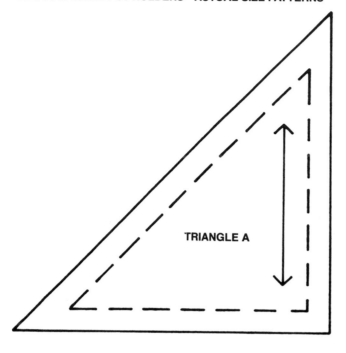

TRIANGLE A

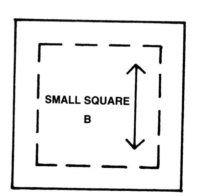

SMALL SQUARE
B

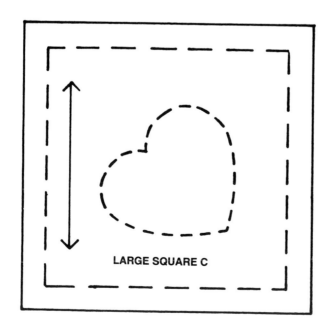

LARGE SQUARE C

# STAR-SPANGLED 4TH OF JULY PICNIC CLOTH

**T**he 4th of July is a fun-filled national holiday. We celebrate with picnics, barbecues, parades, and fireworks. Make every 4th of July picnic special with this star-spangled picnic cloth. Based on the fence rail pattern, machine-appliquéd stars and strip-piecing make this project easy. Use thick batting and tie the layers together to finish it quickly.

*Size: 70″ square*

## MATERIALS

45″-wide cotton fabrics
   3 yards red
   2 yards off-white muslin
   1 yard navy
   1 yard navy print
   4¼ yards backing fabric
   ¾ yard 18″-wide fusible webbing
   74″-square extra-loft quilt batting
   Off-white and red sewing thread
   3 skeins each, red, off-white, and navy embroidery
     floss

## DIRECTIONS

*Cutting*

Following directions under *Templates* (page 15), make templates for pattern A–C and star on page 174. Trace templates to wrong side of fabric and cut out each piece. Measure and draw pieces and strips with a ruler and pencil, or use a rotary cutter. From navy, cut 34 star squares 4½″ by 4½″ and strips 2″ by 45″ (the width of the fabric); from navy print, cut 16 strips 2″ by 45″; from red, cut 24 strips 2″ by 45″ and 36 large triangles (A); from off-white, cut 24 strips 2″ by 45″, 32 large triangles (A), 8 small triangles (B), and 4 small squares (C). Then, following directions under *Machine-Appliqué* (page 22), cut 34 stars backed with fusible webbing.

## Quilt Top

Stitch all seams, right sides together, using ¼″ seam allowance. Fuse stars to center of navy star squares. Zigzag around stars using off-white thread. For striped

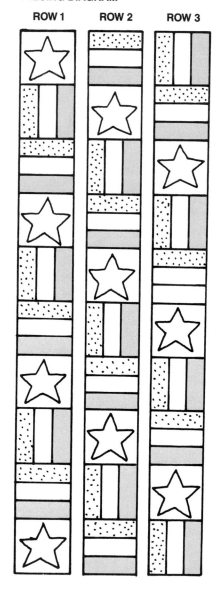

**STAR-SPANGLED 4TH OF JULY PICNIC CLOTH**

**PIECING DIAGRAM**

ROW 1    ROW 2    ROW 3

blocks, stitch red, off-white, and navy print strips together following directions under *Strip-Piecing* (page 18). Make 16 lengths of red, off-white, and navy print. Cut lengths to make sixty-six 4½" squares.

Following piecing diagram, stitch star squares and striped squares together to make 4 of Row 1, and 3 each of Rows 2 and 3. Matching seams, stitch Rows 1–3 together, continuing until all 10 rows have been joined to form center. Stitch 9 red and 8 off-white large triangles together to form 4 inner borders; then join small triangles to ends. Stitch 2 inner borders to opposite sides of center. Stitch squares to ends of remaining inner borders. Stitch these inner borders to center.

Strip-piece remaining strips of fabric together, in this order: red, navy print, off-white, red, navy, off-white until 48 strips have been joined. Cut striped piece into four 10¼" borders so stripes are perpendicular to long edge of border. Stitch borders to sides of center, matching centers and beginning and ending stitching ¼" from edges of center. To miter corners, match seams and stitch borders together diagonally from corners at center to outer edge. Trim edges ¼" from stitching.

### Tying and Finishing

Make backing from 74" lengths of fabric following directions on page 23. Place batting between backing and top, right sides out. Pin the layers together. Thread a large embroidery needle with a 1 yard length of each red, off-white, and blue embroidery floss. For each tie, make a stitch about ¼" long through all three layers of picnic cloth, leaving a couple of inches of thread at end. Tie ends together in a square knot (see Diagrams 1 and 2).

Tie quilt at corners of star and striped blocks, points of triangles on inner borders, and along center of border between red and white stripes. Following directions under *Binding* (page 26), make a 3½"-wide continuous binding from a 30½" square of red fabric. Trim backing and batting even with edge of top. Baste the three layers together ½" from edge. Stitch binding to edges of picnic cloth, using ½" seam allowance.

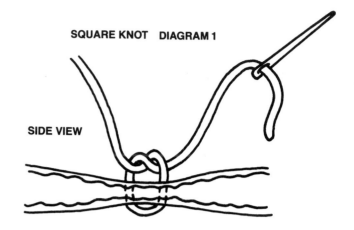

SQUARE KNOT    DIAGRAM 1

SIDE VIEW

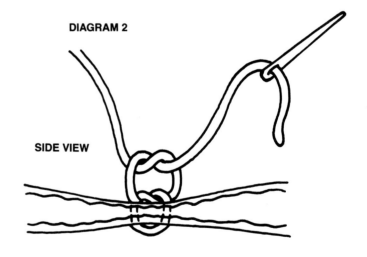

DIAGRAM 2

SIDE VIEW

# STAR-SPANGLED 4TH OF JULY PICNIC TOTE

You can make this oversized tote bag to carry your picnic feast. The stars and stripes that match the picnic cloth are arranged in a block pattern with strip-pieced sides and handles. Machine-quilting makes this bag durable as well as easy to make.

*Size: 18" by 22" by 6"*

### MATERIALS

45"-wide cotton fabrics
  ⅛ yard navy
  1¼ yards navy print
  ½ yard red
  ½ yard off-white muslin
  1½ yards backing fabric
  45" by 54" piece quilt batting
  Off-white and navy sewing thread
  ⅛ yard 18"-wide fusible webbing

### DIRECTIONS

*Cutting*

Measure, then draw, pieces and strips with a ruler and pencil, or use a rotary cutter. Cut four 4½" star squares from navy. From navy print, cut back 21" by 24", 2 side borders 4¼" by 14", lower border 3½" by 24", upper border 4¾" by 24". Cut a 27" strip for striped blocks and 7 strips 1½" by 45" (the width of the fabric). From red, cut a 5" by 7" center, a 2" by 27" strip for striped blocks, and 7 strips 1½" by 45". From white, cut a 2" by 27" strip for striped blocks and 7 strips 1½" by 45". Then cut 4 stars backed with fusible webbing. From backing, cut two 21" by 24" pieces for front and back, two 7" by 30" pieces for side strip, and two 4" by 25" for handles.

## Front

Stitch all seams, right sides together, using ¼" seam allowance. Fuse stars to center of navy star squares. Zigzag around stars with off-white thread. For striped blocks, stitch red, off-white, and navy print strips together, following directions under *Strip-Piecing* (page 18). Cut length to make two 5" lengths and two 7" lengths.

Stitch navy print edge of 7" lengths to long edges of center. Stitch stars to ends of 5" lengths to make sides. With navy print edge of striped blocks toward center, stitch sides to center, matching seams. Stitch side borders to sides of block. Trim ends of borders even with

block. Stitch upper and lower borders to patchwork block. Trim ends of borders even with side borders.

## Sides and Handles

Following directions under *Strip-Piecing* (page 18), stitch 4 strips of red, off-white, and navy print fabric together, alternating colors. Cut this length into six 7" widths. Following color order, stitch these pieces together to form center strip. Stitch 2 strips of red, off-white, and navy print together, alternating colors. Cut this length into eight 3¾" widths. Following color order, stitch 4 pieces together to form each of 2 handles.

### Quilting

Following directions under *Quilting Basics* (page 23), on front, mark a line for quilting 1¼" out from top and bottom edges of pieced block and 1¾" out from side edges to form a rectangle. On back, draw a rectangle 16½" by 19½", beginning 1¾" from lower and side edges. Draw 3 more smaller rectangles, each 2" from outer rectangles. Draw a line through the center of the smallest rectangle parallel to its longest edges.

Stitch backing pieces for side strip together along one end. For front, back, and side strip, place batting between backing and tote bag pieces. Pin the layers together. Baste layers together ½" from outer edge of tote bag pieces. Following directions under *Machine-Quilting* (page 24), stitch along seamlines of stars and stripes block and along line drawn on borders on front. Stitch along lines drawn on back. On side strips, stitch along seamlines between red and navy print stripes.

### Making Tote

Stitch tote pieces together, with right sides in, using ½" seams unless otherwise indicated. Trim batting and backing even with tote front. Cut tote back same size as front. Stitch side strip to sides and lower edge of front, clipping seam allowance of side strip at corners. Stitch remaining side of strip to back in the same manner. Zigzag-finish seam allowance. Turn under ½", then 1", along top edge of tote. Stitch hem in place.

Baste handles right side up to quilt batting. Fold handles in half, right sides in, and stitch edges together, using ¼" seam allowance. Turn right side out. Press lightly so steam is along one side edge. Zigzag-finish ends. Pin ends of one handle under top edge of front hem, 4½" from center. Stitch front to handle along top and bottom of front hem. Attach other handle to back in same manner.

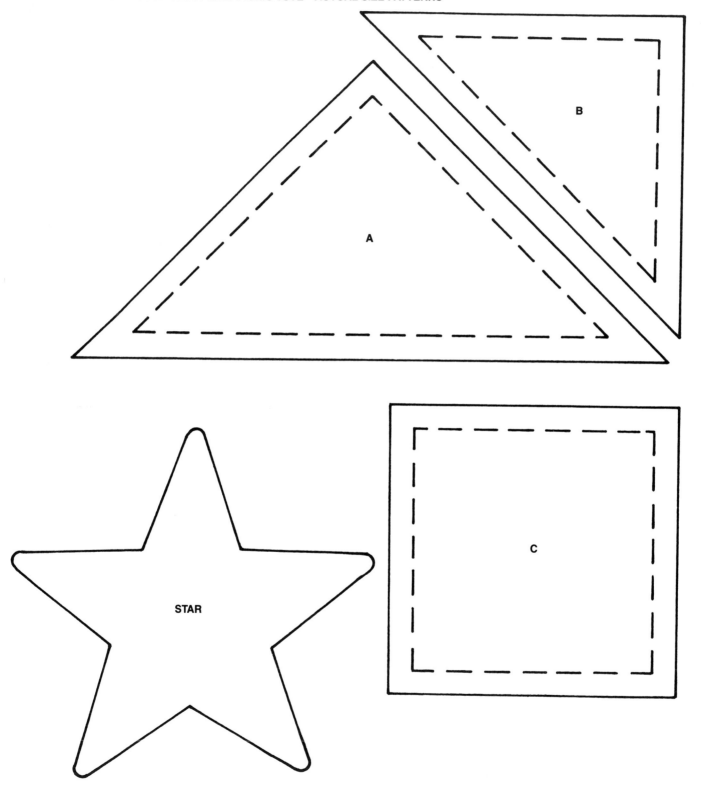

# HOPI KACHINA SASH

Kachinas are dolls made by the Hopi Indians and several other tribes of Pueblo Indians who live on the sandstone plateaus of New Mexico and Arizona. The kachinas are religious symbols representing mostly benevolent beings who control the weather and confer the blessings of rain, good crops, and health that are so important to agricultural peoples. A patchwork representation of a kachina decorates the ends of this strip-pieced sash fashioned in the colors of the Southwest. Embellished with a bead fringe, this sash is a very original accessory for a black, red, white, or sand-colored dress, blouse, or sweater.

*Size: 4½" by 72"*

## MATERIALS

45"-wide cotton fabrics
  ½ yard tan
  ¼ yard turquoise blue
  ⅛ yard each, black and white
  ⅛ yard or scraps of gold and rust
  5" by 74" piece quilt batting
  Tan, black, and white sewing thread
  Tan and turquoise blue quilting thread
  ½ yard each, black and rust embroidery floss
  192 white 4 mm-diameter beads
  32 black 4 mm-diameter beads

## DIRECTIONS

### Kachina Block

To make patterns for patchwork pieces A-N on page 178, trace each shape and add ¼" seam allowance to each edge. Make templates, following directions on page 15. Make patterns for hands and face following directions under *Appliqué Basics* (page 19).

#### Cutting

From turquoise blue, cut 4 squares (B), 8 triangles (C), 2 strips (D), 4 squares (F), 4 rectangles (H), 4 of each background piece (I, K, and L). From black, cut 6 diamonds (A) and feet (N). From gold, cut 6 diamonds (A) and 2 leg pieces (J), and 4 leg pieces (K). From rust, cut 2 torso triangles (G) and 2 lower strips (N). From white, cut 2 arms (E) and 2 torso triangles (G). From tan, cut 2

heads and 4 hands. Transfer markings for features to heads.

#### Piecing

Stitch all seams right sides together, using ¼" seam allowances. Make two blocks, as follows: Matching edges, stitch each gold diamond (A) to a black diamond (A) along one edge, ending stitching at end of stitching line at side corner. Stitch a triangle (C) between each diamond. Alternating colors, stitch 3 pairs of diamonds together along inner edges. Stitch 2 squares (B) between points of diamonds and a triangle (C) between remaining edges.

Stitch strip (D) to lower edge of diamond piece, following piecing pattern. Stitch squares (F) to ends of arms (E) and stitch to lower edge of strip. Stitch white torso triangle (G) to rust torso triangle (G) to make a rectangle. Stitch rectangles (H) to sides of torso. Stitch edge with white triangle to lower edge of arms. Stitch background piece (I) to ends of legs (J). Stitch to lower edge of torso strip.

Stitch gold leg piece (K) to ends of background piece (L). Stitch turquoise background piece (K) to end of leg. Stitch to lower edge of legs. Stitch feet (M) to ends of background strip (L). Stitch to lower edge of legs. Stitch rust strip (N) to lower edge of patchwork piece. Slipstitch head and hands to position on kachina. Using 3 strands of embroidery floss, stitch eyes and nose with black satin stitch (see *Embroidery Basics*, page 32). Embroider mouth with rust satin stitch.

### Sash Center

From tan, cut 4 strips 1½" by 45" (or width of the fabric). Cut 2 strips ¾" by 45" from black. Cut 2 strips ¾" by 45" each from white and turquoise. Following directions under *Strip-Piecing* (page 18), stitch each black strip to a tan strip. Then stitch blue or white strips to remaining edge of black strips. Stitch lengths with blue edge to edge of tan strip with white edge. Cut lengths into 4½" widths (or width of kachina block).

Stitch lengths together to make sash center about 54" long, or length of sash desired minus about 18". Cut a 4½" by 1½" piece of tan fabric, stitch tan strip to white strip at one end of sash. Press all seams in one direction.

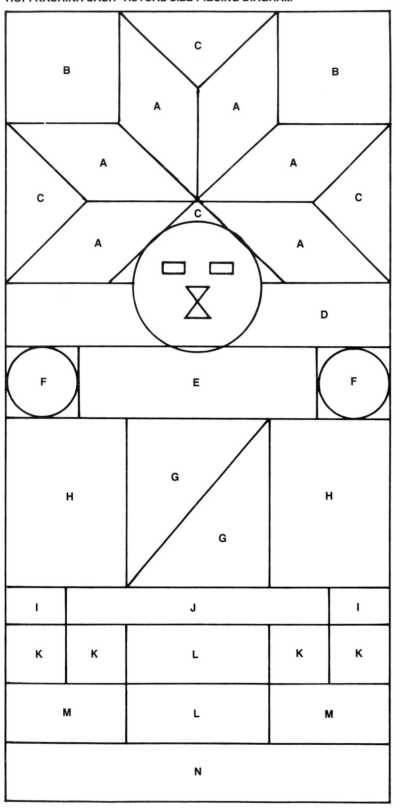

*Finishing*

Stitch kachina blocks to ends of sash. Right side up, pin sash to batting and trim edges even. Baste sash to batting ¼″ from edges. Cut two 4½″ by 9″ (or width of kachina blocks) pieces of turquoise to back kachina. From tan fabric, cut two 4½″-wide pieces one-half the length of the sash center plus ½″ for seam allowances. Stitch tan pieces together at one end, using ¼″ seam allowance. Stitch a turquoise piece to each end to make backing.

   Stitch sash to backing, right sides together, leaving an opening for turning. Trim seam allowance at corners. Turn right side out. Slipstitch edges of opening together. With tan thread, quilt along one edge of tan strips on sash center. With turquoise thread, quilt ¼″ from edge of kachina.

   To make fringe on both ends of sash, thread a needle with a long length of black thread, pull ends even, and knot them together. Bury knot in batting and bring needle out at corner of one end. To make bead fringe, string 12 white beads and one black bead on thread. Insert needle back through holes in white beads, and bring needle out at top of strand. Push beads up close to end of sash. Take a ¼″-long stitch in end of sash and make another bead fringe. Knot ends of thread securely. Repeat across end to make about 15 or 16 strands of beads.

# ROCKY ROAD TO KANSAS PILLOW

**T**his "crazy quilt" of Victorian times reflects the highly embellished style of that era, when many women had more leisure time to devote to needlework that was non-utilitarian. Women's magazines of the day popularized the "crazy quilt" style, and the "rocky road" of the title probably refers to the hardships pioneers encountered on their journey westward. This charming project makes use of favorite scraps of satins, velvets, or pieces of old silk ties embellished with embroidery.

*Size: 15" square*

## MATERIALS

45"-wide fabrics
   ⅝ yard gold satin
   ½ yard black velvet
   ⅛ yard rose satin
   ⅛ yard navy crepe
   Scraps of satin, velvet, velveteen, crepe, or other
      silky fabrics including scraps of old silk neckties
   10½"-square muslin to back patchwork
   2 yards ½"-diameter cotton cording
   14" pillow form
   Sewing thread to match fabrics
   Gold, maroon, blue, and silver pearl cotton yarn

## DIRECTIONS

To make patterns for Rocky Road to Kansas block, divide a piece of tracing paper into quarters. Trace solid lines of pattern on page 180 to each quarter, matching center point. Trace pattern for Rocky Road to Kansas block to center of muslin square. Divide each long narrow triangle into three or four shapes similar to the lines indicated on pattern. Make patterns for each of these shapes, small triangle (A) and large triangle (B), adding ¼" seam allowance to each edge.

### Cutting

From black velvet, cut 2 border strips 3¼" by 16½" and two 3¼" by 12½" border strips. From rose satin, cut 2 inner borders 1¼" by 12½" and 2 inner borders 1¼" by 11". From navy crepe, cut four large triangles (B). From assorted scraps of fabrics and tie silks, cut four small triangles and remaining patchwork pieces.

## Pillow Top

Stitch all seams, right sides together, using ¼" seam allowance unless otherwise indicated. Stitch small triangles together in pairs along short edges. Stitch pairs of triangles together to form a square. Place square in center of muslin backing and hand-baste it in place ¼" from edges. Beginning at edge of center square, turn under ¼" on adjacent edge of first patchwork piece and pin it in position on muslin. By hand, make a row of small running stitches along fold. Hand-baste remaining edges in place. Stitch each patchwork piece in place in this manner.

Turn under ¼" on shorter edges of large triangle (B) and pin each piece in position on muslin over edges of patchwork pieces. Stitch in place with a row of small running stitches. Baste ¼" from outer edge of block. Using pearl cotton, embroider along seams of patchwork pieces with herringbone stitch, blanket stitch, or satin stitch (see *Embroidery Basics*, page 32).

Stitch 11" inner borders to two opposite edges of block. Trim ends of strips even with edges of block. Stitch 12½" inner borders to remaining edges of blocks. Trim ends even with edges of inner borders. Hand-baste, then stitch, 12½" borders to two opposite edges of inner borders. Trim ends even with edges of inner borders. Hand-baste, then stitch, 17" borders to remaining edges of inner border. Trim ends even with edges of borders.

### Finishing

Following directions under *Shirred Cording* (page 28), cut 2½"-wide strips of gold satin and make a shirred cording to cover cording. Hand-baste, then stitch, cording to edge of pillow top. Cut a 17" square of black velvet, or make pillow back as desired according to directions on page 30. Right sides in, stitch top to back, leaving an opening for turning if necessary. Insert pillow form or stuff pillow. Slipstitch edges of opening to close if necessary.

**ROCKY ROAD TO KANSAS PILLOW    ACTUAL SIZE PATTERNS**

**¼ OF PATCHWORK CENTER**

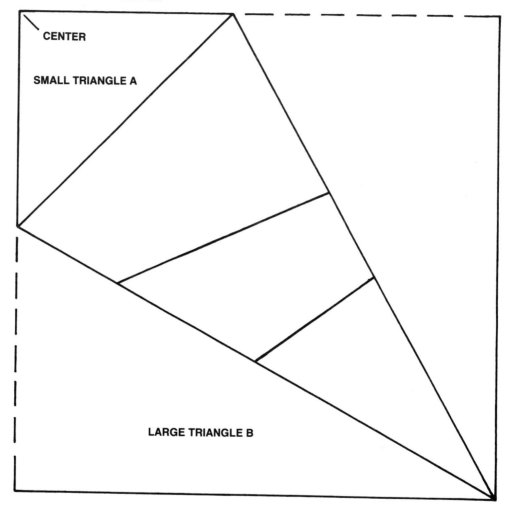

CENTER

SMALL TRIANGLE A

LARGE TRIANGLE B

# ARKANSAS TRAVELER CRIB QUILT

One of the names for this quilt block featuring the popular spool motif is Arkansas Traveler. The other name is Secret Drawer. Many blocks had different names in different parts of the country. Repeated a half dozen times in soft pastel floral fabrics, this block makes a beautiful, delicate crib quilt. The quilt is machine-sewn and hand-quilted. The centers of each block and the border are quilted by following the outlines of the floral motifs on the fabric. This is an heirloom to make and to treasure for many years to come.

*Size: 38" by 50"*

## MATERIALS

45"-wide cotton fabric
   2 yards large green floral print
   ¾" yard off-white print
   ⅜ yard small green print
   1¼ yards pink
   1½ yards for backing
   42" by 54" piece traditional quilt batting
   Off-white sewing thread
   Quilting thread to match fabrics

## DIRECTIONS

Following directions under *Templates* (page 15), make templates for pieces A-E from the patterns on page 184.

*Cutting*

Trace around templates on wrong side of fabric and cut out each piece. From large green floral print, cut 2 side borders 7" by 47", 2 top and bottom borders 7" by 42", with floral motifs of fabric centered along strips. Then cut 6 center squares (C) and 24 corner triangles (D), with floral motifs centered on each piece. From off-white print, cut 24 side triangles (E) and 48 trapezoids (B). From small green print, cut 12 small squares (A) for sashing squares and 48 trapezoids (B). From pink print, cut a 30½" square for binding, 17 sashing strips 2¼" by 11", and 24 small squares (A).

## Arkansas Traveler Block

Stitch all seams right sides together, using ¼" seams. The following directions for one block should be repeated until all 6 blocks are completed. On pink print small squares (A), mark corners of stitching line with small dots ¼" in from the edges. Pin a green print trapezoid (B) to one side on small square. Stitch seam between dots (see Diagram 1). Stitch another green print

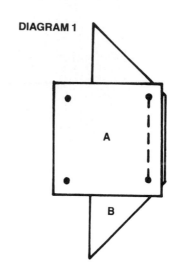

**DIAGRAM 1**

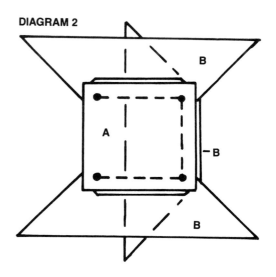

**DIAGRAM 2**

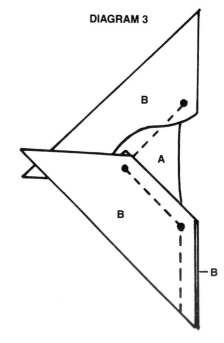

**DIAGRAM 3**

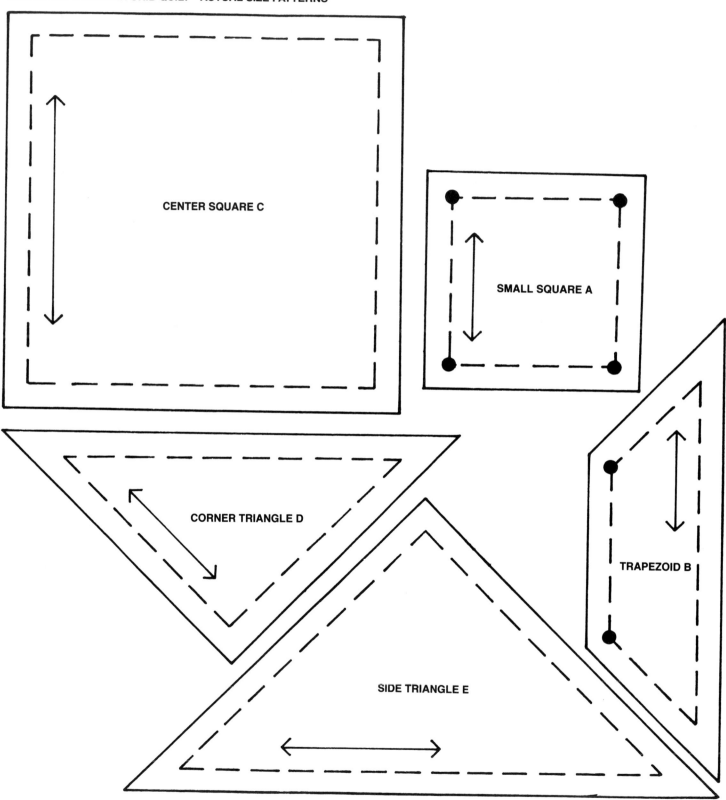

trapezoid to the opposite side of the square in the same manner. Press seams toward trapezoids. Pin an off-white trapezoid (B) to one remaining side on each pink print small square. Stitch seam between dots (see Diagram 2). Stitch another off-white trapezoid to last side of small square in the same manner, (see Diagram 2). Press seams toward center square.

Pin diagonal edges of adjacent trapezoids together. Stitch them together, beginning at corner of small square, to make "spool" section of block. Following Diagram 3, stitch off-white side of "spool" sections to opposite sides of center square (C). Stitch a corner triangle to ends of "spool" sections to make center strip. Stitch side triangles (E) to green print edges of 2 remaining "spool" sections, and stitch these pieces to either side of center strip, matching seams. Stitch corner triangles to off-white edges of "spool" sections.

*Assembling Quilt Top*

Arrange blocks into 2 vertical rows of 3 blocks each. Join them together by stitching one long edge of a sashing strip to the edge of the first block; trim ends of sashing strip even with the edge of the block. Then stitch the other long edge of the sashing strip to the edge of the next block. Join the remaining block in the same manner. Stitch a sashing strip to the end of the row.

Trim ends of remaining sashing strips the length of finished side edges of blocks, plus ½" for seam allowances. Arrange 4 green print sashing squares (A) with strips between them. Stitch strips and squares together to make 3 sashing rows. Stitch the rows of blocks to each side of the corner sashing row, matching seams. Stitch remaining sashing rows to side edges. Press seams toward sashing strips. Stitch side borders to sash-

**ARKANSAS TRAVELER BLOCK    PIECING DIAGRAM**

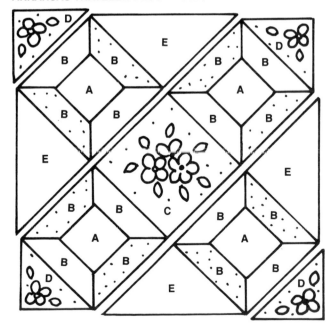

ing strips. Press seams toward borders. Trim ends even with edges of quilt center. Stitch top and bottom borders to quilt center and side borders. Trim ends even with sides.

*Quilting and Finishing*

Make templates for vine and flower quilting motifs below. Mark the vine motif on each sashing strip; it will repeat twice. Mark a flower on each sashing square. If desired, mark quilting lines ¼″ from the edges of each off-white piece on quilt block. Plan to quilt around flo-

ral motifs on borders and center squares, or choose other quilting motifs and mark them on each section.

Place batting between backing and quilt top, right sides out. Pin and baste the layers together (see *Quilting Basics*, page 23). Quilt along all lines of motifs marked on quilt top and ¼″ from edges of off-white pieces, as well as around floral motifs on center square and borders. Quilt along outer seamline of corner triangles. Make a 3½″-wide continuous bias binding from the square of pink print fabric (see directions under *Binding*, page 26). Bind edges of quilt.

**QUILTING MOTIFS**
**FLOWER**

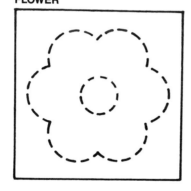

**ACTUAL SIZE PATTERNS**

**VINE**            **1 REPEAT**

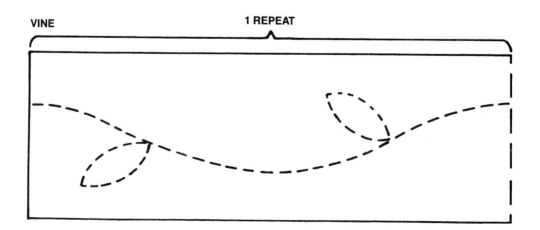

# AMERICAN EAGLE PILLOW

he eagle, our national bird, appears on many symbols and seals of our country. Early 19th century quilters appliquéd stylized eagles to decorate quilts, and blocks with eagles often appeared on album and commemorative quilts. The eagles often were cut from patterned fabric and surrounded with stars, stripes, or elaborately appliquéd borders. A single eagle with a shield is appliquéd in realistic colors on this very masculine pillow.

*Size: 17" square*

## MATERIALS

45"-wide cotton fabric
  ⅝ yard blue
  ⅜ yard red
  ¼ yard brown
  ⅛ yard off-white
  Scraps of gold
  19"-square muslin for backing
  19"-square quilt batting
  Sewing thread to match fabrics
  Off-white, brown, and gold quilting thread
  ½ yard brown embroidery floss
  16" pillow form or polyester stuffing

## DIRECTIONS

*Appliqué*

Following directions under *Enlarging Patterns* (page 15), enlarge appliqué pattern on page 188. Cut an 18" square of blue fabric. Trace outlines of eagle and stars in center of square for pillow top. Following directions under *Appliqué Basics* (page 19), make patterns for eagle's head, body, tail, legs, and beak. Make patterns for corner star, upper shield, and lower shield.

From off-white, cut 4 stars, head, and tail. From brown, cut body; from gold, cut beak and legs; from blue, cut upper shield. From red, cut five ⅞" by 5" strips; from off-white, cut four ⅞" by 5" strips. Stitch strips together, right sides in, using ¼" seam allowance. Trim seam allowance to ⅛". Press seams toward center. Cut lower shield from striped fabric with strips vertical. Stitch upper shield to lower shield.

Pin tail and legs to background and whipstitch edges in place. Pin body to position and whipstitch in place. Whipstitch head, then beak, to position to finish eagle. Whipstitch stars in place. Whipstitch shield to center of eagle's body as indicated on pattern. Embroider eye with satin stitch (see *Embroidery Basics*, page 32) and 3 strands of floss.

*Quilting*

Following directions under *Quilting Basics* (page 23), mark quilting lines on beak, wings, tail, and shield. Place batting between backing and pillow top, right sides out. Pin, then baste, the layers together. Quilt around stars and eagle ⅛" from the edge, using blue thread. Quilt around shield, using brown and off-white thread to match fabric of eagle. Quilt along lines of beak, wings, and tail, using matching thread. Quilt star on upper shield, using off-white thread. Then quilt along center of off-white stripes on shield. Trim batting and backing even with pillow top.

*Finishing*

Following directions under *Cording* (page 28), cover cotton cording with red fabric. Stitch cording around pillow top, ½" from edges. Cut an 18" square for pillow back, or make pillow back as desired following directions under *Pillow Backs* (page 30). Stitch front to back, leaving an opening for turning, if necessary. Turn right side out. Insert pillow form or stuff pillow. Slipstitch edges of opening together, if necessary.

EACH SQUARE = 1"

# INDEX

All of us at Meredith® Press are dedicated to offering you, our customer, the best books we can create. We are particularly concerned that all of the instructions for making the projects are clear and accurate. We welcome your comments and would like to hear any suggestions you may have. Please address your correspondence to Customer Service Department, Meredith® Press, Meredith Corporation, 150 East 52 Street, New York, NY 10022, or call 1-800-678-2665.